GLOBAL GLASNOST
Toward a New World Information and Communication Order?

D0075225

THE HAMPTON PRESS COMMUNICATION SERIES

Communication, Peace, and Development
Majid Tehranian, supervisory editor

Global Glasnost: Toward a New World Information and
Communication Order?
    Johan Galtung and *Richard C. Vincent*

Forthcoming

Restructuring for World Peace: On the Threshold of the Twenty-first
Century
    Katharine Tehranian and *Majid Tehranian* (eds.)

GLOBAL GLASNOST
Toward a New World Information and Communication Order?

Johan Galtung and Richard C. Vincent
University of Hawaii, Manoa

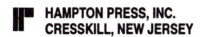

Printed in the United States of America

Library of Congress Cataloging-in-Publication Data

Galtung, Johan.
    Global glasnost : toward a new world information and
  communication order? / Johan Galtung and Richard C. Vincent.
       p.   cm.—(The Hampton Press communication series.
  Communication, peace, and development)
  Includes bibliographical references and index.
  ISBN 0-881303-331-4 (cloth). — ISBN 0-881303-332-2 (pbk.)
    1. Communication—International cooperation.
I. Vincent, Richard C. II. Title. III. Series
P96.I5G35   1992
302.2—dc20   92-20073
                                          CIP

Hampton Press, Inc.
23 Broadway
Cresskill, NJ 07626

TABLE OF CONTENTS

v

PREFACE

This book is about a major process of our time: the New World Information and Communication Order (NWICO). We believe the process derailed, and not only because of First World resistance. The book is an effort to look into the background of the process, as it has unfolded, above all through UNESCO. More important, it is an effort to spell out what NWICO might mean, in concrete terms, in relation to four major international news communication themes: peace, development, ecology and war.

Dr. Galtung is indebted to the University of Hawaii for a professorship in peace studies which rotated among departments, and to Professor Majid Tehranian for an invitation during Spring 1988 to join the Department of Communication of which he was then chairperson. A term spent as visiting professor in the Department of Communication, University of California, San Diego during Spring 1989 was useful as well. These provided unique opportunities to revive the interest in global news communication, in combination with peace, development, ecology and war perspectives. Dr. Vincent continues his work in the area of news communication studies. Recently he participated in the Third MacBride Round Table on Communication in Istanbul, Turkey, and is scheduled to attend the Fourth Round Table in Guarujá (São Paulo) Brazil. He gratefully acknowledges an appointment with the Social Science Research Institute and support from the Office of Research Administration and the Department of Communication, all at the University of Hawaii. These resources allowed him to begin concentrated study on international news flow and the New World Information and Communication Order. Dr. Vincent also welcomes the present opportunity to offer a fresh look at concerns which have plagued world leaders, journalists, and scholars for decades. By engaging in this work, the authors continue the University of Hawaii and East-West Center tradition of major contributions to the dialogue on the World Information Order. Among those who have helped lay foundations in this area are: Erwin Atwood, Wimal Dissanayake, Meheroo Jussawalla, Jim Richstad, Wilbur Schramm, and Majid Tehranian.

We are both grateful to Majid Tehranian, Andrew Arno, and Rodney Reynolds for their helpful comments and assistance, Alan Hancock and Morten Giersing for their aid in locating documents at UNESCO, and the librarians in the Communication and Culture Institute at the East-West Center. We also thank our respective families for their continuing encouragement and tolerance. But a major vote of thanks goes to a person we all know but have not necessarily met personally: Mikhail Sergeyevich Gorbachev. Glasnost, giving voice, openness, that scarce commodity, is probably many things to many persons. We know something about what it meant to the ex-Soviet Union. By using one of the two words Gorbachev brought into universal language, we wanted to explore its implications in a world perspective. His glasnost opened dialogue and was a notable step toward changes now found in the ex-Soviet Union. Perhaps similar open dialogue may one day happen throughout the world.

Honolulu, September 1991   Johan Galtung
                                                          Richard C. Vincent

About the Authors

Johan Galtung is professor of peace studies at the University of Hawaii, Manoa, and professor of social studies at Universitat Witten-Herdecke. In addition he holds honorary professorships at Universidad de Alicante, Freie Universitat Berlin, and Sichuan University. He earned doctoral degrees in mathematics and sociology from the University of Oslo, and is recipient of honorary doctorates from University of Tampere, University of Cluj-Napoca, Uppsala University and Soka University, Tokyo. Dr. Galtung was an early contributor to the news structure literature (1961), and has published widely on peace and security, the environment, political economy, development and research methodology. Prof. Galtung is founding editor of the *Journal of Peace Research*. Among his books are *Theory and Methods of Social Research, A Structural Theory of Revolutions, Toward Self-reliance and Global Interdependence: A New International Order and Global Interdependence, Transarmament and the Cold War, Environment, Development and Military Activity, There Are Alternatives: Four Roads to Peace and Security*, and *Methodology and Development*.

Richard C. Vincent is associate professor of communication at the University of Hawaii, Manoa. He was awarded the Ph.D. in communication from the University of Massachusetts, Amherst. Dr. Vincent specializes in mass communication theory and research with emphasis on media institutions, messages, processes, and effects. He is the author of a monograph on television news, *When Technology Fails: The Drama of Airline Crashes in Network Television News*, and a book on motion picture economics, *Financial Characteristics of Selected "B" Film Productions of Albert J. Cohen, 1951-1957*. He has also published widely in both scholarly journals and book chapters, including "CNN: Elites Talking to Elites," in *Triumph of the Image: The Media's War in the Persian Gulf. A Global Perspective* (Hamid Mowlana, Herbert Schiller and George Gerbner, editors).

Drs. Galtung and Vincent are coauthors of "Krisenkommunikation morgen, Zehn Vorschläge für eine andere Kriegsberichterstattung," in Martin Löffelholz, (ed.): *Krieg als Medienereignis. Grundlagen und Prespektiven der Krisenkommunikation* (War as a Media Event. Perspectives on Crisis Communication) [Opladen, Germany: Westdeutscher Verlag], and the forthcoming book, *Glasnost'—U. S. A.; Missing Political Themes in U.S. Media Discourse* [Cresskill, NJ: Hampton Press, Inc.].

DEDICATION

to our wives, Chris and Fumi

CHAPTER 1

Global Problems
and News Communication*

In the end, we must acknowledge that many of the roots of our trade difficulties lie within the U.S.and that we are partially at fault for being too sure of ourselves and too resistant to the changes we need to make to remain competitive . . . Bashing our competition for their success will not produce any positive end.—From the report of the California-Pacific Year 2000 Task Force [1]

The United States and Japan have already traded places in the global financial hierarchy. Japan's economic surge has made it the world's pre-eminent international creditor.

Now the same shift has taken place in the arena of third world development assistance . . . Japan's program transferred 0.032 percent of its national wealth to the third world, more than twice the share of the United States. The growth of Japan's aid program will gradually but surely erode American influence in the developing countries. It also will erode the image of the United States as a leader in promoting development as a basis for peace, prosperity and political stability.—Victor H. Palmieri, chairman of the Overseas Development Council, Washington, D.C.[2]

. . . [T]he poor man now knows how poor he is. He has his transistor radio.—Carlos Andres Perez, President, Venezuela [3]

GLOBAL PROBLEMS

There are many global problems which ignite cause-effect chains spanning the world, and this chapter begins with an attempt to locate some

* This chapter began as the keynote address delivered by Johan Galtung at the meeting of the International Association for Mass Communication Research, Prague, August 1984. The essay has been expanded and updated by the authors for this book. Professor Galtung extends his gratitude to IAMCR for the invitation to deliver the address, and to the discussants at the meeting for their incisive comments.

1

of them on a political map of the world. The many possible relationships that come out of this classificatory scheme, and the associated possibilities for change in news communication within the old or new world information and communication order (NWICO) are the subjects of this chapter.

The post Second World War world may be divided into four parts, combining the North-South and the East-West axes. The rich multiparty countries found in the Northwest are often called the First World and the formerly socialist, single party countries found in the Northeast are often called the Second World; with a connotation of second class. Then, there is the Third World (TW) consisting of mainly poor countries in the Southwest comprising South America, the Caribbean, Africa, West Asia, the Arab world and South Asia; they are mostly capitalist, some socialist, some both, and some neither one nor the other. In addition, some are democratic, some dictatorial, some both, and some do not fall into any of these categories. To this may then be added a Fourth World, the Southeast, composed of mainly buddhist-confucian countries in East Asia and Southeast Asia. At the top of the Fourth World is Japan, at the next tier down are the mini-Japans/Chinas that are Japanese economically and Chinese culturally (South Korea, Taiwan, Hong Kong, Singapore). The People's Republic of China, the ASEAN (Association of Southeast Asian Nations) countries, the socialist countries in East Asia and finally, as periphery areas in this vast section of the world, the Pacific Islands, Australia and New Zealand then follow.[4] The latter two are actually a First World enclave in a Fourth World; the socialist/former-socialist countries are a Second World enclave in rapid transformation; and the ASEAN, nations with the exception of Singapore and the Pacific Islands, a Third World enclave. What is left is the "Fourth World proper": Japan, the mini-Japans, and China—possibly a formidable future economic bloc, particularly when China and Korea have unified.

With the world divided into these four parts, six possible relationships may be used to look at the geopolitics of this last generation. The six global problem areas of particular interest here are the following:

1. *First World-Second World*: This relationship has been characterized as a nuclear suicide pact with tremendously serious implications, not only for the inhabitants in these two "worlds" but for the rest of humankind. The peace/security/arms race/disarmament issues were of supreme significance including the focus on qualitatively new weapons, on possible disarmament, and on transarmament from offensive to defensive arms. As the socialist systems collapsed at the end of the 1980s, the First World-Second World relation (1) became more similar to the First World-Third World relation (2) below, with Eastern

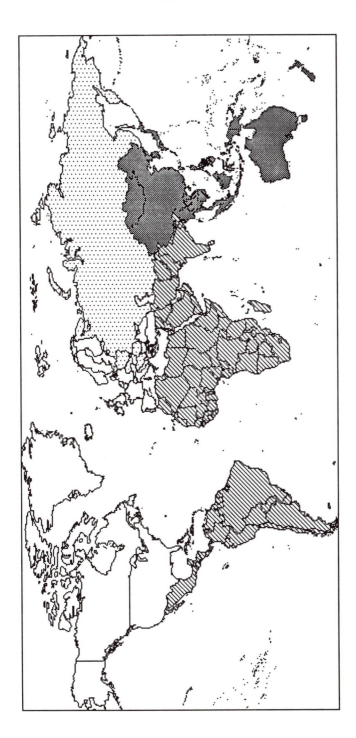

Figure 1. First, Second, Third and Fourth "Worlds." *Copyright with permission, PC Globe, Inc., Tempe, AZ 85282 (602)730-9000.*

Europe/the Soviet Union (later the ex-Soviet Union) playing a role relative to the European community not so different from the role of South America relative to North America.

2. *First World-Third World*: This relationship is characterized by a perennial tendency of the First World to penetrate culturally, economically, politically, and sometimes militarily into the Third World in order to secure its economic grip on raw materials and unskilled labor, plus markets for goods and services for investment. Of major significance recently are military interventions by the U.S. (directly or by proxy) south of the Rio Grande into Mexico, Central America, Panama, the Caribbean, and South America, using both low- and high-intensity conflict strategies, and in the Middle East. In the 1950s and 1960s the focus was more on East and Southeast Asia (Korean and Indonesian wars).

3. *First World-Fourth World*: This relationship is characterized by a new phenomenon, although one that has been coming for a long time: the emergence and consolidation of Japan as the most dynamic economic power in the world. In fact, the whole Fourth World has become a new player in the world capitalist market to the extent that Fourth World capitalism often looks more potent and competent than its First World counterpart, beating First World capitalism in general, and the U.S. in particular, at its own game over an increasing range of goods and services. We have seen the alarm the U.S. expressed when the Japanese electronics giant, Matsushita Inc. bought the Music Corporation of America (MCA) and apparently would acquire the concessions subsidiary operating in Yosemite National Park; negotiations were then made to return control of the concessions to the U.S. in January, 1991. U.S. concerns were again raised when Sony announced plans to buy Columbia Pictures, and when approval was granted to allow the acquisition of the Seattle Mariners baseball team by the Nintendo Corporation. As a result of these First World-Fourth World maneuverings, Japan in economic relation to the U.S. has become increasingly similar to the U.S.'s relation to Latin America and the Caribbean.

4. *Second World-Third World*: This relationship was characterized by Soviet assistance in the fight for liberation from colonialism and neocolonialism. The Soviet goal was to achieve political, military, and economic control after the struggle was over. While the fight for liberation worked, to a large extent, the efforts to achieve various controls did not. Soviet penetration of the Third World was probably coming to an end before socialism collapsed in Eastern Europe. The Second World effort to be First World politically, even if it was to a large extent Third World economically, did not succeed. This was partly because the Soviet Union was its own worst propaganda, partly because the First World had many attractive characteristics beyond its history of colonialism and

interventionism.

5. *Third World-Fourth World*: This relationship is characterized by increasingly heavy penetration of the Third World by the Fourth World, and particularly by Japan. Consequently, many countries of the Third World today look like a Japanese trade fair. Japan, therefore, is not only successful in penetrating economically the First World but is also an economic successor country to the old colonial powers in the Third World, and to the U.S. Will Japan follow up with cultural, political, and military penetration? And will the economic penetration also characterize its relation to the Second World (relation 6 below)?

6. *Second World-Fourth World*: Emptiness was the major characteristic of this relationship; there was little activity. Today it constitutes some kind of safety valve for world interaction. If activity by the U.S. is also considered, however, the Pacific theater of the Cold War could relocate. But such major relationships as ex-Soviet Union-China and ex-Soviet Union-Japan are still undefined, for good or bad, with a relatively open and very dynamic future.

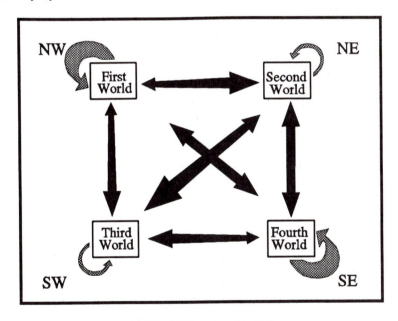

Figure 2. "World" Relationship Patterns.

Much more can be said about these six relations, but this is not the place for that type of extended discussion.[5] Suffice it to mention that the global problems of peace and security, arms races, disarmament and transamament were located above all in the First World-Second World relationship; and the problems of over-and under-development primarily in the First World-Third World relationship. With the "third worldization" of the Second World, this may change. The First World is increasingly over-developed and the Third World increasingly under-developed, with the exception of the tiny elites which have accepted and propagated exogenous models at the expense of endogenous needs and traditions. The center/periphery problem is usually perceived as located between the First and the Third Worlds, although it also has First World-Second World, Third World-Fourth World and, as of late, First World-Fourth World aspects to it, with the U.S. being rapidly "third-worldized" by Japan. As a result of the arms race aspects of the Cold War, some Center/Periphery relations will become the dominant feature of geopolitics. This can be seen in the U.S.-Iraq conflict/war, and the various arms and weapons technology sales made to developing nations by the First and Fourth Worlds.

In all these worlds the exploitation of nature is taking place, depleting resources and polluting the environment, thereby destabilizing a fragile ecosystem. Human beings are also being exploited; they are subordinated to machines which deprive them of some of the sense they might have had of being in control and mastering problems. They are exhausted and frustrated, even if some are materially better off. Poverty and misery hits hardest minorities and women, the very young and the very old and, most particularly, young and old minority women all over the world. The highly avoidable death of children—maybe 40,000 a day, 15 million a year—is an appalling consequence of squeezing weak human beings and fragile nature too hard.

In short, we live in a very problem-ridden world—full of promises, but also of possibilities that it may become worse. The question is: how is all of this reflected in news communication?

NEWS COMMUNICATION AS A FUNCTION OF THE NEWS PARADIGM

Obviously we cannot have all of this at the forefront of mass media or present in our minds every day. A selection of events must take place. There have to be gatekeepers, regulating the flow of information, deciding what should be communicated from the information overload. But what is positively and what is negatively selected? In an effort to explore this gatekeeping process over 30 years ago (in 1961), two simple factors were introduced by Galtung (we will explore this work in greater detail in Chapter 2).[6]

The first factor highlights the *center-periphery structure* of what is being communicated. There are center countries, located in the First, decreasingly in the Second, and increasingly in the Fourth Worlds; and there are periphery countries found mainly in the Third World. That yields three types of relations to be communicated: center-center, center-periphery, and periphery-periphery relations, with top priority given to center-center relations; medium priority to center-periphery relations (but then it should be the periphery of that particular center country, in terms of economic, political, military, and cultural relations); and lowest priority to periphery-periphery relations. All over the world, this hypothesis predicts that when international relations between countries are reported disproportionately much attention will be given to center-center relations, then center-periphery relations, and periphery-periphery relations will come last, heavily under represented.

The second factor concerns *the more precise content of what is being reported*. Twelve criteria events that must be satisfied in order for an event to become news were hypothesized, and the four most important ones in this context will be elaborated here:

1. The more the event concerns *elite countries*, the more probably that it will become a news item.
2. The more the event concerns *elite people*, the more probably that it will become a news item.
3. The more the event can be seen *in personal terms*, as due to the action of specific individuals, the more probably that it will become a news item.
4. The more *negative the event* in its consequences, the more probable that it will become a news item.

As they stand, these propositions look relatively plausible but also somewhat trivial. Writing in 1961, the perfect news item would have been for Khrushchev and Kennedy to kill each other during the Vienna summit meeting that year. The item would have scored high on all dimensions: top elite countries, top elite people, a highly personal relation between specific individuals, and a rather negative event.[7]

These four points have a ring of the obvious, but become less trivial when they are combined. The mock example just mentioned is based on an important point in news selection: *the additivity hypothesis*, suggested by the additive nature of the criteria. The more criteria an item satisfies, the more probable that it will become a news item. This also means that if the event is short on one or some of these dimensions, then it might compensate by ranking extra high on some of the other dimensions. That leads to the *complementarity hypothesis*, suggested by the complementary nature of the criteria. Thus, for non-elite countries or periphery countries to enter the picture they have to be "represented" by highly elite people, preferably heads of state, prime ministers, or possibly foreign ministers. That immediately gives an overly elitist image of periphery countries, as devoid of other human beings, populated only by elite persons and the "masses." The latter will only enter the news when they starve, are killed, or generally perish in great numbers; in other words through super-negative events.

Correspondingly, for center countries, more structural (as opposed to personal, actor-oriented) aspects of events can be mentioned. In periphery countries what happens will much more likely be seen as the actions of a concrete person, "the strongman." Evidently that which has concrete actors behind it is more newsworthy. It is an "event." The slow or quick workings of structures, that is to say processes, are not events but rather "permanents" in the sense of always being there.[8] Nevertheless, a center country is so newsworthy in and by itself that it may be forgiven for producing permanents and not always events. Routine elections, parliamentary proceedings, or cabinet processes are reported in spite of being orderly and institutionalized with no element of the sudden and unexpected. Hence we have what may be considered "press release journalism" in many news items reported by world newspapers and broadcast news.

From the Third World, personalized disorder such as corruption is expected and reported. Most important, if a country is in the periphery, then news must be even more negative to compensate for its periphery origin. As a consequence, we are left with an image of periphery countries as places where negative things happen beyond the ordinary, particularly events rather than permanents—such as tidal waves, earthquakes, hurricanes. When persons are involved it would be in the act of military coups, assassinations, and so forth. Only rarely would we find elections, parliamentary proceedings and cabinet processes reported as a matter cf course.

In the same vein, elite people can have positive events happen to them and they may still be judged newsworthy. Elites marry and have children in the newspapers; ordinary people, will not enter the news through such events. They only qualify through disasters, collective family suicide, or similar occurrences. The masses are gray, with danger spots. Only the irregularities command the attention of news.

In combining these factors, we cannot escape the conclusion that reporting about the periphery countries will be not only scant and quantitatively insignificant, but also highly negative, and even more so for news about periphery people in periphery countries. Of course, attention is drawn to local problems of periphery countries precisely for that reason, and no one would argue that there should be no reporting about drought, famine, and starvation. The point, however, coming out of the theoretical positions taken here, is the following: such reporting is detached from its context, generated by the news paradigm rather than by social reality, projected onto the periphery country as typical of such countries, and not seen in its structural context as partly created and constantly reproduced by strong forces in the relation to the industrialized world in general and to the First World in particular. This type of reporting is probably mainly serving one function: confirming to people in center countries what a miserable life people have in those periphery countries, and consequently how fortunate people in center countries really are for not being there nor being members of periphery countries.

What kind of impact will this type of information-communication paradigm have on our knowledge and perception of global problems? When it comes to peace-security-dis/transarmament issues, the archetype will be the top level disarmament conference, that is, the "summit" meeting. Elite persons from elite countries are meeting. They are addressing each other face to face, in highly personal ways, drawing on a "personal chemistry" presumably above structures. The only news problem is whether the outcome will be positive or negative. As we know, it has usually been negative, thereby making perfect news— though with the rider that the higher the level of the participants, particularly when they are heads of state, the more easily can the camel of positive events nevertheless pass through the needle's eye of the information channel. The sum, the total newsworthiness will still be high, in spite of the news being good.

But isn't this good? Doesn't this mean that such negotiations will simply get adequate coverage? No. The point is that the underlying paradigm for news communication will dominate the perspective on disarmament negotiations much more than vice versa. The structure of arms production, every day, hour, and minute, goes on un- or underreported. And when more ordinary people—such as ambassadors—negotiate, the tendency will be to focus on negative outcomes, and whatever little they may achieve may go under-reported.[9] As a result, pressure will build up for more summit meetings, and whatever they might produce will be overreported in an uncritical manner. Needless to say, public expectations will tend to be disappointed. The game will then be thrown back to the more ordinary level, and here the news will make the results look even more meager. The result is a frustrated public thrown into a cycle of events not of their own making and not knowing what to expect, not to mention what to demand.

There is little reason to defend disarmament conferences organized according to the "balanced, mutual and controlled" arms reductions paradigm. Under these conditions, except when a new weapons system has matured sufficiently to make both parties want to get rid of the old systems, agreement cannot be reached because symmetry will never be perfect.[10] To make progress some elements of imbalance, asymmetry, and unilateralism is needed, as in the INF agreement of December 1987. A first step has to be taken by one of the parties. Since disarmament conferences are actor-oriented phenomena, with individuals participating, they make more news than the process of build-up of arms on both sides and of belligerent attitudes, enemy images, and the piling-up of unresolved conflict material going on simultaneously. Balance makes for a better show, like a sports competition between equals. The traditional disarmament conference provides an excellent stage for the theater model of news to unfold: elite countries and people who are personalized and unsuccessful.

Dramatically underreported was the continuous quantitative and qualitative growth of the peace movement in West and East, in the First and Second Worlds; numerous countries, well prepared, more knowledgeable and able to exert pressure on political decision makers by making the political costs of more armament too high. Only street demonstrations are reported, not the countless small acts of a patient peoples' diplomacy. When demonstrations decrease in numbers the wrong conclusion is derived: the peace movement is dead. Maybe it had moved inside political parties and other corridors of power instead?—for instance, inside the inner circles of power in Moscow and in Bonn, to name two very relevant places, and not in Washington and London. What about the eye-to-eye relation to the state police in Leipzig on October 9, 1989? Perhaps that is the major reason why the Cold War is over—it was symptomatically underreported.

Turning to development issues, the same overreporting of conferences is noticeable since they have the great advantage of being events—a condition underlying the four criteria mentioned earlier. Such conferences mark points in time. Even if they are stretched over months and years, at least the opening and concluding sessions fall between two editions of a newspaper and major newscasts on radio and television. Thus, development issues are projected onto the conference schedules and calendars of the year, while the continuous working of the structures of ecological and human degradation of various kinds, and the heroic efforts by people's organizations to counteract these phenomena usually pass unreported. They may be the subject of articles and books, but they will not appear on the front page of a newspaper under the headline, "Exploitation today the same as yesterday!" or "10,000 children saved by oral rehydration therapy last year!"

Direct violence makes for journalism because it is an event; structural violence for statistics because it is a permanent. Permanents can also be reported in statistical form, and those statistics might not be so unattractive on the front page as news editors seem to think (thus *U.S.A. Today* has a little statistical corner in the left hand bottom of the first page). It might actually be a good idea for a newspaper to have some kind of index of the level of violence, or exploitation, or repression, somewhere on the top of the front page, as a consistent reminder of constant, or only slowly changing, factors. If this is done for meteorological temperature and pressure, why not also for political temperature and pressure?

News as we know it will only reflect the tip of the iceberg, or the crest of the wave, and not the more solid structure/process type of phenomena occurring all the time. This will be even more the case for periphery people, particularly in periphery countries. They will lose their individuality and will be represented as "masses," particularly in communication outlets of the left, where it is often thought progressive to report about people as if they were physical entities. (This is where the unfortunate term "mass" usually comes from.) The structural aspect overshadows the individuality of the actors.

There are, of course, efforts by those who piece together the news to see faces in the crowd, picking out one or two victims of structural violence, with names and addresses. This in itself is praiseworthy because the news becomes more human. News is usually not only individualized but also privatized at the expense of any kind of structural insight into what makes these people victims. The human interest element of the story overshadows any social analysis. Earthquakes and hunger become personalized but the stories are often trivial. There is no mention of such social factors as which parts of the population live in houses that are most easily destroyed by an earthquake, or who are most hit by a drought when water is used for grazing cattle for beef export, and not for the farming population in general. The individuality of the actors overshadows the structural aspect. As Helder Camara is reported to have said: "When I help the poor, people call me a saint. When I say why they are poor, they call me a communist." It should be possible to do both; to understand both the actor and the structure.

Due to the highly dramatic confrontation of the First and Second Worlds in most of the Cold War period, this particular type of center-center relation will tend to penetrate and overshadow all other kinds of news generated from all other relations among the four worlds. News stories were usually seen in "East-West" terms. In other words, it was not only a question of center-center relations dominating quantitatively, but also of qualitative penetration into other news categories with efforts to see the other five relationships in terms of the first one. Of course, this was above all a U.S.-style reductionism, used during the Cold War to attribute all problems to "communism." Partly due to the power of the U.S. in general, and the U.S. press (agencies) in particular, this also became the Western style.

The perspective taken here also explains certain features of how the Fourth World, particularly Japan, is reported. The build-up of the Japanese economy has gone on for a very long time. It went unreported, or at least underreported, because it was a process, not an event; moreover, it happened in a periphery (at the time) country. Then, suddenly Japan was discovered, because the First World began to worry about foreign competition and even to initiate actions, such as demands for "voluntary restraint." Just as the underpayment by the First World for oil supplies went undiscovered until prices were forced up in 1973, so too the high level of Japanese industrial achievement went unnoticed until the country's export prices were suddenly seen as very low, meaning highly competitive. This was in addition to the quality being very high—a fact not exactly overreported.

What comes suddenly is tainted with an air of the devious, of a plot, a sudden conspiracy, concocted by oil sheikhs or by "Japan Incorporated." In a similar vein, the concern for the "debt burden" is hardly motivated by sympathy for poor people in the Third World as much as for what this means for the "World Banking System," Third World revolts, "instability," and so forth. The truth is that all of this was predictable to anyone knowing anything about the issues involved and the processes under way; in other words, all that is effectively hidden by the pseudo-reality created by the news paradigm.

The argument is not that news communication should become an article service written by social scientists; that would be tantamount to introducing the opposite bias. The point is that the world image we receive through this pattern of news communication has a built-in bias in not reporting the continuity in distant phenomena. As a result, when there are social explosions, they appear as incomprehensible and (hence) unnecessarily threatening because the prehistory has gone unreported, and the more so the further removed from us they are. The Middle Eastern Gulf crisis of late 1990 and early 1991 is a typical example. Contributing to this, of course, are the usual misunderstandings about Japan and the Arab and Islamic worlds. Japan is often seen as a capitalist country, even as a part of the West, with no understanding of the country's cultural and structural specificities. The fact that Japan, just as China, might have her own agenda and strategies, different from, and even at variance with, those of the West (and is entirely entitled to this), is also rarely mentioned or explored except as something devious. The same applies to the Arab and Islamic strivings for unity and autonomy, ridding themselves of what is seen as remnants of colonialism.

NEWS COMMUNICATION AS A FUNCTION
OF OCCIDENTAL COSMOLOGY

Let us now try to delve more deeply into the structure of news communication. The general thesis is that it cannot be detached from its sociocultural context. News communication is also shaped by an occidental deep ideology and deep structure in general, a characteristically Western "social cosmology"[11] which also shapes Western technology, foreign and domestic policy, art and science, work and leisure, and so on. Whereas the news paradigm of the preceding section was specific to news communication, occidental cosmology is not.

Within that social cosmology six themes with articulations in the field of news communication can be singled out:

1. *Space.* There is a Western inclination to see the world as divided into three parts: Center, Periphery, and an outer periphery of Evil, with the West, of course, in the Center. This perspective is not only found in the Center, however, but also in any Periphery under Western influence where many people see themselves as living in a Periphery with the West as the center. News communication is one expression of this, making it normal for an African or Latin American country to find very little about its neighbor country in the newspapers, and then only as seen through the eyes of the metropolitan country. This situation has been improving in recent decades, though, with an increasing tendency for developing countries to report what happens in and to other developing countries (see review of the literature in Chapter 2).[12] However, in the Center that trend will be overshadowed by the fight against Evil, "Communists," "Muslim fanatics," and "Blacks." Who ever read about "Christian," or "Shinto," or "White" terrorists?[13]

2. *Time.* There is a tendency in the West to believe not only in progress, but also in the possibility of a crisis, and after that crisis some kind of *Enduzustand*, a final state of affairs, or catharsis. This applies only to the Center, however. The Periphery is not a part of the progress, particularly not any obstinate evil part of the Periphery that refuses to be incorporated. In part, this accounts for the negative color of news communication. The Periphery is a place where, by definition, things go badly and/or where Evil originates or has more of a bite. Hence, it is correct and objective when news from the Periphery is negative.

How does this relate to the fact that news from the Center also tends to be negative? The following hypothesis is one possible answer: negative events are overreported in spite of a general faith in progress, precisely because when progress is normal, being negative they constitute news. If events had been positive, they would have been uninteresting, merely a part of the general move in the direction of something better—

perhaps believed in today somewhat less than before, due to the general idea that there is a crisis occurring.

In short, negativism can derive from four sources: the Periphery as a source of evil; the Periphery as a place where life is negative; the crisis as a phase in which life is negative; and the noncrisis Center where negative events are exceptional and become news for that very reason.

3. *Knowledge.* There is a general inclination in the West to see knowledge in terms of atomism and deductivism, a tendency to present reality in a fragmented, scattered way, dividing it into small bits that can be understood and "digested" one at a time. On top of this comes the tendency to try to tie all these bits and fragments of knowledge together in contradiction-free theoretical frameworks. The first tendency is certainly satisfied through news communication via the day in and day out reporting of what can be referred to as "news-atoms"—events that are limited in space and time to the there/then that through the communication channel are brought to the here/now of the printed page, the television screen or the newscast, usually with one or more actors whose actions, and possibly also motivations, are reported. The classical Greek dramatic unity of space, time and action is adhered to, and is highly compatible with the notion of atomism. In practice this means a never-ending subdivision of the world into small parts, some of them overselected and some underselected, projected onto the news media with no connecting links, be they deductive or otherwise. Instead the social cosmology is that connecting clue. Atomism, the basic detachability of events, is the basic underlying message, not the content. There is killing of trade union leaders one month; the signing of an International Monetary Fund agreement months later. No connection, not even the report that some people suspect a connection is presented via the news media.[14]

4. *Nature.* The occidental theme of person-over-nature is reflected in turning nature into a nonactor, reporting nature only *für mich* and not *an sich*, not in terms of nature's own balances, pain and pleasure, and development potential. The objection to this alternative view would be that such modes of reporting would be anthropomorphic; the counter-argument being that because nature is seen as so different from human beings, reporting becomes anthropocentric. Again, the projection of the problems of nature becomes like the projection of the problems of disarmament and development, perhaps onto a conference room that satisfies the dramaturgical rules of news reporting, in this case, some environmental conference.

5. *Persons.* There is a tendency to see people according to two general occidental themes, individualism and verticality, joined synergistically in competition: who is best, who is the worst, who is the winner,

who the loser? Whenever a social problem of any kind can be defined by this archetypical form, considerable advances have already been made toward it becoming news. Elections are not seen in terms of whether aspirations, hopes and interests are adequately articulated but of "who wins, who loses." Politics in general tends to be presented this way, focusing on whether political actors get their way in the struggle based on their power resources rather than on the validity of the politics they advocate. Even in the field of culture, music is reported as the pretext for a contest; art and literature are evaluated in terms of "Who is our leading artist," and so on. Thus, perspectives of both personalization and negativism can be served, since the focus is often as much on the loser as on the winner, on the fading star as on the rising one.

6. *The transpersonal*: A perennial occidental theme sees humans as subordinate to the supernatural, the Supreme Being. However, we live in a secularizing world so Supreme Being becomes Supreme Value. This makes us ask: what is the supreme value of news communication? Who is the god of news? Probably just the three letters, that it is *new*. Olds are blasphemy. News should not be olds; it is about as simple as that. With limited space this leads to a detachment of the recent from the lasting, of the event from the permanent, of today from yesterday and from time itself—the exception would be when new data, or "revelations," are unearthed about old events. Typographically, this tendency can be counteracted by having analytical articles on the front page and news items inside as is done in some newspapers of very high quality (e.g., *International Herald Tribune, The Guardian, The European, Le Monde*). Another idea would be to place reports on elite persons and/or elite countries deep inside the paper or in the middle rather than the beginning of a newscast. But generally, the newness and prominence of the news will serve as the basic guideline and distort the image of the world in the direction of the closest neighbors in time, space, and social space only.

More concretely, if the focus is on violence and on events rather than processes, the primacy of newness would direct attention towards direct violence rather than structural violence. People will be trained to conceive of the world in terms of the former rather than the latter. In order to see political or economic structural violence at work—commonly referred to as injustice, repression, or exploitation—a higher level of education would be needed to compensate for the difficulties in reporting and conceiving of structural categories undergoing slow processes of change.[15]

A conclusion to be drawn might be that we have the news communication we deserve. It sells on the market and is demanded by people in the occidental world because it is in strict conformity with the underlying occidental social cosmology. If so much in our societies can be seen as competitive struggles between concrete persons for elite positions, and between countries struggling for elite positions, with no scarcity of negative aspects to these struggles, then we get news reflecting such struggles. The opposite is equally true: because of our social cosmology we compete and struggle. And the media become major carriers of the cosmology, because they reflect above all that which is cosmology compatible. What is seen is seen because it fits. It is fit to print because it fits the cosmology; it is news because it is fit to print.

People demand what their collective subconscious commands them to demand. Ironically, that ongoing production, distribution, and consumption of distortions of reality of which one is not even aware—because the underlying cosmology is exactly that, deep in the collective subconscious—is often referred to as "freedom." The same could be said about a person born inside a prison, living among others of the same kind, with no check on his/her consciousness: s/he will certainly not refer to the prison as a prison, but as freedom, as it is the only known reality. The North American Hutterite Community writ large?

There is another consequence of this. What happens when people become conscious of the nature of the constraints on news communication, in terms of quantitative over and underrepresentation of certain structural categories, relations, and filters favoring certain types of dramatically constituted news compatible with the underlying cosmology? What happens when a body like UNESCO points out all of this and tries to pry the mass media loose from the extended family of occidental social cosmology articulations? The answer is obvious: any such effort would be referred to as "interference with freedom," or even as "censorship," forcing people out of their beloved thought prisons.[16]

On the other hand, there is reality to the metaphor. There could additionally be censorship at work in the second case. Having no choice, people can be forced to see only that which is compatible with the underlying filters—as is generally the case today. But they could also be forced to digest only that which is less compatible or even incompatible with the filters. A "high quality" news media, as argued in Chapters 4, 5, 6, and 7 would give more attention to periphery people in periphery countries, to how structures operate day in and day out, and to reporting positive factors that might demand a higher educational level of its readers. So what? Would that not be an argument for giving people that higher educational level? Is it not rather ethnocentric to assume that the image of reality compatible with certain prejudices of one's own civilization is necessarily correct, and that all other images can only come about because of lack of freedom?

This is a problem of consciousness and education, and not only of the reader/listener/viewer, but also of the journalist/editor. In addition, it is a market problem. Does it not stand to reason that there will be more demand for the cosmology-compatible than for the cosmology-incompatible? Is it strange if the night editor, as the final filter or gate-keeper, makes the headlines super-compatible, cuts out what is less fitting from a compatibility point of view, or gives it low visibility, hiding it deep inside the article? Is it strange that in the former socialist countries, in an effort to articulate some counter-cosmology, there were efforts to make news more periphery and more structure/process oriented, with the proverbial reporting of apple harvests and dam construction complete with land and industrial workers? Is it strange that the result is inexpensive since it costs less to report olds than news; but also somewhat boring because it is so monochromatic?

Much of this boils down to one precise problem: the more global the problems, the more we need a new global journalism. Clearly something has to be done about these massive biases; biases probably so massive that news can be better predicted knowing the sociocultural contexts than knowing actual events. Still is it possible to achieve a new journalism conscious of cosmological constraints, and be able to transcend one thought prison without entering another? Is it not better to be forced with than against one's will? The question may be more important than the answer and undoubtedly, the question will stay with us for some time. We will return to it at the end of this chapter. First, after having explored the structure of news, we look at the structure of world society again (and then once again, in more detail, in Chapter 3).

TOWARD A NEW WORLD INFORMATION AND COMMUNICATION ORDER

Structure and process, power, and underlying culture, provide the background against which the struggle for a new world information and communication order can be understood. It is generally assumed that the New International Economic Order (NIEO), initiated through the OPEC action in 1973 and the resolutions of the U.N. Special Sessions in the mid-seventies (1974-5), might provide a model for this process. More than a model, it might also pave the way for a new order, due to a certain primacy of economic matters.[17] It is then assumed that the New World Information and Communication Order (NWICO), above all, will deal with the more quantitative aspects, and not so much with the qualitative dimensions, of news communication.

Awareness of the underlying factors of the "social cosmology" type discussed above will probably be relatively low. NWICO will be a new "order," but not a new journalism. It would parallel the new international economic order as essentially a structural rearrangement, not challenging capitalism as such, but improving the position of the Third World (usually called "South") relative to the First World (usually called "North") on the world capitalist market.

NIEO can be conceived of as a process with the following five elements:

1. Better terms of trade for the Third World (leading to improved and/or decreased North-South trade);
2. More Third World control over productive assets in their own countries (nature, labor, capital, technology, management leading to import-substitution);
3. More Third World interaction (leading to increased South-South trade; Technical Cooperation between Developing Countries, TCDC as an example of ECDC, Economic Cooperation between Developing Countries);
4. More Third World counter-penetration (investment in "rich" countries, etc.); and
5. More Third World influence in world economic institutions, such as the World Bank, the International Monetary Fund, and UNCTAD, as well as in transnational corporations.

How far this total process has come is difficult to determine. It often looks as if the Third World has not even entered the first stage, except for the price of oil from the OPEC countries. The so-called North-South conflict is essentially a dialogue about the first phase, with the Third World very slowly becoming less convinced that the First World has any intention of structural change at all. The First World seems to be using the "dialogue" for anything but exactly that; in other words, using each conference for little more than preparing the agenda for the next, always pushing the issue ahead and never tackling it.

This does not mean, however, that there is no process of the NIEO kind going on in the world. On the contrary, the NIEO process could be seen as a recapitulation of the history of Japanese economic evolution, in line with the "flying geese theory."[18] Having carefully watched the terms of trade for their early export products, having kept control over productive assets, and having interacted with neighbors in East Asia, the Japanese are now certainly in the stage where counter-penetration into the First World has gone very far, including Japan-directed "joint ventures" cooperating with First World partners inside transnational corporations (such as automobile manufacturers). Plus, Japan for a long time has been able to claim the number two rank in the World Bank and will possibly one day be Number One (*ichiban*) there also, unless the European Community in the coming European Union is counted as one actor.

Perhaps it is not only Japan, but the Fourth World in general that could be viewed as the analytical category going through the NIEO stages. With world attention focused on the Third World's claims on the First World, the Fourth World proper—Japan, the Four Dragons, China—simply does it, forging ahead, translating the words into action as a split-off movement from the Third World, in the wake of Japan the pioneer. This is one major reason why they are classified as a separate world in this chapter; another is cultural (buddhist-confucian).

Imagine now the five points of the NIEO process, as described above, used as a predictive model for what will happen in the field of the NWICO. If this is a valid model, we might expect to find strong efforts to improve the First World-Third World terms of news exchange, with more symmetric representation; increasing Third World influence over information-communication assets; increasing news about other Third World countries in Third World media and lessening news about the First World; and increasing both Third World influences over First World communication institutions such as the "international" wire agencies, and attempts to control U.N. agencies in the field, such as the UNESCO and ITU. The recently proposed sale of UPI to the Arabic television network, Middle East Broadcasting Centre, Ltd. is one example.

Suppose, for a moment, that this process is carried out to its full range of consequences. Would we then get a balanced picture of the world, or an equally biased picture with the world turned upside down? There is some evidence for the latter interpretation. Anyone familiar with the Indian press will know how India-centered it is. The Indian press writes almost exclusively about India. But then, it can be argued, India is, if not a continent, at least a sub-continent. Nevertheless, the rest of the world, including the classical center countries, feature in very small news items, and usually in a rather unfavorable light; they are treated as if they were a periphery of India. Today, the Malaysian press and the Caribbean press, to take two other examples, also tend to write about their own regions, and much less about the "mother" countries than used to be the case there. This view is supported by some recent studies reviewed in Chapter 2.

In other words, the transformation process in this field of news exchange seems to be under way already, and has been under way for some time. But there is one major difference where the NWICO process went much further than the NIEO process: UNESCO. There is little

Third World control over international wire agencies at the moment. Efforts to set up international wire services, such as Prensalatina and the Inter-Press Service (IPS)[19] are not the same as penetrating, or even partially controlling, the world's major wire services, such as Reuters (originally designed for stock exchange reports), Associated Press (AP), United Press International (UPI), Agence France-Presse (AFP), and TASS (Telegrafnoye Agentstvo Sovietskovo Soyuza). Where NWICO is ahead of NIEO is in the Third World influence in UNESCO, the forum chosen for this structural transformation, as opposed to no or very little control over the World Bank and the International Monetary Fund. Third World control of UNCTAD (United Nations Conference on Trade and Development) is inconsequential because the First World can escape into WIPO (World Intellectual Property Organization) and GATT (General Assessment on Tariffs and Trades). But UNESCO is the only organization of its kind. The consequence of this instance of Third World control is well known: the Western accusation, led by the United States, that this control constitutes an intolerable case of anti-Western "politicization;" the outcome was the withdrawal of the United States (followed by England, et al.) from UNESCO, a process to be explored in Chapter 3.[20]

Clearly, the United States fully understood the significance of what was happening. In one sense, a truly New World Information and Communication Order would be even more important than a New International Economic Order. It has the potential of making people all over the world look at world politics in new ways. People would be much more interested in their own countries and regions and less mesmerized by center powers and superpowers. Positive and negative colorations of what happens in the world would be distributed differently. The (former) First World could be seen as a dangerous, violent place, exposed to sudden and unexpected events, partly stemming from nature (ecological degradation) and partly from wicked people inside the social structure. Inhabitants of developing countries (or countries in the other three worlds) might see their own countries as being in closer continuity with the past, changing or unfolding in sometimes slow, sometimes quick, processes. Instead of seeing the present Center as the part of the world from which salvation comes, it could be seen as a risky, even vicious place from which dangers originate, among them the possibility of a war with nuclear weapons or other means of mass destruction. The view of the Third World would thus be much more benign, that of the First World more highly critical. Generally speaking, this upside-down picture might be a more realistic perception, given the realities of today's world.

As a consequence of withdrawing from UNESCO, the U.S. was forced to react to preserve status quo by preserving status quo imagery.

To the extent political actions come out of political imagery one might argue that a whole world order, and not only an economic order, was at stake. A NWICO might pave the way not only for NIEO but for any other new international orders (technological, military, political) built and maintained by a new order of information and communication.

The strategy of the First World to prevent this from happening seems to be the same as in the economic field: control over the production, distribution, and consumption of news. What counter-action could the Third World take? As an example, consider First World control of what goes into producing a newspaper. There is, above all, newsprint (the paper itself); labor needed in the form of trained journalists; capital needed to finance the paper and the media in general; research underlying the transformation of events into news; and finally, information-communication management which is often the most difficult. This makes a strong combination.

The only answer to First World control over these resources would be for Third World countries to become independent on all five production factors listed above, singly or together with other countries in the same predicament.[21] Of course, this can be done in a pluralistic manner, with different types of news orientation within any given Third World country, and several newswire agencies coexisting. Each one would have a particular specialty or tendency rather than one common recipe and they would achieve this without governmental control. Why should the world labor under one monolithic recipe, an occidental tradition that has the gall to refer to itself as freedom, in spite of all the constraints under which it operates? The solution is not to substitute one prison for the other. If each discourse or metadiscourse is some kind of mental prison, then at least there should be several of them with some possibility of choice.

One further speculation might be ventured. Let us assume for the sake of the argument that the economically successful part of the world right now is not the First World with its multiple crises, nor the Second World with a rigidity that turned into stagnation and hence had to be loosened up, nor the Third World with its bottomless misery and increasing discrepancy between elites and the general population, but the Fourth World, where both elites and the populace seem to be undergoing processes of economic growth, in a more parallel manner (with the important exception of China). If this is the case, how would it be reflected in a New World Information and Communication Order?

Any analysis of the structure of foreign news during the last 20 years would reveal very clearly how much more prominent the Fourth World has become in First World news reporting (see Chapter 2). It has probably also become much more prominent in its own news reporting.[22] But what about the Third World? Has the Third World really discovered what goes on in East Asia? Or, are these countries basically so obsessed with First World-Third World relations, with occasional attention to First World-Second World events, that they exclude the Fourth World from their news horizon? Does the Third World see Japan as just a part of the West, which it evidently is not, and the other Fourth World countries as part of the South, which they equally evidently are not, as witnessed by their very rapid industrialization and increasing share in the world market? In short, does the Third World make the specificity of the Fourth World, the Southeastern corner of the world, invisible, much like the First World does with the fatness of the NIC (Newly Industrialized Countries) formula?

It should be remembered that the West is not the only civilization that sees itself as the center of the world. So does China, perceiving the rest of the world less as a Periphery than as "barbarian," dangerous, uninteresting, possibly exotic, sometimes useful, but definitely not as something of which China is a part.[23] And so does Japan, with a tendency to see the rest of the world as one big "resource," in terms of markets and access to advanced technologies in the earlier stages, and in terms of markets and access to raw materials in later stages.[24] Would that not lead to a news image of other parts of the world as exotic, distant, dangerous places that exist *für mich* and not *an sich*? And if this is coupled with a possible major revolution in telematics, given the ascendancy of Japan in teleprinters, telex, facsimile, and other voice and data transmission technologies, would the conclusion not be that the New World Information and Communication Order could be very much like the old one, only with the center in the Fourth World rather than the First, and certainly not in the Third?

One argument put forth in the New Information Order debate holds that new, emerging technology will help place Third World countries on a more "equal" footing with the rest of the globe, and its people on a more equal footing with the elites.[25] The assumption here is that such technology will be extremely affordable and accessible to a larger population than older technology (e.g., mass media). Given the many countries of the world where large portions of the population still do not own television sets, radios, and telephones, this position can be criticized. Computers will most likely continue to be much more expensive than television receivers, at least for the foreseeable future. Use of many voice and data transmission devices also would require higher levels of literacy than that which currently exist. The net result is that the Third World, and the less privileged layers of the First and Second World, will probably not gain markedly through the use and adoption of many of these new technologies. Even with the hardware better distributed, the gap between senders and receivers of communication remains difficult to bridge. Yet as Sean MacBride observed, "I would not like anything . . . to be construed as advocating a slowing down in the use of technological developments. I would rather urge that, concurrently with the utilization of technology, there should be a constant assessment of the moral and social implications that will result from modern technology."[26] Perhaps this is the area that has been most overlooked. The zeal to implement new technology-based communication processes often exceeds efforts to study all-important societal effects!

While Fourth World Centers might dominate technologically, in other realms they do not. This is for one simple reason. The Centers in the Fourth World do not labor under the same missionary zeal to propagate themselves, their cultures, and structures worldwide, as does the First World. Marketing of economic products is certainly done, out of commercial interest; but that is something different and much more limited. If anything, it is more likely that the countries in the Fourth World will have a relatively self-contained news system, circulating detailed news among themselves, less interested in what goes on inside "Barbaria" and "Resourcia," except insofar as it is directly relevant to their own operations.

The future statistical distribution of news items will probably become less First World centered. But neither the Second nor the Third World will command enough economic/political/cultural power to say "We are the new Centers," and even if they may say so they will not convince anyone, including themselves, of the truth of any such statement. The countries of the Fourth World have economic power, as well as considerable political and cultural *Ausstrahlung*. But their world concept is different. They may be less interested in being seen by others as the Center, content with their own judgment to that effect—with the possible exception of Japan.

Hence, the prospects are perhaps not so bad. The current First World Center is slowly being dethroned, relatively speaking, and there is no single obvious successor. A more symmetrical pattern of global communication might become possible. What a challenge for a truly global newspaper, and not only one but many! But not one like the *International Herald Tribune*, so biased toward the West, in general, and the United States, its country of origin, in particular. A *new* journalism, a *global* journalism, a problem-conscious, socially conscious journalism, at home in the world as a whole, is still far away.

CONCLUSION: TOWARD GLOBAL AND HUMAN JOURNALISM

In this effort to find some major trends in the structure and process of international news information and communication, two phenomena warrant closer examination.

First, there appears to be little doubt that a *quantitative* transformation is taking place, with somewhat less relative emphasis on the former Center and somewhat more on the former Periphery. It is difficult to tell, however, whether this is being accompanied by a similar *qualitative* transformation, changing the character of what is regarded as news itself. More power to the Periphery, both on the printed page, in the loudspeaker, on the television screen, and in the production of news, does not mean that the product has changed. It might, in fact, have become even worse, as is been evidenced by junk newspapers (e.g., tabloids in the U.S., Great Britain, Germany and Scandinavia), and junk radio and television reporting (e.g., "happy talk" news and other entertainment-based program formats in the U.S. and elsewhere as the line between information, advocacy, and entertainment becomes increasingly blurred) in the First World, with even more elitism, personalization, and negativism than ever before. This is often justified by appeals to "human interest," as when the front page of a newspaper or lead story of a telecast degrades itself and its journalists—not to mention its readers and viewers and those involved—by presenting rape, murder, natural disasters, and elite scandal as the major components of the world news that day.

Second, communication has become more relevant to global problems than ever before, but it may also have become increasingly counterproductive. A vast array of detached space/time events or "atoms" presented as news constitute a set of events, not a set of problems. A problem has a beginning in its roots and a possible end in its solution. It is a "molecular," a composite, and not an atom. A global problem spaces the world. On the complex way from problem to solution, alternatives have to blossom and the carriers of those alternatives, strategic actors, must be mobilized or at least identified and noticed. But this is not the way reporting is done. All such linkages are regarded as "ideological," "biased," not worthy of attention, or as consuming too much valuable news space.

In short, little progress is being made toward global and human journalism. The structure of news is sliding and jumping all over the globe. But the product remains basically the same. The content is about the same, relevant but biased. This seems not so strange given the universality of the news paradigm and the diffusion of occidental cosmology. Yet precisely because a New World Information and Communication Order is not enough, we need a new global and hunan journalism, liberated from visible and invisible repression, capable of reflecting in its social communication the dialectic between the global nature of our problems and our perception of them.[27]

But how? The 1976 Nairobi UNESCO General Conference resolved that the mass media should play a critical role in the spectrum of international relations. There is no reason why news media cannot significantly advance the causes of peace, international relations, global resource protection, and promote the needs of the disadvantaged.[28] Riding on this theme, the final chapters of this book are an effort to say something concrete about this new global and human journalism in four major issue areas: peace (Chapter 4), development (Chapter 5), environment (Chapter 6), and war reporting (Chapter 7). We hope to help set an agenda for international journalism in the upcoming years. By working to fulfill these journalistic goals, we may find that world journalism is indeed moving closer to the press the Nairobi delegates envisioned.

Before we move to our universal values, we must first go deeper into the two major themes explored so far, international news flow (Chapter 2) and the new international order (Chapter 3). In doing so there will inevitably be some repetitions to make the chapters more self-contained. Just as they tell the passengers when the flight is arriving late: thanks for your patience.

NOTES TO CHAPTER 1

1. Teresa Watanabe, "Report Blames U.S. for Own Trade Ills," *Los Angeles Times*, August 21, 1990, p. D1.

2. Victor H. Palmieri, "U.S. Takes a Back Seat in Third World," *New York Times*, August 26, 1990, sec. 3, p. 13.

3. John Moody and Strobe Talbott, "On Drugs, Debt and Poverty," *Time*, November 27, 1989, p. 14.

4. Despite the slower growth pace of some countries in Asia, the region as a whole continues to dominate world economic growth figures: 9.3% in 1988 and 5.4% in 1989 (versus world economy growth of 3.2%). Examples of some individual nation performances: Thailand, over 10% in 1988 and 1989; Vietnam, 5.9% in 1988 and 8.2% in 1989; Indonesia, about 5% in 1988 and 1989; Laos: 2.1% in 1988 and 4% in 1989. "Asian Development Outlook 1990," Asian Development Bank report; see Maria L. LaGanga, "Asia's Economic Growth Tops Rest of World," *Los Angeles Times*, April 30, 1990, p. D2.

5. See Johan Galtung, *World Politics of Peace and War* (forthcoming) for a detailed discussion of this geopolitical typology.

6. See Johan Galtung and Mari Holmboe Ruge, "The Structure of Foreign News: The Presentation of the Congo, Cuba and Cyprus Crises

in Four Norwegian Newspapers," in *Essays in Peace Research, Vol. IV* (Copenhagen; Christian Ejlers, 1980), pp. 118-151. Originally published in *Journal of Peace Research* (1965), pp. 64-91.

7. For generations Western historians were faulted for similar short-comings. The tendency to write only histories of elite individuals is known as the "great man" tradition. The French *Annales* school, focusing on the structure and process of daily life and common people, can be seen as a reaction to this tendency.

8. See Johan Galtung, *Methodology and Ideology* (Copenhagen: Christian Ejlers, 1977), Chapters 8 and 9.

9. Thus, negative outcomes are seen as normal and are compatible with the anonymity of some disarmament functionaries, such as ambassadors. When top people are involved, positive news may be more easily permitted, and even should appear. Consider, for example, the overly positive reporting of the Geneva meeting between two superpower foreign ministers, Schultz and Gromyko, in early January 1985, leading to nothing. For a fine study of how news thrives on the combination of elite, person, and negative, see Karl Eric Rosengren, Jay G. Blumler, and Denis McQuail, "Special Issue On News Diffusion," *European Journal of Communication*, 2 (2) (1987), focusing on the assassination of the Swedish Prime Minister, Olof Palme, in 1986.

10. Johan Galtung, *There Are Alternatives: Four Roads to Peace and Security* (Nottingham: Spokesman, 1984), also in German, Norwegian, Swedish, Dutch, Italian, Spanish and Japanese editions.

11. See Johan Galtung, T. Heiestad and E. Rudeng, "On the Last 2500 Years in Western History," in *The New Cambridge Modern History, Companion Volume*, ed., P. Burke (Cambridge: Cambridge University Press, 1979), chapter XII, for a discussion of Western cosmology in a historical perspective.

12. But this was certainly not the case in 1961 when the famous study by the Wilbur Institute for Communication Research of Stanford University and the *Institut francais de presse* of the University of Paris of the flow of news among 13 countries was conducted. See Wilbur Schramm's classic book, *Mass Media and National Development* (Urbana, Il: University of Illinois Press, 1964), pp. 60-63, for major findings and interpretation. The study by Tapio Varis, "The International Plan of Television Programs," *Journal of Communication* (Winter 1984), is summarized with the following words: "A major study covering 69 countries finds few overall changes since 1973 in the pattern of program flow, but does indicate a trend toward greater regional exchanges along with the continued dominance of a few exporting countries." That the structure of international news coverage is quite similar across systems is mentioned in the literature, for instance in Annabelle Sreberny-Mohammadi,

"The 'World of the News' Study," *Journal of Communication* (Winter 1984).

13. See Mohamed Kamal, "Why Tar Arabs and Islam," *New York Times*, February 16, 1987: "The U.S. media never say 'Christian' or 'Shinto' terrorists."

14. See Helga Theunert and Bernd Schorb, *Gewalt im Fernsehen und Ihre Sozialien Folgen.* (Munich: Institut Jugand-Film-Fernsehen, 1983).

15. See David Pion-Berlin, "The Political Economy of State Repression in Argentina," in *The State as Terrorist: The Dynamics of Governmental Violence and Repression*, eds., Michael Stohl and George A. Lopez (Westview, Conn.: Greenwood Press, 1984), Chapter 5.

16. We are, of course, thinking of the UNESCO debate in connection with the very important report by the MacBride Commission, entitled *Many Voices, One World* (Paris: International Commission for the Study of Communication Problems, UNESCO, 1980). The title is beautiful, but given the argument that the press has been standardized by the Western style, the opposite title, *One Voice, Many Worlds* might have been more appropriate.

17. Johan Galtung, "The New International Economic Order and the Basic Needs Approaches: Compatibility, Contradiction and/or Conflict?," *Alternatives* 4 (1978), pp. 455-476; and Johan Galtung, "Towards a New International Technological Order?," *Alternatives* 4 (1979), pp. 277-300.

18. For reference to Akamatsu Kaname's "Flying Geese Development Theory," see Okita Saburo, "Japan, China and the United States: Economic Relations and Prospects," *Foreign Affairs* (Summer 1979), p. 1102.

19. In due time the creation of the IPS will stand out as a watershed in the entire history of international news reporting, and the audacious and important work of people such as Roberto Savio and Marc Nerfin in that connection will be duly appreciated. They are successfully counter-acting the type of reporting so well analyzed in the study by Mort Rosenblum, *Coups and Earthquakes: Reporting the World to America* (New York: Harper Colophon Books, 1979). Coups and earthquakes are seen as typical and even endemic in the Third World. But accidents and certain other tragedies are seen as atypical and avoidable in the First World, and elite responsibility is underplayed as demonstrated by the research of the Glasgow News Group [their series: Glasgow University Media Group, *Bad News* (London: Routledge & Kegan Paul, 1976); Glasgow University Media Group, *More Bad News* (London: Routledge & Kegan Paul, 1980); Glasgow University Media Group, *Really Bad News* (London: Writers and Readers, 1982)] and by Richard C. Vincent, Bryan K. Crow and Dennis K. Davis, "When Technology Fails: The Drama of

Airline Crashes in Network Television News," *Journalism Monographs*, (1989), No. 117.

20. The withdrawal of the U.S. became effective January 1, 1985. UNESCO still had the opportunity to continue to work on these important matters, however. In addition, UNESCO could have contemplated slashing staff salaries by the 25% that corresponded to the U.S. contribution mainly by eliminating top, overpaid positions. At present, these salaries are often too high and easily attract money-oriented, rather than task-oriented, people. But nothing like that happened. In fact, the number of top, overpaid positions may actually be increasing, while the future of some long-standing programs now hangs in jeopardy of elimination. As for the U.S., the Reagan administration got massive media support knowing that UNESCO-baiting went well with their worry about their "freedom of access" to Third World events. A larger review of these activities can be found in Chapter 3. For an excellent historical analysis, with thoughtful emphasis on events surrounding the U. S. withdrawal from UNESCO, see William Preston, Jr., Edward S. Herman and Herbert I. Schiller, *Hope & Folly: The United States and UNESCO 1945-1985* (Minneapolis, Minn: University of Minnesota Press, 1989).

21. Again, IPS stands out as a concrete effort in that direction. For examples, see chapter 5.

22. Thus, the boisterous, quite self-conscious, Japanese reporting about their country today is rather different from what it was only 15 years ago.

23. Johan Galtung, "The Chinese Path to Development," *Review* 3 (1982), pp. 460-486.

24. Johan Galtung, "On The Possible Decline and Fall of Japan," *East Asia*, Vol. 1 (Frankfurt : Campus Verlag, 1983), pp. 1-26.

25. Pool and others have argued that new communication technologies may help resolve problems in the Third World; see Ithiel de Sola Pool, "The Influence of International Communication on Development," *Media Asia*, 6(3) (1979), pp. 149-156. Schiller, on the other hand, cautions against such technologies noting that they could result in increased dependency by Third World countries on the industrialized world; see Herbert I. Schiller, "Whose New International Economic Information Order?" *Communication*, 5(2) (1980), pp. 299-314.

26. Sean MacBride, "Foreword" to *The Myth of the Information Revolution*, ed., Michael Traber (London: Sage, 1986).

27. Johan Galtung, "On the Dialectic Between Crisis and Crisis Perception," *International Journal of Comparative Sociology*, 1-2 (1984), pp. 4-32.

28. Kaarle Nordenstreng makes similar observations in his article, "Bitter Lessons," *Journal of Communication*, 34 (Winter 1984), pp. 139-142.

Also see forthcoming book by authors on news as an agent of discourse: Johan Galtung and Richard C. Vincent, *Glasnost—U. S. A: Missing Political Themes in U.S. Media Discourse* (Cresskill, N.J.: Hampton Press, forthcoming).

CHAPTER 2

The International News Flow: Reflections on a Debate*

We must conclude that the flow of news among nations is thin, that is unbalanced, with heavy coverage of a few highly developed countries and light coverage of many less developed countries, and that, in some cases at least, it tends to ignore important events and to distort the reality it presents. — Wilbur Schramm, 1964 [1]

TWO ATTITUDES TO "NEWS"

Let us begin in a light vein, with two anecdotes.

During the years 1962-1965, one of the authors was living in Chile as UNESCO professor. As a Norwegian he would sometimes scan Chilean newspapers for news about his own, rather stable, rather well organized country. But all he could find about Norway in the news were two reports during September 1963.

The first was a report that the Norwegian government had fallen in connection with an issue related to the safety of mines in Spitsbergen. The Labor government, instead of apologizing which they could easily have done, tried to belittle the issue. Against them were not only the conservative parties (not usually that concerned with workers' safety), but also the small Socialist People's Party that was holding the balance of power in parliament, (the *Storting*). Exit the Labor government.

Three weeks later Norway was again in the news. The conservative government had fallen. After presenting its budget proposals they were outvoted both by the Labor Party and the Socialist People's Party together, for obvious reasons. Enter the Labor government.

---

* Portions of this chapter began as a paper by Richard C. Vincent and Dennis K. Davis. See Richard C. Vincent and Dennis K. Davis, "Trends in World News Research and the Implications for Comparative Studies," Paper presented at the 39th annual conference of the International Communication Association, San Francisco, May 26, 1989.

Student reaction was interesting: "We did not know that Norway had such an unstable political system." Well, this was about as much instability as there had been since 1945, shaking Norway for certain, but not exactly typical of the country. As a far away place, not much was reported anyhow. For anything to be worth reporting it would, of course, have to be an *event*, by definition the difference between the state of affairs today and the state of affairs yesterday. The two governments that collapsed both satisfied that criterion. In addition, there was also something negative in the events reported, at least to someone.

The second anecdote is from 1969 and from a very different country, Burma. The same author was on a brief visit, actually on his honeymoon, and hungry for news. There was a kiosk in a main square in Rangoon with newspapers displayed in the window. He went in and asked for a foreign paper and got one immediately, *The Observer*. Full of expectations he started reading the paper as soon as he was out on the street. Finding the news familiar yet somewhat strange, it called for a closer inspection. The newspaper was 3 years old. A visit back to the shop in a somewhat complaining mood offered little restitution. With considerable justification the shop owner replied: "You asked for a newspaper didn't you? When you try to buy a book does it really matter to you whether the book was printed yesterday? I sold you a newspaper. Moreover, if you have a closer look at the news you may not find it that different from the newspaper you were looking for." A further glance at *The Observer* confirmed his general point of view. But there might have been some specifics about the current week in which we were living, possibly somewhat different from that week reported in *The Observer* 3 years earlier. And we were not living in that week.

Morale: it is not that obvious what constitutes a newspaper in general and news in particular. Nor is it that obvious what kind of relationship there is between "news" and the "real world," however we choose to conceive of that rather complicated relation.

EARLY NEWS FLOW RESEARCH

News professionals, government leaders, and academics have long been interested in studying and discussing the topic of news. This has resulted, in part, from an increasing awareness of the role and responsibility the news media play in the exchange of information in the contemporary world. Extensive research and writings have been generated on the topic of news, and these range from general commentaries and practitioners' experiences, to field and laboratory experiments. Since World War II, we also have become increasingly interested in the news process on the international level. It is on this level that print and broadcast information is exchanged across the globe, by a complex web of correspondents, editors, and news agencies. The implications are enormous and far-reaching. Much is at stake, including the control of international policy-making and economic stability, according to some critics. In 1963, one author wrote in his book, *The Press and Foreign Policy*: "[The press] may not be successful much of the time in telling its readers what to think, but it is stunningly successful in telling its readers what to think about. The editor may believe he is only printing the things that people want to read, but he is thereby putting a claim on their attention, powerfully determining what they will be thinking about . . ."[2] The recognition that the press does indeed have the power to command attention and help mold and tailor public opinion has not changed with time. While some 30 years have passed since this observation was made, it is just as appropriate a comment now as it was then. If anything, the power of the news media has become greater. Consider, for example, the increased level of dependence many had for print and electronic news media during the Persian Gulf War and its aftermath.

The nature and function of the international news process are topics that have garnered wide interest in contemporary society. World leaders have come to realize the potential power of news media, and a number have demonstrated their ability to use, even manipulate, the press in efforts to sway public opinion. Others in government and various public leadership positions frequently discuss and debate the role of the press in society. We will look more closely at the formal debate as it has been conducted by government and industry leaders on a worldwide scale in the next chapter. At the moment we will concentrate on attempts, largely by the scholarly community, to come to some general understanding of the information flows between nations. This process is often referred to as "news flow."

Audience study (readership/viewership analysis) is another research perspective, but will not be discussed here. Audience studies assess the volume of news read/viewed/listened to by newspaper subscribers or broadcast audience members (mostly television), and analyze corresponding attitudes and motives. The news learning literature cited later in this book fits into this category of research.

In examining the existing literature, we find that content analysis and gatekeeping research have been the two principal approaches employed by news flow researchers. Content analyses tend to group news story or wire service content systematically into sets of predetermined categories. Gatekeeper studies are interested in various social and circumstantial matters which seem to influence editors in their selection of stories. Another form of research, agenda setting, combines content study with audience analysis to ascertain how the press influences the prominence of issues and the priority viewers and readers give to certain news items. Given the trends reviewed below, we find mostly content analysis represented in the news flow literature.

News flow researchers are interested in audience patterns of news consumption. While there has been scholarly interest in international communication and news flow or transaction as early as the 1920s, a major emphasis in research on the subject came only in the late 1940s and early 1950s.[3] In one of these studies, the purpose was to examine the flow of news involving the United States, Western Europe, West Germany, and India. It was found, not surprisingly, that news agencies were a paramount source of news for the average newspaper, and coverage tended to center on only a few dominant countries. It also found that newspaper editors did very little editing of stories from news agencies. As for international news, the study demonstrated that while the average United States newspaper was publishing a mere four columns of international news daily, European and Indian newspapers were printing even less. The International Press Institute (IPI) concluded that the average reader worldwide reads little foreign news in newspapers, and her/his knowledge of major foreign events is quite low.[4] This early research by the Institute was one of the studies which began to document that which would later be known as a "one-way flow" of information from developed to developing nations. We must keep in mind, however, that the IPI was established for the promotion of the more liberal notions of press freedom normally associated with the Western press. Its objective was also to help foster the growth of journalism in developing countries (meaning by that essentially "Western style" journalism).

Much of the early news flow research has been faulted for lacking a systematic theory. This did not change markedly until the introduction of two works by the late Wilbur Schramm.[5] Schramm concluded that international news flow was unbalanced and tended to favor "a few highly developed countries." He went on to criticize the international news process for its inability to identify important events and the tendency in some cases to "distort the reality it represents.[6] Schramm's work focused on a review of types of international news coverage and flow and institutional considerations which impact on international news flow. Following Schramm, researchers examined one or more of these variables.[7] In one study, Jim Hart measured the portion of international news published in eight English language newspapers, the *New York Times*, the *Washington Post*, the *Minneapolis Tribune*, and the *Philadelphia Inquirer* in the United States; and the *Manchester Guardian*, the *London Daily Telegraph*, the *London Daily Express*, and the *Times* of

London in Great Britain. The content analysis found that the British papers all devoted greater space to foreign news than did their American counterparts. The only positive finding that Hart could stress for the American sample was that the newspapers which allotted more space to foreign news (the *Times* and the *Post*) were "close" to the lower frequency British papers (*Guardian* and *Daily Express*). Actually, the *Times* was slightly ahead (.3%) of the *Guardian* whereas the *Post* fell behind the *Daily Express* (1.2%) in space allocations.[8] Ironically these findings seem to be quite different than those from the IPI study 20 years earlier. IPI's relations with the Western press, of course, presumably had some influence on the questions asked and the research design used in that analysis.

Worth mentioning here is a methodologically interesting 1970 article by L. Erwin Atwood. It combined portions of news flow and audience research perspectives. Correlated in the study were story preferences broken down by both readers and journalists. He did not examine international news flow or story preferences, however.[9]

PREDICTING "FLOW" VERSUS UNDERSTANDING OF DETERMINANTS

The international news flow literature is generally divided into two categories.[10] The first paradigm attempts to understand and predict volume and direction of news.[11] In Hester's work it is assumed that volume and direction are influenced by independent variables, involving various levels of national hierarchy, cultural affinities, and economic relations dominances and weaknesses. Hester hypothesizes, for example, that international information flow would move in greater volume from "high" ranking nations to "low" rather than the converse order, would be tempered if one nation is considered a threat to another, would be influenced by cultural and historical affinities and active economic relations and dependence, and would be markedly affected by current and historic relations between mother countries and colonies or former colonies.[12]

The second construct proposes to understand and predict factors and values determining news flow.[13] This notion was developed in an earlier work (1965) by one of the present authors in which the objective was to explore how "'events' become 'news'."[14] As presented in the preceding chapter, the basic notion was that the world is divided into two areas—a center and a periphery—with the center accounting for the majority of news reported in the world press and for the large difference existing between central and peripheral nations in terms of news exchanged. In all, 12 factors are offered as determinants of an event's newsworthiness (frequency, threshold, unambiguity, meaningfulness, consonance, unexpectedness, continuity, composition, relevance to elite nations, relevance to elite persons, personalization, and negativity). Within this tradition, Rosengren suggested other related factors— importance, physical/cultural distance, and event predictability.[15]

The center-periphery notion was further developed by Galtung in a later article (1971) on structural imperialism in which he concluded that cultural interaction means that "center news" dominates both "center" and "periphery" media, "center-periphery" news exchange is not equal, "center" news occupies larger portions of foreign news in "periphery" nations than "periphery" news does in "center" media, and relatively little flow exists between periphery nations, particularly when colonial based block borders are involved.[16] In this research tradition international events and news coverage both are treated as dependent variables while position in the world structure implicitly is seen as independent variable, but specific independent variables are not formally considered.[17] We will examine news structure later in this chapter.

Fitting into these general traditions, an assortment of empirical studies emerged which studied news flow in a variety of nations and regions.[18] For example, Hester provided a detailed analysis of news flow by examining international news over the Associated Press domestic trunk wires down to the Wisconsin state wire and then demonstrated how it filtered down to 15 Wisconsin dailies. The study documented how few subjects and a relatively small number of nations were actually covered by AP on its United States wire. State wire and local newspaper editors changed stories only a little. While developing country stories were generally at a minimum, when they did run they often emphasized war news and U.S. involvement. Stories on social and economic development were rare.[19]

Through a study of three Swedish morning newspapers, the Swedish news agency (TT), and other media outlets, we see how news flows from the Middle East into Sweden. The project found that while the national newspaper used TT material only irregularly, its distribution of news by editorial disposition was roughly the same as TT's output in many categories. Hard news (war, foreign relations, defense) dominated while soft news was under-represented (compared to other parts of the world, at least). The authors also found evidence for the existence of consensus in news evaluation, a "common standard" upon which "Swedish news carriers seem to evaluate news from the Middle East."[20]

Still another example is Skurnik's study of foreign news coverage by *Fraternité Matin*, the daily newspaper of the Ivory Coast.[21] Findings were that most foreign news was from sub-Saharan Africa, although a few other countries were found to dominate the news. The newspaper also tended to rely on news agency material. Interestingly, former colonial ties were not judged important in this analysis.

Traditionally, it was the newspaper that was studied here, but researchers soon expanded their work to include news agencies and television.[22] Hester, as an example, studied Latin American news flow over the AP wire, this time concentrating on AP staff and editors in Latin America and New York. Fewer occurrences of reports giving emphasis to the United States were found when Latin American copy was examined, but the number increased for the outflow of New York copy to United States AP members. Once again, only a few subjects were covered. This seemed to be largely due to the stereotyped perceptions that AP editors had of their AP member interests.[23]

GEOGRAPHIC IMBALANCE AND CULTURAL AFFINITY

The New World Information and Communication Order debate also helped to spur research in the area.[24] Literature fell on both sides of the debate (i.e., pro-Western perspective vs. anti-Western perspective). Concerns about potential imbalances of information flow were generated and these concerns were directed toward newspapers and wire services. Regarding the news agencies, Elliot and Golding summarize:

> The history of colonialism had an equal impact on the growth of the international news media. Towards the end of the nineteenth century the newly established European news agencies concluded a series of cartel agreements by which they divided the world between them, according to prevailing imperial spheres of influence. These first links in the international media system set a precedent for much that was to follow as the media in developed and developing societies alike became progressively more involved in the corporate capitalist economy.[25]

The New World Information and Communication Order debate helped to cultivate these arguments further as much literature has been devoted to the topic of uneven communication flow. Larson summarizes the principal findings of this research. Third World countries receive less coverage, the proportion of crisis stories is higher, they typically appear when the U.S. or other developed nations are also mentioned, and they are less likely to appear in stories on single countries.[26]

Masmoudi takes the problem specifically found with old colonial ties and sets out to clarify problems in such relational imbalances including: Western media indifference, news resource inequality, North-South information flow imbalances, a literate-biased media, negative news emphasis, and Western dominance in socioeconomic and cultural systems.[27] All of these topics, of course, deal with dependence and inequality in various ways and disguises.

Communication Flows: North-South, West-East, West-West, South-South

To illustrate, take as one of these points: the North-South information flow. While we have already touched on this earlier, the contention is that news flows from developed, industrialized nations (North) to developing nations (South). The North-South flow question has guided many news flow studies. For example, Naemeka and Richstad, in their study of 15 nations in the Pacific, found that former colonial networks still held importance in the flow of news across islands [28] Likewise, Dajani and Donahue made similar, but qualified, observations in their study of six Arab dailies. "The persistence of cultural affinity established by former colonial ties is borne out to a certain degree by Algerian and Syrian reporting on France, and Kuwait's reporting on Great Britain." They go on to note that in the case of the former two, "relatively more attention" was given to Socialist countries.[29] Other studies on cultural affinity provide similar findings including analyses by Ostgaard and Hester.[30] In explaining these trends of news dominance by the former mother country, Galtung and Ruge conclude that newspaper readers seek the familiar and culturally similar.[31] We should note that there is some research, however, which paints a more positive picture. One recent article concludes that U.S. dominance may be much lower than previously reported in a region such as Latin America.[32] It remains to be seen if these trends continue and can be replicated in other portions of the world.

The potential impact of news flow becomes apparent even when we look at inter-nation news communication limited to First World countries. In one analysis, U.S. and Canadian newspapers where studied. Canadian daily newspapers were found to cover U.S. news over 50 times more than the U.S. dailies covered Canadian issues.[33] Another study, again based on Canadian newspapers, found that there were "remarkable cultural affinities toward their readers' respective cultural homelands, the French-language newspapers towards France and the

English-language ones towards the United Kingdom. In that part of New Brunswick where people of both cultural groups live, the newspaper examined provided a more even balance of news from the two cultures."[34]

First World-Second World flow can also exist, but it is analogous to First-World-Third World flow more than it is like First World-First World.[35] In a study by Kressley, for example, European television programs were observed to move from Western to Eastern European countries more than they flowed conversely.[36]

As we suggested in Chapter 1, Fourth World-Third World relations are similar to that which we find in First World-Third World scenarios, but with some variation. News flow follows this trend. Note the findings reported by Schramm and by Giffard in two different studies on Asian prestige press and the AP and UPI Asian news wire services.[37] Schramm found that considerable space was devoted to Asian news while items on developing countries was no greater than that found in the Western press. Giffard also found an Asian emphasis on news reported, but found longer stories for developing nations than developed ones.

Looking at the influence of proximity on news flow within the Third World, Sreberny-Mohammadi, et al. have shown that more than one-half of the news tends to come from the immediate geographic region.[38] Stevenson and Cole report similar results.[39] Vincent and Riaz found much the same in their analysis of Bangladesh Television news.[40] On the other hand, it has been estimated that some 25% of the Third World's news still comes from four Western news agencies.[41]

Of course, not all world flows fit neatly into the North-South and East-West paradigms. A modification of these is the triangular flow hypothesis which suggests that the North is divided into (North-) East and (North-) West.[42] We used a comparable concept in our discussion of geopolitics in Chapter 1. While one can conceptualize news flow in a variety of ways with a range of models, the net effect is that such geographic flow patterns simply underline the problems which can exist in communication efforts between nations.

Western Dominance

In a major UNESCO-IAMCR (International Association of Mass Communication Researchers) study, mass media outlets in 29 countries were scrutinized.[43] The study found that while different levels of development and many political perspectives could be found in the various nations, the overall results were at times remarkably alike.[44]

. . . (N)ews everywhere appears to be defined as the "exceptional event," with coups and catastrophes being newsworthy wherever they occur. That the South is so often portrayed in such a manner is a function of the limited amount of attention paid to developing areas outside their own regions. The media of the South both exhibit less interest in covering and are less a source of "soft" news items such as human interest stories, culture, entertainment; further, the fewer the number of international news items, the more those items are concentrated in a few subject areas and reflect very immediate events. Only in the Eastern European media is any significant amount of attention paid to what might be termed "positive" news about culture and science.[45]

General findings included the observations that (1) politics dominated international reporting, and (2) regionalism was still prominent; "peripheral nations do not read much about each other, especially not across bloc borders."[46]

Using some of the same data from the UNESCO-IAMCR study, Stevenson and Cole try to correct the misnomer that Western news totally dominates world media. In 17 countries, including an examination of data on some 25 other nations, they report that in only one newspaper was the greatest attention not given to the local region.[47] They also assert that "dependence" on Western news agencies by developing countries is not as extensive as many critics maintain.[48] They do acknowledge, however, as does Sreberny-Mohammadi, et al. that there are still imbalances.

It is clear that the flow of news and information is overwhelmingly from North to South, and from a handful of industrialized nations in the West to the developing nations. Most of the news is supplied by the four Western news agencies and their broadcast counterparts, although alternatives do exist. Most of the popular culture of mass media also has a strong Anglo-American look. But the aggregate data measuring the flow of information and entertainment around the world can be misleading. Many of the data are also out of date.[49]

Yet elsewhere Stevenson argues that news agencies should not be faulted, per se, since political disruptions simply are more prevalent in the Third World.[50] Another study by Stevenson and Thompson measured news from five countries—the United States, the Soviet Union, Algeria, Brazil, and Zambia—and concludes that there is little reason to believe that developing countries are being exclusively targeted for negative reporting by Western press and the TNAs.[51] Similar findings were reported by Stevenson and Smith when they looked at coverage on Mexico and Lebanon in two American news magazines.[52] In an examination of the AP and UPI wire services, for example, significant differences were found between the number of stories on less developed and more developed countries, with the less developed accounting for more stories and longer story length.[53] In another study they report that 60% of the foreign news carried on U.S. domestic regional wire services comes from the Third World.[54] On the other hand, Weaver and Wilhoit go on to acknowledge that "less developed" countries outnumber their counterparts, 3 to 1, obviously contributing to the results.[55] Yet even this heavily pro-Western research often ends with caveats, exceptions, and disclaimers. As Stevenson and Cole conclude, "regional proximity is clearly the dominant characteristic of foreign news" with North America and Western Europe most visible, and Eastern Europe and developing areas of the globe receiving the least attention.[56]

Empirical studies involving general news flow between countries has also been fairly popular among researchers.[57] Schramm and Atwood, for example, studied 19 Asian daily newspapers in various languages in order to map out the movement of news from origin to newspaper reprints to reader consumption.[58] Another study by Kawatake looked at eight countries (Japan, U.S., U.K., Australia, Malaysia, Hong Kong, Brazil, and Ghana) and uncovered "an imbalance" by Third World countries, but also a shortage of Japanese news items sent abroad.[59]

Many researchers have documented the major news influence the U.S. alone exerts on other countries. Among these is research on news in Japan[60], Nigeria[61], and Yugoslavia.[62] The United States was found to be the nation appearing with the greatest frequency with respect to each nation's foreign news coverage, although not necessarily with the most positive disposition. In the previously mentioned Arab press study, the U.S. was the most covered foreign country in Lebanon, Saudi Arabia, Egypt, Algeria, and Syria. Only in Kuwait was Israeli news more dominant. Interestingly, the United States was the sole country where the attitude toward it had a negative imbalance coefficient for each daily; this was attributed to "political animosity . . . not cultural rejection." Great Britain was next closest in negative rankings.[63]

In many of the above studies we find that the Third World often appears to be dominated by communication from highly industrialized nations. This conclusion about Western and Japanese influence is basically the same as that proposed by Galtung. Information flow has been unidirectional. Access tends to be controlled by national wealth, and the many development problems facing Third World nations are not perceived as important relative to other industrial nation concerns. Complicating this is the self-image many First and some (former) Second World countries have as crusaders for world freedom and human rights.[64] As Mowlana concludes in his analysis of international communication literature: "studies in specific cultural and geographical areas have corresponded roughly to United States involvement in those areas. This factor of involvement seems to have influenced heavily what domestic studies have been undertaken and what foreign works translated."[65]

INTERNATIONAL NEWS IN THE U.S. MEDIA

We have already examined the influences of geographic/cultural relationships (North-South, East-West, Northeast-Southwest, etc.) on international news flow. We saw how imbalances in news flow can be attributed to such relationships. In terms of the U.S. media, this type of influence appears to have much to do with the level of attention the media assign to various nations and regions of the world. This is the case for both the print and electronic media, but television news seems to be the most pronounced. Larson and Hardy found all three U.S. networks devoted significantly more stories to developed rather than developing nations. The difference was greatest for NBC.[66] Hester found that U.S. television network news most frequently reported on Western Europe (28.81%), Indo-China (26.32%), and the Middle East (19.15%) between 1972 and 1976. Markedly less frequent, in descending order, were Africa (6.50%), Asia (6.13%), Eastern Europe (4.82%), and Latin America (3.32%).[67] Weaver, Porter and Evans took this data and added newscasts from 1977-1981. They found a 22.9% drop in Asian stories (Indo-China and Asia combined), a 7.2% decline for Western Europe, a 13.2% rise in Middle Eastern stories, a 6.0% jump for Eastern Europe, a 2.9% increase for Latin America, and a 0.1% increase for Africa. Overall, the Middle East was now highest, followed by Western Europe. But in these results, the authors observe, one can see that "emphasis was often afforded those news items originating from countries and concerning topics which were directly related to the vital economic and strategic interests of the United States overseas. As a result, these findings suggest much so-called 'foreign' news is in fact news of the U.S. from a foreign dateline." We can see the influence of the decline of interest in Asia as U.S. involvement in Vietnam ended, and an increase in the Middle East via peace initiatives and the Iranian hostage crisis.[68] Within a much larger data set, we get another glimpse of U.S. media, this time in six U.S. newspapers (*New York Times, Washington Post, Los Angeles Times, New York Daily News, Minneapolis Tribune,* and *Charlotte Observer*). Here Sreberny-Mohammadi reports that for the articles scrutinized in a six day sample (full sample = 2,675 articles), 35% contained news of a North American origin. The next largest region represented was Western Europe (17%), followed by Asia (13%), the Middle East (11%), Eastern Europe (7%), Africa (7%), and Latin America (6%).[69]

Similar trends are seen in analyses of natural disaster coverage. One study on U.S. network television news found that while 6.72 minutes were spent per 1,000 deaths when the disaster occurred in Western Europe, this figure dropped to 2.53 minutes for Eastern Europe, .92 minutes for Latin America, .83 minutes for the Middle East, and .63 minutes for Asian disasters. The greatest number of major natural disasters (total of 27 versus 3) occurred in Latin America, the Middle East, and Asia, however.[70] Another study examined earthquake coverage on television and in newspapers. Most occurred in the Third World. Still there was an imbalance between the number of earthquakes, and how often they were reported; while only 65% of the world's earthquakes during the period occurred in the Third World, 71% of all earthquake reports were centered there. And the trends are fairly consistent. Schoemaker, Chang and Brendlinger in yet another study in the area, report that the more deviant an international event, the greater the likelihood that that event will be covered in the U.S. mass media.[71] So, while largely under-reported in the U.S., the more catastrophic events appear to be unrepresentatively reported. This lends to the notion that much of the reporting on the developing world concentrates on "bad" news.[72]

NWICO DEBATE

Not only did the NWICO help direct attention to the international news flow process, but interest also centered around the debates themselves. Specific research efforts explored whether the press, particularly the American press, was allowing its own biases/dispositions to affect the manner in which it covered UNESCO debates. Also of interest was the degree in which they covered UNESCO news other than that involving the NWICO debate. UNESCO, after all, has a full agenda that addresses numerous world problems annually.

An article by Raskin proves particularly revealing as it reviews research on the United States press's coverage of the 21st UNESCO General Conference in Belgrade. The meeting served as a forum for extensive debate on the information flow proposals and helped create the International Commission for the Study of Communication Problems (MacBride Commission). The article is useful since it provides information on two UNESCO analyses: a study independently conducted by UNESCO, and a separate staff report on newspaper clippings. In the former, some 448 news articles and 206 editorials were found in newspapers from across the country by checking files of major newspapers and scores of others through a press clipping service in Washington, D.C.[73] In the latter, UNESCO analyzed 302 clippings from U.S. publications in September and October 1979.[74] In both, not one report of any non-communications issue was found. Other research has produced similar findings.

Another internal report, this one by communication study commission staff member John G. Massee, evaluated 185 clippings from around the world collected between February and September 1980.[75] Most were from newspapers and raw dispatches from AP, UPI, Reuters, Agence France Presse (AFP), and the Press Trust of India. Many of the newspaper clippings credited wire services as their source. Massee concluded that news reports were "largely negative" toward the MacBride Report. Fifty-five were considered "negative, hostile and/or defamatory." Massee noted that even those articles which offered "straight reporting without commentary . . . often contained critical comments on the (MacBride) Report, giving a generally unfavorable impression of the report or stressing controversy about it." *The International Herald Tribune* and the *Washington Post* were said to be "the most critical."

Offering a useful comparative frame of reference, Roach conducted similar research on French press coverage of UNESCO following the 1980 Belgrade conference. Ninety-seven Parisian and regional dailies and monthly magazine articles, and 99 dispatches from Agence France Press (AFP) were collected between mid September and early November 1980. The communication debate was the subject of half of the dispatches, and slightly more than half of the articles. As Roach concludes, "The 'neglected party' in the French coverage of the Belgrade conference was the Third World. Very few Third World spokespersons were quoted on their reactions to the MacBride Report . . ."[76] She goes on to note how a key resolution made by the Venezuelan delegation calling for formal studies "'necessary for the formulation of specific and practical proposals on the establishment of a new world information and communication order'" was not mentioned in the sources studied during the entire period.[77] Likewise, there was no mention of "collective self-reliance" and "South-South" realignment, major Third World discussion topics at the time.

> Generally speaking, the coverage devoted to the call for a New International Information Order was at best incomplete and at worst openly biased. Although the "information imbalance" was acknowledged, there were hardly any details on this situation. But an even more serious charge may be leveled against the French press: the presentation of this new order solely in quantitative terms, i.e., technical and financial assistance. In summary, analysis of the French

coverage of the UNESCO conference at Belgrade leads to the conclusion that only one side of the New International Information Order story is being told.[78]

Studies such as those reviewed above offer a fairly grim assessment of Western press treatment of the NWICO. Journalists responded that charges of their slanted treatment of events were unfair. Mort Rosenblum, editor of the *International Herald Tribune*, when learning of the Massee survey retorted:

> We have been fair and balanced in our news columns and have attacked the MacBride Report in our editorials. I think UNESCO has seized on this international news issue to build its own power. If any one doesn't think that press repression is intended he should read section 58 of the MacBride Commission Report . . . A free press is not a matter for compromise. It's a matter of principle. Either there is credibility and honest reporting or there is none. You can't have partially free reporting. An agency as biased as UNESCO should not be supervising reporting. To UNESCO, fair comment is unbalanced criticism.[79]

Michel Saint-Pol, the director of international affairs at Agence France Press reacted in a similar way.

> We have no objections to the legitimate aspirations of the Third World but we stand on the fundamental principal of a free exchange of information . . . We also are prepared to accept Third World regional or national news agencies and are willing to help them set up such organizations. However, we will not compromise on freedom of information for all parties . . . Freedom of information is not an abstract concept. More than two-thirds of the world are developing countries and all are governed by strong regimes. Certainly there is a suspicion of state control in the MacBride Report.[80]

Rather than speaking to the issue of imbalance in reporting, these press leaders seem to have been caught up in highly defensive rhetoric. One UNESCO aide noted that "The MacBride Report is as balanced as it's possible to achieve in an international organization." Commenting on the highly critical charges made by Reuters director Gerald Long, he added:

If Mr. Long's view prevails the confrontation between the west and the Third World on news dissemination will continue . . . Actually, UNESCO has done a great deal to help reporters function more freely in developing nations. The MacBride recommendations can create a better understanding of the journalists' problems . . . We know that sinister motives are being ascribed to the resolutions but, in fact, UNESCO has done much over the years to help the cause of journalism . . . It has given assistance to media in developing countries and had made the world more aware of press problems, including controls, in those nations.[81]

While the New World Information and Communication Order debate has come under attack by (particularly American) critics, there is no question that the movement helped to direct much attention to the issue of news flow imbalances. Yet the notion of communication imbalance is complex. It is difficult to come to quantitative agreement on the degree of imbalance.[82] The larger question may be does such research represent the only or best way to explore the news flow question.

SOME ENCOURAGING DEVELOPMENTS IN NEWS RESEARCH

Despite the voluminous literature, news flow research still is faulted for use of a mechanistic model in which the emphasis is on a type of passive gratification or effect. The presupposition, according to some, is that audiences are inactive participants in the consumption of international news. There are other types of news content research methods that are available, however.

News content research takes on a variety of formats and approaches. While some are exclusively quantitative in approach, others are qualitative, and still others combine quantitative and qualitative research techniques in the same study. The latter two categories have been influenced to a major degree by a variety of techniques borrowed from sociology, linguistics, literary studies, and rhetorical analysis. Typically this research is being conducted by researchers in either North America or Western Europe.

One group of studies we wish to call attention to looks at news from a thematic perspective. Among these Nimmo and Combs use traditional rhetorical criticism, and Breen and Corcoran study the presence of "myths" in news.[83] Taking a somewhat different approach, an article by Barkin and Gurevitch, and a monograph by Vincent et al., offer analyses of the discourse aspects of television news via narrative theory.[84] Narrative theory is an appropriate analytic mode for event-oriented news studies. It provides insights into the influence and function of TV news stories through an examination of their narrative structure and dramatic content. Narrative theory traces its origins to literary theory and rhetorical analysis, but it has recently received attention from scholars throughout the social sciences and humanities.[85] While there is no central theory, the basic assumption is that story-telling is an important human activity. It is through a pedestrian understanding of the narrative process that individuals decipher the nebulous information found in society. What is revealing in a social world created by narrative is the inherent link among its elements. The who, what, where, why, how, and when provide acts and events within a narrative frame. A choice among alternative settings or among origins of political development also determines morality, reward systems, and the range of effective solutions to life's problems.[86] In other words, according to Barkin and Gurevitch, "narrative becomes . . . a means of understanding the social world."[87] It acknowledges that humans are story tellers, and concedes that we can better understand ourselves and our social milieu by examining our story construction methods. One assumption is that our proficiency in deciphering the world improves as we learn assorted narratives and start to utilize them.[88] Unfortunately, this research has not been applied in many international news story analyses.

Another approach is that employed by the Netherlands-based researcher van Dijk.[89] He looks at linguistic structures, but in a very different way than the traditional linguist would approach language. His work begins with the assumption that language has use and social practice. Using discourse analysis and cognitive psychology, he does word counts and then determines how many times particular structures occur. His textual coding techniques, unfortunately, lack consistency across and even within analyses.

Other Amsterdam researchers such as Kleinnijenhuis and Scholten do work distantly related to van Dijk's, but better controlled.[90] By taking a type of systems approach, they set out to study numerous variables by using sophisticated computerized content analysis techniques. A basic objective is to differentiate positive from negative news. In Sweden, Findahl and Hoyer do detailed content analyses of television pictures and spoken text, and then combine these observations with audience survey data.[91] Essentially, these are processing studies. Another Swedish researcher combining quantitative and qualitative methods is Dahlgren.[92]

An interesting variation on the news effects literature is a qualitative/theoretical approach offered by Jensen.[93] What is intriguing about his work is that it begins with a very different set of assumptions than that of traditional news effects researchers. From the outset, most of the studies of news reception assumed that people will learn or be able to use information. The difference comes when trying to assess what that something is exactly. Most news learning studies attempt to measure precisely what and how much viewers could recall following exposure to news reports. Jensen's work on news reception instead asks if there are other benefits from receiving news (similar to questions gratifications researchers traditionally have asked). His research seems to be in response to the tendency in uses and gratifications research where it is assumed that if television and other kinds of news media do not teach people, then media consumption has no value. Jensen instead posits the notion that individuals can receive more than just learning gratifications from news. He challenges the notion that viewing television solely for entertainment might be bad. This, he says, is a negative assumption. As a result, he might look at news as a source of daily living—a conversation piece, if you will. Conceptualized this way, television viewing can be thought of as something necessary for social, cultural, and political identity—an aspect of legitimization. Hence, the concern shifts from specific information being transferred to a type of agenda or forum-setting. It can be viewed as simply one more information input or source. Jensen believes that news audience research separates audience from news. He looks at this relationship and asks what the effect might be. In a way, this approach places emphasis on individuals rather than on the news institution. Cultural assumptions are made about news and its purpose. In some ways the New Information Order did nothing to help turn attention away from the "individual" (not necessarily journalists, but news organizations). Jensen proposes that we look at economic and organizational factors governing the kind of news available. News flow studies, of course, are interested in documenting what is actually getting through. By looking at economic factors, Jensen's method offers alternatives for Third World concerns (versus the question of passing on control over information to someone else).[94]

In Jensen's *Critical Studies in Mass Communication* article, an attempt is made to link the empirical tradition (survey research) with the more textual approach found throughout Europe. He argues for looking at empirical factors relevant to any audience study, but then proposes that they be combined with qualitative textual analysis. It is an argument directed toward both camps. To the quantitative camp, he is saying that there is explanatory value to this approach. Yet the argument is also directed against them.[95]

THE STRUCTURE OF FOREIGN NEWS

The study by Galtung and Ruge briefly alluded to above was an early effort to focus more on the quality—and less on the quantity—of bias in news flow. In 1960 the fledgling International Peace Research Institute in Oslo, founded January 1959, decided that one of the major approaches in peace studies would have to be "the structure of foreign news." Publication of a working paper came the following year. It was not published as an article until the *Journal of Peace Research*, founded by the institute in 1964, had cleared a sufficient amount of other manuscripts; hence the journal article dates from 1965.

The basic hypothesis was that foreign news has a "structure." The word "structure" should not be taken lightly. First, "structure" connotes a certain invariance, that there are certain features that recur. They appear and reappear with a certain automaticity regardless of where in the world we are located. They act like laws of nature, unless they are consciously counteracted. Second, "structure" connotes absence of intent, that there is not necessarily any personal will, at least in the explicit, deliberate sense of that word, underlying those recurring features. Third, "structure" as used here defines some countries as Center and some as Periphery. But this is not always permanent. A Center country may slip into the Periphery, and vice versa.

This article[96] obtained a certain circulation, particularly in schools of journalism around the world. Otherwise, it has probably been totally forgotten, except for its most important feature which we shall come to immediately. There were actually five ideas explored in the article. The first four were fairly trivial, but the fifth idea was more important.

First, there was the commonly held idea that events constitute some kind of raw material and that news is the outcome of the processing of events. For news to be reported, events have to be sifted and sorted. They have to be "processed," made "fit to print," and "ready to serve." This particular aspect was then developed somewhat further in the much broader context of another article published in 1971.[97]

Second, there was the rather obvious idea of a parallel between processing of events into news and processing of raw materials into manufactured goods. This is where the Third World enters the picture. Just as the First World descends upon the Third World mining those countries for raw materials to be processed into manufactured goods—either in the Third World in factories owned or at least controlled by the First World, or in the First World itself—the First World also descends upon the Third World in the guise of international news agencies, five of which are rather famous or infamous (Associated Press, United Press International, Reuters, Agence France-Presse, and Tass), mining for events that can be processed into news. The selection of raw materials in general, and events in particular, and how they should be processed, would by and large be decided by the tastes of the First World in both cases. The added value, the profits, would generally go to the First World. Beyond this comes a rather important aspect of news processing: by doing so the First World would have the upper hand in deciding what kind of image should be presented of the Third World. These particular aspects were then developed into another article written in 1979.[98]

Third, there was one more listing of factors that supposedly operated in selecting events for their "newsworthiness." As noted above, a list of 12 such factors were identified; rather than quoting from the original article we take them from Hartley, *Understanding News*,[99] where the original article is summarized as a basis for further commentary.

1. *Frequency*. The time-span taken by an event.
2. *Threshold*. The size of an event.
3. *Unambiguity*. The clarity of an event.
4. *Meaningfulness*. Cultural proximity and relevance.[100]
5. *Consonance*. The predictability of, or desire for an event
6. *Unexpectedness*. The unpredictability, or rarity, of an event.
7. *Continuity*. The "running story."
8. *Composition*. The mixture of different kinds of event.
9. *Reference to elite nations*.
10. *Reference to elite persons*.
11. *Personalization*. Events are seen as actions of individuals.
12. *Negativity*. Bad news is good news.

As in the preceding chapter, we will examine only the last four factors from the original article (referred to as F9, F10, F11, F12; (F = factor). Of course, any list of such factors is in and of itself a rather low level intellectual activity. This does not constitute a theory, only raw material for a theory.

Fourth, there is the additivity hypothesis. At this point there is an effort to improve the level of intellectual activity somewhat. The obvious hypothesis was the higher the number of these 12 factors being satisfied, the higher the likelihood that the event would pass the threshold and be processed into a news item. The simplest way of expressing this would be to count the number of factors satisfied and give each an equal weight of "1." The additive index of newsworthiness would then run from 0 to 12, with events having higher totals being the leading candidates for news.

Fifth, there is the complementarity hypothesis or the effort to say something new: The idea is simply that if an event falls short on some factors it may nevertheless qualify as news if it is particularly pronounced on some of the other factors. In other words, a particularly high factor may complement another particularly low factor, and the sum total may nevertheless be sufficient. This actually means that factors are no longer scored with equal weights, but cumulatively as well.

The numerous implications of the complementarity hypothesis as an analytical perspective are rather important. To illustrate, we use the last four factors, F9-F12. (Once more we ask the reader to pardon us for a slight overlap with Chapter 1 above as a different point is being developed this time.)

Imagine that an event is low on both F9 and F10; it involves very ordinary people in very ordinary countries. Nevertheless, the event can qualify as news if it scores extra high on F11 and F12; it is both highly personalized and highly negative. Concretely, this means that for anything to appear as news about ordinary people in the Third World it has to be personalized and negative. An enormous accident killing a great many people, compensating for the ordinariness of the individuals by their numbers is an obvious example. But this could also take the classical form of a political takeover, a military *golpe* or *Putsch*. Elite persons, in non-elite countries, but both personalized and negative. Hence, news, even top news.

Compare this to news about elite persons in elite nations. By definition, the point of departure is already so high that the event can be low on other dimensions. If, in addition, it is about concrete individuals, then even the most positive event can be included, such as the happy birth of a royal child. In this particular case good (positive) news is good (printable) news.[101] Moreover, events that are institutionalized and not necessarily personalized, such as a change of government according to a completely regular election process and parliamentary rules, would be reported even if everything that happens is positive, simply because it is from an elite nation and concerns elite persons.

The net conclusion is very clear, given in Table 1 in which all 16 combinations based on the four factors are spelled out, with examples (the numbers are the additive index values). From non-elite (Third World) countries for news to be reported, there will have to be an overabundance of highly dramatic events, including but not limited to vast quantities of individuals, but with no coverage of how structures are operating to produce these unhappy circumstances for poor people. There will also be news about people high up, highly personalized, and occasionally with happy tidings, but then preferably about elite countries. The news could also be entirely depersonalized, in terms of structure in the form of institutionalized processes. For countries high up in the system, this means that there will be an over-representation of elections or transfer of power as parts of news reporting, focusing on regular or institutionalized processes. In other words, a structural perspective is given for elite countries, but then as the orderly workings of institutions. For non-elite countries the rule will be the scandals and mega-accidents; the riots and the military takeovers.

Table1. A four factor news communication model

	Person Negative	Person Positive	Structure Negative	Structure Positive
Elite countries; elite people	No problem: any gossip; however false (4)	Happy family events (3)	Cabinet falls change (3)	Elections, even minor (3)
Elite country; non-elite people	Accidents lottery, wealth (3)	Prizes crashes (2)	Economic growth (2)	Economic (1)
Non-elite country; elite	Scandals (drugs) wealth (3)	Prizes lottery change (2)	Coup d'etat but major (2)	Elections, (1)
Non-elite country; non-elite people	Mega-accidents (2)	Miracles (1)	Revolutions "trouble," riots (1)	No chance; however true (0)

This, then, is what is referred to as the "structure of foreign news," as something invariant given our pattern of news communication. At no point is there any hypothesis of conspiracy or intent. Nor is there any hypothesis to the effect that these factors should be operating only in today's First World countries with the First World countries as Center, elite countries. In short, the theory is entirely structural. It is not even a theory of imperialism, cultural or structural. It would operate pretty much the same way in the Periphery and in locations other than Western Centers. The basis of the theory is simply this: the news paradigm, *the very idea of news,* as already indicated above, carries with it certain characteristics. On the other hand, the way the news paradigm operates is entirely compatible with any kind of imperialism, with Center and Periphery producing pretty much the same, highly compatible images of the world, because the Periphery is so successfully penetrated by the Center. That both the news paradigms and Western imperialism are compatible with occidental cosmology, as pointed out above, goes without saying; even to the point that the cosmology can be seen as the basic underlying factor.

REFLECTIONS ON A DEBATE

Let us now contrast this perspective with those of other researchers who have entered the debate.

In a paper for the *Communication Yearbook* 1990,[102] Ito documents in admirable detail the Japanese transition from importer to exporter: "At present, however, there are only three countries in the world where the media coverage of Japan is less than the Japanese media coverage of those countries. They are the United States, the Soviet Union and China. The coverage of Japan in the rest of the world is either about the same as or more than the Japanese media coverage of those countries." He also has very interesting comments on the type of imports: ". . . the programs featuring American domestic life, human relations and humor disappeared at an early stage, while programs featuring war, crime and violence remain. For this reason some Westerners living in Japan believe that the Japanese public sees the West through a prism of violence and sex, and that the Japanese are likely to form inappropriate images of the West and its people." Ito makes the point that Japan imports from the West "high quality culture" and "violence and sex" with the latter emphasizing "action dramas." In-between categories like *Dallas* apparently are not successful.

A problem with Ito's article comes when he moves from data to theory. He constructs an image of "the so-called cultural imperialism," "media imperialism," and "dependency" theories. According to his image of these theories, the world consists of a "center" (economically advanced capitalist exploiting countries) and a "periphery" or "satellite" (the economic and political exploitee). Then, there is "the second approach to explaining the international flows of information [which] are based on all non-Marxist theories and hypotheses." There is an abundance of effort spent at explaining news flow in terms of geographical proximity, the presence or not of news agencies, etc. Summarizing theoretical discussion, Ito adds that Japan "provides a unique case because it changed from information importer to information exporter, from 'peripheral country' to 'central country,' during the past twenty years."

The difficulty here is in the apparent assumption that a country can be classified as either-or. Those who use "center" and "periphery" as analytical categories never thought of them as static or absolute. Marxists use theories of uneven development to explain how a country can get an edge over another. Non-Marxists talk about rank disequilibrium, equilibration of rank profiles, and mobility in the world system, up and down, from periphery to center, and vice versa.

Actually, Japan's growth has been more complex than Ito appears to acknowledge. Japan has moved from marginal (Tokugawa) to regional center (Meiji, Taisho); then, to the center of the world stage (the Pacific War period 1931-1945). After the Pacific War, Japan moved from latent center in the early occupation period to regional center, then, to world center again, this time using economic rather than military aggression. There is little question that Japan is becoming more newsworthy to the point of becoming a net information exporter. This is precisely what one would expect according to Center/Periphery theory.

As its international status increases, more is written about Japan abroad. Yet what is written? Unfortunately, Ito has not analyzed of the quality of information about Japan. With no systematic content analysis backing, we propose that there are two basic types of information about Japan: (1) news about Japan's phenomenal rise in economic power including analysis of why and how; and (2) news about Japan's penetration of the economies of other countries, and about other countries' non-penetration of Japan.

Whereas the former appear as like positive information, the latter is mainly negative to the point of Japan-bashing. A limitation of Ito's analysis may be that it does not seem to be concerned about the "what" of information, only about the "how much." As we have already demonstrated, "quantity" studies have been a staple of U.S.-influenced news flow analysis from Wilbur Schramm onward (as opposed to a more qualitative approach).

The by and large negative, often misleading, information about Japan should be seen in the light of Japan's former status as a non-elite country, in other words, as a lag phenomenon; and in terms of the conflicts inevitably accompanying rapid upward mobility. From the flow perspective of the preceding section, the elite status of Japan should lead to the general hypothesis of more positive news content. This is impression (1) above. But the hypothesis has to be modified to accommodate impression (2). And in the U.S., the Soviet Union and China, relative to which Japan still has some periphery characteristics, the events will still have to be negative to be processed into news. The U.S. will set the tone for the rest of the world. As Japan starts to substitute for the U.S. as a Center country in, for instance, Thailand, we might expect the negative coloring of the news to decrease. But not down to zero, and not in Thai newspapers essentially written for Americans.

As Ito very rightly points out, in order to become a net information exporter there is also the strategy of limiting imports. His cultural "competition theory" focuses on Japanese cultural identity. "It was suggested that the cultural identity problem consisted of three elements, i.e., weakness in the "competitive sector of culture," "lack of things to be proud of," and "continuity between past and present." He then shows what Japan did to overcome these problems, whereupon he suggests that "the cultural imperialism, media imperialism, and dependency theories explained neither Japan's change nor the situation in East Asia."

On the contrary, it may show precisely the strength of these approaches. What Ito shows is how a country can successfully fight against cultural and media imperialism through a strategy of cultural self-reliance, by being proud of its own past, and particularly by constructing bridges between past, present, and future. "It was shown how this phenomenon, especially the retreat of Western popular cultural products, is now occurring throughout East Asia. It was suggested that the major factors which reduced the share of foreign cultural products were: (1) strengthening of the mass media infrastructure including the advertising industry, and (2) the existence of cultural peculiarity that functions as a barrier against foreign cultural products."

Precisely. That is exactly what media and cultural self-reliance are about and it is very similar to the way Japan built her economic strength. Ito has actually delivered arguments for the cluster of theories he thinks he has refuted. Consequently, there is much to learn from Japan in this field when East Asian countries in due time also seek to overcome the phase of overabundance of information import from Japan, as they are now learning to become economically independent of Japan. In that connection, it might be worth noting how Japan handles information import. Japan has taken not only the best from the West, including high culture, but also the negative (violence and sex), building a positive self-other gradient in favor of Japan. The best is useful for elite consumption; the worst solidifies the negative image of the U.S. In doing so, East Asia is merely confirming a basic hypothesis for Chapters 1 and 3 in this book: the salience of the Fourth World as a new world center.

But Ito is not alone in misunderstanding the Center-Periphery hypothesis. Ahern also proceeds along the classical U.S. quantitative line in trying to come to grips with the problem.[103] In the very opening sentence of his study, he says that "a number of theoretical studies of international news flow proposed that the economic, social, political, and geographic characteristics of nations helped determine the amount of coverage one country received in the press of another (Galtung and Ruge, 1965 . . .)." He then goes to make a quite statistically complicated study in which the dependent variable is "the quantity of coverage a nation receives in the U.S. press,"[104] specified two pages later as "quantity of coverage, measured as the number of articles."

This is the easy approach. No qualitative coding is involved, only a count of articles.[105] But the approach misses the whole point: not how much is written,[106] but what is written. Similar problems occur in other news flow studies. The use of simple coding schemes can be potentially misleading and shallowly interpreted.[107] The news paradigm has a built-in logic that decides in advance how the biases are going to come out, independent of what happens in the real world.[108] The study of the quantity of coverage is not entirely without merit; it is only that this alone is not what the New World Information and Communication Order agenda is about, but only a trivialization of that agenda.

Incidentally, Ahern does mention the critique made by Rosengren,[109] who points out: "Newsfactors could not be shown to operate as selection criteria without a comparison between events reported and events rejected," and this was not done in Galtung and Ruge's article. The criticism is appropriate; hopefully someone will do that rather painstaking job sooner or later! An indication of how to proceed is given in Table 1—study the extent to which what would have been news from a First World country does not qualify when coming from a Third World country.

A third example of misunderstanding the issue is illustrated in an article by Ravault, "International Information: Bullet or Boomerang?"[110] Ravault is critiquing the "bullet theory," which sees communication as something that hits and is absorbed. He substitutes a "boomerang theory," where the recipient of communication is reacting, even throwing the "bullet" back to the center. The recipient can exit from a passive mode and enter an active mode.

So far, so good. Where Ravault seems to go astray is in believing that the proponents of a New World Information and Communication Order are themselves of the opinion that the receivers are always passive. In other words, once the structure has been operating it cannot be changed. If this were true, where would those people—and they are rather numerous—fighting for a New World Order ever get the idea that such a struggle is not doomed in advance? On the contrary, the struggle goes on precisely because the condition is seen as changeable, modifiable, with receivers not forever doomed to remain receivers, and interaction not forever doomed to remain vertical.

Ravault goes quite far in characterizing NWICO as an "extremely radical solution" (which, amazingly, presents striking similarities with the economic and cultural solutions of the "have not" or Fascist countries opposing the "haves" just before World War II). Of course, there are some similarities among all people or countries wanting in one way or another to get further onto the front of the world stage, to get more of the limelight so to speak. For that reason, Ravault should not be surprised if he finds some similarities in rhetoric. But the differences in methods are considerably more important. The New World Information and Communication Order has essentially been fought verbally in the UNESCO, with some consequences around the world. Fascism operated in a rather different way.

Ravault "contends that the cultural dissociation proposal is based upon the victimizing view of the communication process in which the receiver is considered to be passive and totally receptive to the 'messages' broadcast or diffused by powerful producers or senders." Of course, believing that the other side in a debate, where Ravault basically lines up with the status quo forces, believes in what Ravault believes they believe in makes it easy to debunk them. Ravault points to a number of ways in which the recipient turns the situation around, all of them methods used by Third World countries today. In short, Ravault's study, which is more theoretical and more polemical than Ito's analysis, suffers essentially from the same basic misunderstanding. There is the same failure to understand critical social science that uses empirical methods not to understand the status quo, assuming it will remain so forever, but to change it.

CONCLUSION

At this point we prefer to stop, as we are not sure that the debate has come much further. But something can be said about how the research could or should continue.

The first point would be to get out of the quantitative mind-set that has dominated much of the debate, by adding a more qualitative approach. One is reminded here of the corresponding debate about international trade that shows important similarities. On the one hand there are those who seem happy and content to analyze trade in terms of quantity, measured in physical volume or monetary value. It is easy to count and easy to compare by subtracting one from the other: if the difference is positive there is a trade surplus; if it is negative there is a trade deficit. Net exporter, net importer.

Yet this may be very misleading. The qualitative approach, that is, an analysis of what kinds of products (goods and services) are exchanged, from the totally raw and crude to the most sophisticated integrated circuit, gives a much more profound insight into the relationship between countries and regions. Countries communicate through their products: a sophisticated product communicates sophistication and a crude product communicates something crude; it is about as simple as that. It is better to have a trade deficit, while exporting sophisticated products, than a trade surplus based on exporting the crude and unprocessed, the scrap metal and the waste paper, the hamburgers and the fried chicken franchises, and so on.

Second, work in this field would probably benefit greatly from turning to discourse analysis in addition to the more atomizing types of content analysis of which quantitative counting of numbers of articles or inches is the bottom level in terms of intellectual crudeness. The context, and the individual frame of reference (not to mention the collective frame of reference of the entire journalist culture, and from there to the culture of the country and the region) in general will give us many more profound insights in how the discourse defines a script. The script in turn defines what has to be done to an event in order for it to become news. We do not think that this necessarily will contradict the news factor approach.[111] But it will definitely make for a deeper understanding, rooting news in culture, thereby enabling us to see connections that are not included in the news flow debate we have had so far.[112]

NOTES TO CHAPTER 2

1. Wilbur Schramm, *Mass Media and National Development* (Stanford, CA: Stanford University Press, 1964), p. 65.

2. Bernard C. Cohen, *The Press and Foreign Policy* (Princeton, N.J.: Princeton University Press, 1963), p. 13.

3. Walter Lippman and Charles Merz, "A Test of News," *New Republic* No. 296, (Supplement)(August 1920); Walter Lippman, *Public Opinion* (New York: Macmillan, 1922, 1961); Julian L. Woodward, *Foreign News in American Morning Newspapers: A Study of Public Opinion* (New York: Columbia, 1930; London: P.J. King & Son, Ltd., 1930). A major emphasis in research on the subject came in the late 1940s and early 1950s: see Scott M. Cutlip, "Content and Flow of AP News — From Trunk to TTs to Reader," *Journalism Quarterly* 31 (1954), pp. 434-446; Jacques Kayser, *One Week's News: Comparative Study of 17 Major Dailies for a Seven-Day Period* (Paris: Unesco, 1953); International Press Institute, *The Flow of the News* (Zürich: International Press Institute, 1953).

4. International Press Institute, *The Flow of the News.*

5. Wilbur Schramm, *One Day in the World's Press* (Stanford, CA: Stanford University Press, 1960); Schramm, *Mass media and National Development.*

6. Schramm, *Mass media and National Development.*

7. Jim Hart, "The Flow of News Between the U.S. and Canada," *Journalism Quarterly* 40 (1963), pp. 70-74; Jim Hart, "Foreign News in U.S. and English Daily Newspapers: A Comparison," *Journalism Quarterly* 43 (1966), pp. 443-447; James W. Markham, "Foreign News in the United States and South American Press," *Public Opinion Quarterly* 25 (1961), pp. 249-262; Stig Thoren, "Datelines of Foreign Wire Service News into Sweden," *Cooperation and Conflict* 4 (1969), pp. 312-316.

8. Hart, "Foreign News in U.S. and English Daily Newspapers: A Comparison," pp. 443-448.

9. L. Erwin Atwood, "How Newsmen and Readers Perceive Each Others' Story Preference," *Journalism Quarterly* 47 (1970), pp. 298-302.

10. K. Kyoon Hur, "A Critical Analysis of International News Flow Research," *Critical Studies in Mass Communication* 1 (1984), pp. 365-378; Hamid Mowlana, *International Flow of Information: A Global Report and Analysis* (Paris: UNESCO, 1985).

11. Albert Hester, "Theoretical Considerations in Predicting Volume and Direction of International News Flow," *Gazette* 20 (1973), pp. 82-98.

12. Al Hester, "Theoretical Considerations in Predicting Volume and Direction of International Information Flow," *Gazette* 19 (1973), pp. 239-247.

13. Einar Östgaard, "Factors Influencing the Flow of News," *Journal of Peace Research* 2 (1965), pp. 39-63.

14. See Johan Galtung and Mari Holmboe Ruge, "The Structure of Foreign News: The Presentation of the Congo, Cuba and Cyprus Crises in Four Norwegian Newspapers," *Journal of Peace Research* 2 (1965), pp. 64-91; reprint: *Essays in Peace Research*, vol. 4, ed., Johan Galtung (Copenhagen: Chistian Ejlers, 1980), pp. 120-130, 690-691; reprint: *Media Sociology: A Reader*, ed., Jeremy Tunstall, (London, 1970), pp. 259-298; Johan Galtung, "A Structural Theory of Imperialism," *Journal of Peace Research* 8(2) (1971), pp. 81-118. For a test of the Galtung and Ruge theory, see Raymond S. Smith, "On the Structure of Foreign News: A Comparison of the *New York Times* and the Indian White papers," pp. 23-36.

15. Karl Eric Rosengren, "International News: Intra and Extra Media Data," *Acta Sociologica* 13 (1970), pp. 96-109.

16. Galtung, "A Structural Theory of Imperialism," pp. 81-117

17. Hur, "A Critical Analysis of International News Flow Research," pp. 365-378.

18. Albert Hester, "An Analysis of News Flow from Developed and Developing Nations," *Gazette* 17 (1971), pp. 29-43; Claus-Olof Olsson and Lennart Weibull, "The Reporting of News in Scandinavian Countries," *Scandinavian Political Studies* 8 (1973), pp. 141-167; William A. Payne, "American Press Coverage of Africa," *Africa Report* 11 (1)

(1966), pp. 44-48; Karl Erik Rosengren and Gunnel Rikardsson, "Middle East News in Sweden," *Gazette* 20 (1974), pp. 98-116; Wilbur Schramm and L. Erwin Atwood, *Circulation of News in the Third World: A Study of Asia* (Hong Kong: Chinese University Press, 1981); W. A. E. Skurnick, "Foreign News Coverage in the Ivory Coast: A Statistical Profile of *Fraternite-Matin*," *Gazette* 24 (1978), pp. 99-112; W. A. E. Skurnick, "Foreign News Coverage in Six African Newspapers: The Potency of National Interest," *Gazette* 28 (1981), pp. 117-130; John H. Sigler, "News Flow in the North African International Subsystem," *International Studies Quarterly* 13 (1969), pp. 381-397.

19. Hester, "An Analysis of News Flow from Developed and Developing Nations," pp. 29-43.

20. Rosengren and Rikardsson, "Middle East News in Sweden," pp. 98-116.

21. Skurnick, "Foreign News Coverage in the Ivory Coast: A Statistical Profile of *Fraternité-Matin*."

22. Cutlip, "Content and Flow of AP News—From Trunk to TTs to Reader;" Richard L. Barton and Richard B. Gregg, "Middle East Conflict as a TV News Scenario: A Formal Analysis," *Journal of Communication* 32 (2) (1982), pp. 172-185; Robert L. Bishop, "How Reuters and AFP Coverage of Africa Compare," *Journalism Quarterly* 52 (1975), pp. 654-662; Albert Hester, "Five Years of Foreign News on U.S. Evening Newscasts," *Gazette* 24 (1978), pp. 86-95; Albert Hester, "The News from Latin America via a World News Agency," *Gazette* 20 (1974), pp. 82-98; Stig Thorén, "The Flow of Foreign News into the Swedish Press," *Journalism Quarterly* 45 (1968), pp. 521-524; Stig Thorén, "Datelines of Foreign Wire Service News into Sweden," *Cooperation and Conflict: Nordic Studies in International Politics* (Sweden) 4 (1969), pp. 312-316; William C. Adams, ed. *Television Coverage of the Middle East* (Norwood, N.J.: Ablex, 1981); James F. Larson, *Television's Window on the World: International Affairs Coverage on the U.S. Networks* (Norwood, N.J.: Ablex, 1984); Kaarle Nordenstreng and Tapio Varis, *Television Traffic: A One-Way Street*, Reports and Papers on Mass Communication, No. 70 (Paris: UNESCO, 1974); Waltraud Quieser-Morales, "Revolution, Earthquakes and Latin America: The Networks Look at Allende's Chile and Somoza's Nicaragua," in *Television Coverage of the Middle East*, ed., William C. Adams (Norwood, N.J.: Ablex, 1981); Tapio Varis, "Trends in International Television Flow," *International Political Science Review* 7 (1986), pp. 235-249; Tapio Varis, "European Television Exchanges and Connections with the Rest of the World," *Instant Research on Peace and Violence* 1 (1973); Tapio Varis, "The International Flow of Television Programs," *Journal of Communication*, 34(1) (1984), pp. 143-152.

23. Hester, "The News from Latin America via a World News

Agency," pp. 82-98.

24. UNESCO, *Report and Papers on Mass Communication: News Dependence, No. 91* (Paris: Unesco, 1980); D. R. Mankekar, *One-Way Free Flow: Neo-Colonialism via News Media* (New Delhi: Clarion Books, 1978); Mustapha Masmoudi, "The New World Information Order," *Journal of Communication* 29 (2) (1984), pp. 172-185; L. Erwin Atwood and Stuart J. Bullion, "News Maps of the World: A View from Asia," in *International Perspectives on the News*, eds., L. Erwin Atwood, Stuart J. Bullion and Sharon Murphy (Carbondale, Il: Southern Illinois University Press, 1982), pp. 102-132; Breda Pavlic and Cees J. Hamelink, *The New International Order: Links Between Economics and Communication*, Reports and Papers on Mass Communication, No. 98 (Paris: UNESCO, 1982); Annabelle Sreberny-Mohammadi, "The 'World of the News' Study," *Journal of Communication* 34 (Winter 1984), pp. 121-134; Robert L. Stevenson and Donald Lewis Shaw, eds. *Foreign News and the New World Information Order* (Ames, Iowa: Iowa State University Press, 1984).

25. Phil Elliot and Peter Golding, "Mass Communication and Social Change: The Imagery of Development and the Development of Imagery," in *Sociology and Development*, eds., Emanuel de Kadt and Gavin Williams (London: Tavistock Publications, 1973; New York: Harper & Row, 1974), p. 235.

26. James F. Larson, "International Affairs Coverage on U.S. Network Television," *Journal of Communication* 29 (Spring 1979), pp. 136-147.

27. Masmoudi, "The New World Information Order," pp. 172-185.

28. Tony Nnaemeka and Jim Richstadt, "Structural Relations and Foreign News Flow in the Pacific Region," *Gazette* 26 (1980), pp. 235-257.

29. Nabil Dajani and John Donohue, "Foreign News in the Arab Press: A Content Analysis of Six Arab Dailies," *Gazette* 19 (1973), pp. 155-170.

30. Einar Östgaard, "Factors Influencing the Flow of News," *Journal of Peace Research* 2 (1965), pp. 39-63, based on an analysis of data by Frederick W. Frey, *The U.S. Mass Media and the Newer East*, mimeograph (Cambridge, MA: M.I.T. Center for International Studies, 1963), and the International Press Institute's *The Flow of News* (Zürich: International Press Institute, 1953); Al Hester, "Theoretical Considerations in Predicting Volume and Direction of International Information Flow," *Gazette* 19 (1973), pp. 239-57.

31. Galtung and Ruge, "The Structure of Foreign News."

32. Louise F. Montgomery, "Images of the United States in the Latin American Press," *Journalism Quarterly* 65 (1988), pp. 655-660.

33. Vernone M. Sparkes, "The Flow of News between Canada and the United States," *Journalism Quarterly* 55 (1978), pp. 260-268.

34. Herbert G. Kariel and Lynn A. Rosenvall, "Cultural Affinity Displayed in Canadian Daily Newspapers," *Journalism Quarterly*, 60 (1983), pp. 431-436.

35. See general review of topic in Mowlana, *International Flow of Information: A Global Report and Analysis*.

36. Konrad Kressley, "East-West Communication in Europe—The Television Nexus," *Communication Research* 5 (1978), pp. 71-86.

37. Wilbur Schramm, "Circulation of News in the Third World: A Study of Asia," in *Mass Communication Review Yearbook*, Vol. 1, eds., G. Cleveland Wilhoit and Harold de Bock, (Beverly Hills, CA: Sage Publications, 1980), pp. 589-619; C. Anthony Giffard, "Developed and Developing Nation News in U.S. Wire Service Files to Asia," *Journalism Quarterly* 61 (1984), pp. 14-19.

38. Annabelle Sreberny-Mohammadi, with Kaarle Nordenstreng, Robert L. Stevenson and Frank Ugboajah, *Foreign News in the Media: International Reporting in Twenty-nine Countries*, Reports and Papers on Mass Communication, No. 93 (Paris: UNESCO, 1984); Robert L. Stevenson and Richard R. Cole, "Foreign News Flow and the Unesco Debate," Paper presented at the annual meeting of the International Studies Association, Los Angeles, 1980; Robert L. Stevenson, Richard R. Cole and Donald Lewis Shaw, "Patterns of World News Coverage: A Look at the UNESCO Debate on the 'New World Information Order,'" in *Assessing the New World Information Order Debate: Evidence and Proposals*, ed., Gertrude J. Robinson (Chapel Hill, N.C.: International Communication Division, Association for Education in Journalism, 1982).

39. Robert L. Stevenson and Richard R. Cole, "Patterns of Foreign News," in *Foreign News and the New World Information Order*, eds., Robert L. Stevenson and Donald Lewis Shaw (Ames, Iowa: Iowa State University Press, 1984), p. 37.

40. Richard C. Vincent and Ali Riaz, "Foreign News on Bangladesh Television: An Analysis of News Content and Selection," Paper presented at the 40th annual conference of the International Communication Association, Dublin, Ireland, June 27, 1990.

41. Sreberny-Mohammadi, *Foreign News in the Media: International Reporting in Twenty-nine Countries*, see general review.

42. George Gerbner and George Marvanyi, "The Many Worlds of the World's Press," *Journal of Communication* 27 (1) (1977), pp. 52-66.

43. Sreberny-Mohammadi, *Foreign News in the Media: International Reporting in Twenty-nine Countries*, p. 126.

44. Annabelle Sreberny-Mohammadi, "Results of International Cooperation," *Journal of Communication* 34 (Winter 1984), p. 126.

45. Ibid., p. 128.

46. Ibid., pp. 126-127; see also Annabelle Sreberny-Mohammadi, *Foreign News in the Media: International Reporting in Twenty-nine Countries;* Stevenson and Cole, "Foreign News Flow and the Unesco Debate;" Stevenson, Cole and Shaw, "Patterns of World News Coverage: A Look at the UNESCO Debate on the 'New World Information Order.'"

47. Stevenson and Cole, "Patterns of Foreign News," p. 37.

48. Ibid., p. 59.

49. Robert L. Stevenson and Richard R. Cole, "Issues in Foreign News," in *Foreign News and the New World Information* Order, eds., Robert L. Stevenson and Donald Lewis Shaw (Ames, Iowa: Iowa State University Press, 1984), p. 17.

50. Robert L. Stevenson and Gary D. Gaddy, "'Bad News' and the Third World," Paper presented at the annual conference of the International Communication Association, Boston, 1982.

51. Robert L. Stevenson and Kirsten D. Thompson, "'Contingencies' in the Structure of Foreign News," in *Foreign News and the New World Information Order*, eds., Robert L. Stevenson and Donald Lewis Shaw (Ames, Iowa: Iowa State University Press, 1984), pp. 71-87.

52. Robert L. Stevenson and J. Walker Smith, "Cultural Meaning of Foreign News," in *Foreign News and the New World Information Order*, eds., Robert L. Stevenson and Donald Lewis Shaw (Ames, Iowa: Iowa State University Press, 1984), pp. 98-105.

53. David H. Weaver and G. Cleveland Wilhoit, "Foreign News Coverage in Two U.S. Wire Services," *Journal of Communication*, 31 (Spring 1981), pp. 55-63.

54. Ibid., 55-63.

55. David H. Weaver and G. Cleveland Wilhoit, "Foreign News in the Western Agencies," in *Foreign News and the New World Information Order*, eds., Robert L. Stevenson and Donald Lewis Shaw (Ames, Iowa: Iowa State University Press, 1984), pp. 153-185.

56. Stevenson and Cole, "Patterns of Foreign News," pp. 37-62.

57. George Gerbner and George Marvanyi, "The Many Worlds of the World's Press," *Journal of Communication* 27 (1) (1977), pp. 52-66; Peter Golding and Phil Elliott, *Making the News* (New York: Longman, 1979); Wilbur Schramm and L. Erwin Atwood, *Circulation of News in the Third World: A Study of Asia* (Hong Kong: Chinese University Press, 1981); Anthony C. Giffard, "Developed and Developing Nations News in U.S. Wire Services to Asia," *Journalism Quarterly*, 61 (1984), pp. 14-19; Anthony C. Giffard, "Inter Press Service: News from the Third World," *Journal of Communication*, 34(4) (1984), pp. 41-59.

58. Schramm and Atwood, *Circulation of News in the Third World: A Study of Asia.*

59. Kazuo Kawatake, "A Week of TV News—Comparative Study of

TV News in Eight Countries," in *Studies of Broadcasting*, eds., G. Kurono and K. Sata (Tokyo: Radio & TV Culture Institute of the Nippon Hoso Kyokai, 1982, No. 18), pp. 51-68.

60. S. Iwao, "Study of the International TV News in Japan," *KEIO Communication Review* 2 (March 1981), pp. 3-16; Kenji Kitatani, *Assessment of the New World Order: A Content Analysis of International Affairs Coverage by the Primary Western Television Networks* (Tokyo: Hosa Bunka Foundation, Inc., 1981).

61. O. E. Nwuneli and E. Udoh, "International News Coverage in Nigerian Newspapers," *Gazette* 29 (1/2) (1982), pp. 31-40.

62. Lee B. Becker, I. Sobowale and W. Casey, "Newspaper and Television Dependencies: Effects on Evaluations of Public Officials," *Journal of Broadcasting* 23 (1979), pp. 465-475.

63. Nabil Dajani and John Donohue, "Foreign News in the Arab Press: A Content Analysis of Six Arab Dailies," *Gazette* 19 (1973), pp. 155-170. The United States is also faulted for its dominance of other media usage abroad. Seventy percent of the foreign films brought into Morocco for its television, cinema, and videocassette markets, for example, came from the United States; Alan Woodrow, "North's Communication Channels Go Only One Way," *Le Monde*, reprinted in *Guardian Weekly*, October 21, 1990, p. 16.

64. William A. Hachten, *The World News Prism* (Ames, Iowa: State University Press, 1981).

65. Hamid Mowlana, "Trends in Research on International Communication in the United States," *Gazette* 19 (1973), p. 82.

66. James Larson and Andy Hardy, "International Affairs Coverage on Network Television News: A Study of News Flow," *Gazette* 23 (1977), pp. 241-256.

67. Al Hester, "Five Years of Foreign News on U.S. Television Evening Newscasts," *Gazette* 24 (1978), pp. 86-95.

68. James B. Weaver, Christopher J. Porter and Margaret E. Evans, "Patterns in Foreign News Coverage on U.S. Network TV: A 10-Year Analysis," *Journalism Quarterly* 84 (1984), pp. 356-363.

69. Annabelle Sreberny-Mohammadi, "Results of International Cooperation," *Journal of Communication* 34 (Winter 1984), pp. 121-134.

70. William C. Adams, "Whose Lives Count? TV Coverage of Natural Disasters," *Journal of Communication* 36 (Spring 1986), pp. 113-122.

71. Pamela J. Shoemaker, Tsan-Kuo Chang and Nancy Brendlinger, "Deviance as a Predictor of Newsworthiness: Coverage of International Events in the U.S. Media," in *Communication Yearbook*, vol. 10, ed., M. L. McLaughlin (Newbury Park, CA: Sage, 1987), pp. 348-365.

72. See also Emile G. McAnany, James F. Larson and J. Douglas

Storey, "News of Latin America on Network Television, 1972-1982: Too Little Too Late?" Paper presented at the annual conference of the International Communication Association, Boston, May, 1982; Al Hester, "Theoretical Considerations in Predicting Volume and Direction of International Information Flow," *Gazette* 19 (1973), pp. 239-247; James F. Larson, "International Affairs Coverage on U.S. Network Television," *Journal of Communication*, 29 (Spring 1979), pp. 136-147.

73. A. H. Raskin, "U.S. News Coverage of the Belgrade UNESCO Conference," *Journal of Communication* 31 (Autumn 1981), pp. 165-167.

74. Joseph A. Mehan, "U.S. Media Coverage of UNESCO General Conference, Belgrade," UNESCO Memorandum, New York, December 16, 1980.

75. M. L. Stein, "UNESCO Defends MacBride Report," *Editor and Publisher*, January 10, 1981.

76. Colleen Roach, "French Press Coverage of the Belgrade UNESCO Conference," *Journal of Communication* 31 (Autumn 1981), pp. 164-187.

77. Ibid., pp. 164-187.

78. Ibid., pp. 164-187.

79. Stein, "UNESCO Defends MacBride Report."

80. Ibid.

81. Ibid.

82. For example, some of the research outlined above offers findings which partially refute the notion of exclusive negative treatment of the Third World by Western media. Stevenson and Cole, "Patterns of Foreign News," pp. 37-62; Robert L. Stevenson and J. Walker Smith, "Cultural Meaning of Foreign News," in *Foreign News and the New World Information Order*, eds., Robert L. Stevenson and Donald Lewis Shaw (Ames, Iowa: Iowa State University Press, 1984), pp. 98-105; Robert L. Stevenson and Kristen D. Thompson, "'Contingencies' in the Structure of Foreign News," in *Foreign News and the New World Information Order*, eds., Robert L. Stevenson and Kristin D. Thompson (Ames, Iowa: Iowa State University Press, 1984), pp. 71-87.

83. Dan D. Nimmo and James E. Combs, *Nightly Horrors: Crisis Coverage by Television Network News* (Knoxville, TN: University of Tennessee Press, 1985); Myles Breen and Farrel Corcoran, "Myth in the Television Discourse," *Communication Monographs*, 49 (1982), pp. 127-136.

84. Richard C. Vincent, Bryan. K. Crow and Dennis K. Davis, "When Technology Fails: The Drama of Airline Crashes in Network Television News," *Journalism Monographs* (1989), No. 117.

85. W. R. Fisher, "Narration as a Human Communication Paradigm: The Case of Public Moral Argument," *Communication Monographs* 51 (1984), pp. 1-22; also see Richard C. Vincent, Bryan. K. Crow and Dennis

K. Davis, "When Technology Fails: The Drama of Airline Crashes in Network Television News," for a discussion. Also see W. R. Fisher, "Narration as a Human Communication Paradigm: The Case of Public Moral Argument," *Communication Monographs* 51 (1984), pp. 1-22.

86. W. L. Bennett and M. Edelman, "Toward a New Political Narrative," *Journal of Communication* 35 (4) (1985), pp. 156-171.

87. S. M. Barkin and Michael Gurevitch, "Out of Work and on the Air: Television News and Unemployment," *Critical Studies in Mass Communication* 4 (1) (1987), p. 5.

88. Dennis K. Davis and John P. Robinson, "Newsflow and Democratic Society in an Age of Electronic Media," in *Public Communication and Behavior*, ed., George Comstock (New York: Academic Press, 1989).

89. Teun van Dijk, *News as Discourse* (Hillsdale, N.J.: Lawrence Erlbaum Associates, 1988); Teun A. van Dyke, ed., *Discourse and Communication: New Approaches to the Analysis of Mass Media Discourse and Communication* (Berlin and New York: Walter de Gruyter, 1985); Teun A. van Dyke, "Discourse Analysis: Its Development and Application to the Structure of News," *Journal of Communication* 33 (2) (1983), pp. 20-43.

90. Jan Kleinnijenhuis, "Images of Cold War: Effects of Press Opinion in the Netherlands," *European Journal of Communication* 2 (1987), pp. 311-336; O. Scholten, "Selectivity in Political Communication," *Gazette* 35 (1985), pp. 157-172.

91. Ole Findahl and Brigitta Hoijer, *On Knowledge, Social Privilege and the News* (Stockholm: Sveriges Radio, 1974); Ole Findahl and Brigitta Hoijer, "Effects of Additional Verbal Information on Retention of a Radio News Program," *Journalism Quarterly* 52 (1975), pp. 493-498; Ole Findahl and Brigitta Hoijer, *Fragments of Reality: An Experiment with News and TV Visuals* (Stockholm: Sveriges Radio, 1976); Ole Findahl and Brigitta Hoijer, "Studying Media Content with Reference to Human Comprehension," in *Scandinavian Studies in Content Analysis*, ed., Karl Eric Rosengren (London: Sage, 1981).

92. Peter Dahlgren, "TV News as a Social Relation," *Media, Culture and Society* 3 (1981), pp. 291-302; Peter Dahlgren, "Beyond Information: TV News As a Cultural Discourse," *The European Journal of Communication* 2 (1986), pp. 125-136; Peter Dahlgren, "What's the Meaning of This? Viewers' Plural Sense-Making of TV News," *Media, Culture and Society* 10 (1988), pp. 285-301.

93. Klaus Bruhn Jensen, *Making Sense of the News* (Aarhus, Denmark: Aarhus University Press, 1986); Klaus Bruhn Jensen, "Qualitative Audience Research: Toward an Integrative Approach to Reception," *Critical Studies in Mass Communication* 4 (1987), pp. 21-36; Klaus Bruhn

Jensen, "News as Ideology: Economic Statistics and Political Ritual in Television Network News," *Journal of Communication* (Winter 1987), pp. 9-27; Klaus Bruhn Jensen, "The Politics of Polysemy: Television News, Everyday Consciousness and Political Action," *Media, Culture and Society* 12 (1990), pp. 57-77.

94. Ibid.

95. Klaus Bruhn Jensen, "Qualitative Audience Research: Toward an Integrative Approach to Reception," *Critical Studies in Mass Communication* 4 (1987), pp. 21-36; also Klaus Bruhn Jensen, "The Politics of Polysemy: Television News, Everyday Consciousness and Political Action," pp. 57-77.

96. See Johan Galtung and Mari Holmboe Ruge, "The Structure of Foreign News: The Presentation of the Congo, Cuba and Cyprus Crises in Four Norwegian Newspapers," *Journal of Peace Research* 2:1 (1965), pp. 64-91.

97. See Johan Galtung, "A Structural Theory of Imperialism," in *Essays in Peace Research*, Vol. IV, chapter 13. For a discussion, see R.D. Haynes, Jr., "Test of Galtung's Theory of Structural Imperialism", in *Foreign News and the New World Information Order*, eds., Robert L. Stevenson and Donald Lewis Shaw (Ames, Iowa: The Iowa State University Press, 1984). Among his conclusions: "It seems, as Galtung suggests, that Third World newspeople have readily absorbed the journalistic lessons of the developed world" (p. 213); and "The findings indicate that the international system is not a simple feudal structure as Galtung suggests" (p. 214).

98. See Johan Galtung, "The New International Order: Economics and Communication," in *Communication, Economics, and Development*, eds., Meheroo Jussawalla and D.M. Lamberton (Elmsford, N.Y.: Pergamon, 1982), pp. 133-143. Portions of the article appear in a modified version as part of the present volume, in Chapter 3.

99. See John Hartley, *Understanding News*, (London and New York: Methuen, 1982), pp. 76-79. "In a famous study, Galtang [sic] and Ruge (1973) isolated a series of conditions which have to be fulfilled before an event is selected for attention" (p.76), whereupon he reformulates them masterfully.

100. Among the twelve criteria for newsworthiness, two of them were actually more holistic: F4 focused on "meaningfulness" and F5 on "consonance," in other words, on *contexts* for the news item. These two hypotheses were tested in an interesting way by Jan Kleinnijenhuis ("Structure of Discourse and the Selection of Foreign News," Paper presented at a Vrije Universiteit workshop, Amsterdam, April 27, 1988) who concluded:

that the NET-method for discourse analysis looks useful to investigate news selection hypotheses. The substantial conclusion should be that Johan Galtung's early news selection hypotheses F4 and F5 are supported strongly by empirical evidence. To a large extent the selection of news is dependent upon structural characteristics of the discourse already presented (p. 6).

It should be noted that what Kleinnijenhuis is saying here actually goes beyond "The Structure of Foreign News" analysis. That analysis was essentially atomistic, trying to correct for atomism with the additivity and complementarity hypotheses. But only discourse analysis can bring in the context.

101. For an example of precisely this logic consider this excerpt from *The Jerusalem Post*, June 9, 1988, in the midst of the *intifadah*:

Good news is supposed not to be news at all. But that hoary old notion is long *passe*, and it is especially out of place at a time of pain and self-doubt and daily expectation of more of the same. In such a time, even the holding of a regular, annual affair may qualify as good news. It is thus right that the opening of Hebrew Book Week should be hailed with satisfaction, even pride.

And even if bad news is normal news, good news is nevertheless evaluated positively:

GORBACHEV OUTDOES REAGAN IN 'GOOD' NEWS

During the study period — last November through April:

-Gorbachev got 4.5 percent of national media attention — the equivalent of 153 pages of USA TODAY or 14.9 minutes of network TV per week — more than half of it positive.

-Reagan got 3.5 percent of national coverage — equivalent of 119 pages of USA TODAY per week — less than half of it positive.

(From USA TODAY, May 24, 1988, p. 1A.)

102. Youichi Ito, "The Trade Winds Change: Japan's Shift from an Information Importer to an Information-Exporter, 1965-1985" *Communication Yearbook 13* (Newbury Park, Calif.: Sage Publishers, 1990), pp. 430-465.

103. Chapter 14, Thomas J. Ahern, Jr., "Determinants of Foreign Coverage in U.S. Newspapers," in Stevenson and Shaw editors, *Foreign News and the New World Information Order*, pp. 217-236.

104. Ibid., p. 226.

105. Kaarle Nordenstreng:

> The final project [the "World of the News" study] was dominated by "vulgar" categories that capture *ad hoc* aspects of the media context, rather than a comprehensive message carried by the content. In other words, it became more of a quantitative than a qualitative exercise, whereas the original idea was to make it more "intensive" than "extensive."

(from Kaarle Nordenstreng, "Bitter Lessons," *Journal of Communication* (Winter 1984).

106. Robert L. Stevenson, in "Pseudo-Debate," *Journal of Communication* (Winter 1984), found that "the attention given to disruptive news in the Third World is characteristic of all media systems, particularly those in the Third World itself." We have no problem with that finding since our approach deals with the news paradigm as such, not with the Western wire agencies. See the excellent book by Robert L. Stevenson, *Communication, Development and the Third World: The Global Politics of Information* (White Plains, N.Y.: Longman, 1988).

107. The concern is that simple content analyses, in their effort to reduce data to categories, potentially ignore many of the larger and more important trends. Many studies on U.S. network television news do not even bother to examine the actual programs, but instead use the brief story descriptions listed in the *Television News Index and Abstracts* as the unit of analysis. This index is published monthly to guide users of the videotape archives at Vanderbilt University. For one example of such an approach, see James Larson, *Television's Window on the World: International Affairs Coverage on the U.S. Networks*.

108. See W. Lance Bennett, Lynne A Gressett and William Haltom, "Repairing the News: A Case Study of the News Paradigm," *Journal of Communication* 35 (Spring 1985), pp. 50-68.

109. Karl Eric Rosengren, "International News: Methods, Data, and Theory," *Journal of Peace Research* (1974), pp. 145-156.

110. René-Jean Ravault, "International Information: Bullet or Boomerang?" in *Political Communication Research: Approaches, Studies, Assessments*, ed., David L. Paletz (Norwood, N.J.: Ablex Publishing Corporation, 1987), Chapter 15, pp. 245-265.

111. Teun A. van Dijk of the University of Amsterdam, a specialist on news discourse, puts it this way:

> An account of news production in terms of the well-known "news value" criteria, first proposed by Galtung & Ruge in 1965 may now

> be complemented with a theory of social cognitions of journalists. These socio-political and cultural representations, shared by journalists as a group, influence the so-called "models" journalists construct of (news) events. An interdisciplinary discourse analysis of news, featuring such a social cognition component, enables us to specify in detail how these models influence the actual production (and understanding) of both source texts and news reports.

In other words, to the atomistic focus on lists of news value criteria, a holistic focus on the total representation or mode is added. (From "Discourse Analysis and News Analysis," Paper presented at a Vrije Universiteit workshop, Amsterdam, April 27, 1988, p. 1). For a detailed exposition of van Dijk's position, see "Discourse Analysis: Its Development and Application to the Structure of News," *Journal of Communication*, 33 (2) (1983), pp. 20-43. For an excellent use of discourse theory, see R.K. Mandoff, *Narrative Strategy and Nuclear News*, Occasional Paper no. 1 (New York: Center for War, Peace and the News Media, New York University, 1987).

112. For a general survey, including "content as resulting from social and institutional forces," see Pamela J. Shoemaker and Elizabeth Kay Mayfield, "Building a Theory of News Content: A Synthesis of Current Approaches," *Journalism Monographs* (June 1987), No. 103.

CHAPTER 3

The New International Order: Economics, Information and Communication

If a free society cannot help the many who are poor, it cannot save the few who are rich.
　　　—*John F. Kennedy, Inaugural Address, 1961*

The nature of bad news infects the teller.
　　　—*William Shakespeare, Anthony and Cleopatra*
　　　Act I, sc. 3, 1. 99.

THE SEARCH FOR AN UNDERLYING WORLD PROCESS

The basic thesis of this chapter, elaborating a theme touched in Chapter 1 above, is that it may not be so fruitful to explore the direct relations between economics and information-communication. No doubt these relations exist. Economic surplus can be invested in a communication infrastructure which can then be used to build and expand economic cycles, involving nature, production, and consumption nodes. Improved communication/information will serve to increase the volume that passes through the economic cycle, to increase the speed with which it passes, to increase the depletion of nature through extraction, and to increase the pollution of nature with industrial waste from production, and consumer waste from the consumption node. As enough surplus is generated and invested at various points, the cycle will be expanded and deepened further. The second component, information, in principle reduces uncertainties and makes us see opportunities that otherwise might get lost. On the other hand, information may also make us sensitive to risks and dangers that might prevent us from taking action. In general, there is hardly any doubt that economic growth and information-communication growth go hand in hand.

But precisely because they go hand in hand we might also explore the nature of the body carrying these hands. Is there an underly-

71

ing factor that directs both economics and information-communication, making it look like one is causing the other, when it might actually be more fruitful to see them as two different manifestations of the same underlying phenomenon? If this is accepted as a working hypothesis, what, then, is the nature of that phenomenon? And given its nature, how is it likely to affect the future shape of the relation between economics and information-communication?

EARLY UNESCO ACTIONS

Activities within the United Nations provide some of the basis for looking more closely at these phenomena. The United Nations, of course, was not the first to examine imbalances and inequities which stood in the way of the "free-flow of ideas" throughout the world. For example, Bullion notes that in 1934 the world's intercontinenal radio cable network was 90% controlled by Britain, the United States, France and Italy.[1] International interest in seeking agreements regarding journalism can be traced back to international congresses held in the late 1800s, and League of Nation meetings in the 1920s and 1930s.[2]

In its first session (1946), the United Nations General Assembly accepted the notion that communication was a fundamental human right. According to Article 19 of the Universal Declaration of Human Rights, adopted in 1948: "Every individual has the right to freedom of opinion and of expression, which entails the right to be free from harassment for his opinions and the right to seek out, to receive and to communicate, regardless of frontiers and ideas, by whatever means of expression he may choose." This theme continued to play a role in U.N. Conferences and General Assembly discussions.[3]

The United Nations Educational, Scientific and Cultural Organization (UNESCO) was first involved with freedom of information issues through the Beirut and the Fiorenze Accords. In the 1950s, UNESCO was associated with some of the early studies being conducted on one-way information flow between developed and developing nations.[4] In 1951 the Economic and Social Council appealed to governments by passing Resolution 387(XII), calling for the safeguarding of correspondent rights in gathering and transmitting news.[5] The United Nation's first news study was conducted in 1953 and offered a comparative review of one week's news in seven major dailies, and a review of news agencies. A second study, in 1956, further examined press messages and the role of foreign correspondents. In 1954, through Resolution 522C(XVII), the Economic and Social Council transmitted these studies to states, members, and nonmembers, requesting that addressed measures be implemented.[6]

The 1950s and 1960s also saw a series of conferences on various worldwide imbalances and inequities which were seen as standing in the way of the "free-flow of ideas."[7]

At the Ljubljana meeting of 1968 it was noted that:

> The system of manipulating man's thinking is getting accomplished in such a way that a contemporary individual with his 'freedom' is often becoming, without realizing it, a prisoner of foreign concepts of the world for they are being incessantly and systematically forced upon him. Where the information media are treated as a privilege of the ruling elite, the money and the authority, they represent a power which is out of the influential sphere of the public... In the present conditions the safeguarding of independence and of freedom of information has to be treated from new aspects and in a new, modern way....

In June 1969, participants of the Montreal meeting on news media and society were even more blunt when they offered this summary:

> News media are capable of improving and broadening international understanding, but inter-cultural communication does not necessarily or automatically lead to improved international understanding. We believe, on the contrary, that at the present time, what is known as the 'free flow of information' is in fact a 'one-way' flow rather than a genuine exchange of information.

Because the meeting was aware of the dangers in attempting to restrict free flow of information, they closed by simply noting that the matter merited further attention.

Around this time an interest in satellite communications and a fear of modern technology developments generally, lead to a concern among some nations about the role of satellites in communication and the use of broadcast satellites to transmit signals across borders.[8]

> The objective of satellite broadcasting for the free flow of information is to ensure the widest possible dissemination, among the peoples of the world, of news of all countries, developed and developing alike.... Cultural programmes, while promoting the enrichment of all cultures, should respect the distinctive character, the values

and the dignity of each, and the right of all countries and peoples to preserve their cultures as part of the common heritage of mankind.[9]

As we can see from the above chronology, while information flow was being discussed, no radical proposals were put forth, nor were major demands made. All of this was important, however, for it was part of the decolonization discourse which was gaining momentum at the time. By the early 1970s, notes Nordenstreng, the developing countries had acquired some "political power and economic potential." It is not by chance, then, that the term "new order" became popular.[10]

It was at the Sixteenth Session of the UNESCO General Conference (November 1970, Paris) that several developing nation delegations, lead by India, outlined the problems of unequal information flow. According to the Report of the Programme Commission: "Delegates from a number of developing countries stressed the need to ensure that the free flow of information and international exchanges should be a two-way operation. They asserted that the programme must continue to emphasize the rights of less privileged nations to preserve their own culture . . . ," and to help Member States formulate mass communication policies.[11] UNESCO followed this by helping to map out a research agenda on news flow.[12] A variety of areas were proposed and these included the establishment of "international communications networks," obstacles to "free flow of information," news exchange, the "one-way 'pipeline'," "cultural autonomy," and problems with "isolationist" policies.[13] Following the mandate that it address policy matters, a meeting of experts called by UNESCO identified a variety of "cultural neocolonialism" problems which were largely a result of the rapid developments of communication technology.[14]

This 1970 Paris meeting is also generally recognized as the starting point for the UNESCO Mass Media Declaration.[15] The resolution called for all States to take "necessary steps . . . to encourage the use of information media against propaganda on behalf of war, racism and hatred among nations . . ."

At the next General Conference of UNESCO, the debate over Direct Broadcast Satellites intensified when the Soviet Union proposed that "a binding convention of principles for television transmission from satellites" be approved.[16] The draft on DBS (Direct Broadcast Satellites) was originally written by the Soviets in New York in September 1972, during the Seventeenth General Assembly of the U.N., and was presented there as a declaration of UNESCO on November 15.[17] The declaration endorsed the notion of prior consent when dealing with broadcasts coming from satellites. The resolution was adopted by the Assembly, 102 to 1 (the United States cast the lone dissenting vote). At the same meeting the Soviets introduced another resolution, addressing "fundamental principles governing the use of the mass media." The United States's position on these resolutions was that such moves would be a threat to its longstanding tradition of unrestricted information flow.[18]

In such an environment attention was becoming increasingly focused in two major areas. The New International Economic Order[19] and the New World Information and Communication Order[20] were the labels given to these approaches advocated by the Third World (TW) countries. Emerging as they did from the same context they may be seen as carriers of the same deep structure.

THE NEW INTERNATIONAL ECONOMIC ORDER

The first formal new order adopted by UNESCO was an economic one (the communication new order followed). The call for a new economic order was partly a reaction to the installation of the International Monetary Fund, the World Bank (International Bank for Reconstruction and Development), and the General Agreement on Tariff and Trade during the post-World War II period. During post-war negotiations, unsuccessful proposals by poorer nations for national sovereignty and management of economic development systems were later developed into a campaign for international economic revision.[21] The New International Economic Order was a campaign launched by UNESCO to help provide greater balance between developed and developing nations economically. At the time of its initiation, the NIEO was reacting to conditions in which 75% of the world's population represented only 30% of its income. While the average per capita income for industrialized nations was $2,400 annually, in developing countries it was a mere $180, and in the 24 poorest nations, annual per capita income was less than $100. Making matters even worse, the share of world trade enjoyed by developing countries had dropped from 32% in 1950 to 17% by the mid 1970s, and this had been coupled by an enormous increase in Third World Debt ($233,000 million in 1977 to $1,340,000 million in 1990). The inequities were alarming, and fostered grave concern. A call for action proposed that developing and industrialized nations engage in joint economic and social activities. Stabilization of raw material prices and increased grants of aid were encouraged. The objective was to help raise living standards in the Third World, thereby nurturing new markets for industrialized nations. The mass media was seen as a useful tool in helping to "condition" public opinion in developed countries.[22]

NIEO interests received a major boost when the Organization of Petroleum Exporting Countries (OPEC) called for a new economic order in 1974, and the United Nations General Assembly adopted the "Declaration of the Establishment of a New International Economic Order" along with the "Program in the Establishment of a New International Economic Order" to help insure economic sovereignty for Third World countries in April 1974. The formal start of the NIEO, however, is believed to have come when delegates at the Fifth Conference of Heads of State or Government of the Non-Aligned Countries convened in Colombo in 1976. There were concerns about the disparity between Western wealth and Third World poverty, and the inequity of wealth distributions, with imbalances forming along the lines of old colonial ties. It was recognized that true political and economic independence was not possible under the current system of information and communication dependence. This link between communication and economic concerns was made at the UNESCO General Conference held later that year (Nairobi, 1976).[23] As the MacBride Commission report noted:

> . . . the new communication order must be considered as an element of the new economic order. . . There is a coherent correlation between these two orders stemming from the fact that information is now a specific kind of basic economic resource (and not just a commodity) which performs an essential social function but which is today unequally distributed and badly used. In some other respects, the new communication order is a pre-condition of the new economic order, just as communication is the *sine qua non* of all economic activities between groups, peoples and nations.[24]

NIEO is a process of historical importance. It has been the basic project of the Third World—and the majority of humankind and of the U.N—but they are operating with a considerable deficit relative to their objective power base when it comes to exercising control over the world economic and information and communication orders. The underlying idea is quite simple. There is actually no challenge to the old international economic/communication order at all except for one rather important point: the Third World wanting to have (much) more of a say in running these international orders. Thus, under NIEO, the world economy will still undoubtedly be a capitalist world economy (a system we have seen expanding with the changes in the Eastern Bloc and the Soviet Union); under NWICO, the world information and communication system will still be dominated by news about elite people in elite countries, and will still be actor-oriented and basically negative, focusing on events rather than on structures and processes. There may be rhetoric to the contrary in both cases. But what has been seen so far emanating from TW centers looks very similar to what we see from the West. There is hardly a change in what flows in the economic and information-communication cycles. The debate is over power rather than substance.

In our view the debate is not over the form of the structure of the economic and information cycles either, at least not in the longer run. The First World, and in a more limited sense also the (former) Second (socialist) World, has always seemed so overwhelmingly powerful that it is hard to imagine a world run from the Third World. The Third World is still very much in the Periphery; marginalized, fragmented, with only sectorial participation, penetrated, and exploited. Today the 103 member nations of the Non-Aligned Movement, for example, account for almost half of the globe's population, two-thirds of the United Nations seats, but a mere 8% of the world's economic yield. The Third World looks so incapable of being a partner in equitable, symmetric interaction with the First and Second Worlds. One additional reason appears to be that the Third World always underestimates both its own power and the vulnerability of the First World, so dependent on raw materials and cheap labor. Yet the Periphery as the First World is absolutely conceivable today, if not exactly around the corner. Just look at what not only Japan, but also the mini-Japans/Chinas—all of them very poor countries in 1945—are doing economically to the U.S. today.

The answer to the question *what is NIEO all about* is found neither in the substance, the form, nor in the structure of the economic cycle. It is the *location* of the structure that is at stake. World capitalism is not in a crisis; the position of the U.S. within that system is. The center of gravity of the system is moving and perhaps also dividing. It is painful for those who lose control, delightful for those who gain it after having fought for it. Later on, the delight in the pain may become as obvious as the pain in the delight. More particularly, those who gain are less likely to be found in South America, Africa, and West and South Asia than in Southeast and East Asia.

To understand this more clearly, NIEO should be seen as a process, not as something static, and certainly not merely as a demand for better terms of trade. More precisely, five phases can be reasonably inferred from the U.N. resolutions, debates, and actions of the NIEO. The NIEO, as it was planned, included the following points (there is some overlap with the corresponding section in Chapter 1, for the sake of completeness and because other points are being developed):

1. Better terms of trade for the Third World (possibly leading to decreased North-South trade;
2. More Third World control over productive assets (nature, capital, labor, technology; leading to import and export substitution);
3. More Third World interaction—South-South trade (TCDC, ECDE);
4. More Third World counter-penetration (investment in "rich" countries, etc.); and
5. More Third World control over world economic institutions, including TNCs, The World Bank, and the International Monetary Fund.

Thus, in the first and conservative phase the only thing at stake is the terms of trade between the commodities produced by the Third World from the colonial period onward, and the processed goods produced by the First World. The focus is on the quantity of goods and money, not on the quality of goods exported. There is no basic challenge of the infamous "division of labor" conventionally legitimized by the principle of "comparative advantages."

In the second phase, the Third World tries to do something about this by gaining control over productive assets. This is a political rather than a (neo)classical economic question. It may boil down to nationalization, and the legitimizing preparation was already done in the 1974 U.N. General Assembly CERDS resolution (Charter of Economic Rights and Duties of States). This is what the mini-Japans/Chinas did, and with considerable success—but it did not come without very hard work, and with heavy human costs.

In the third phase, then, this is translated into increased South-South trade and interaction in general. In the old order there were almost no links of this kind. With this move the structure changes and becomes more symmetric because there is now trade in all kinds of geographic directions. But this is on the surface; the reality is different. The First World still penetrates the Third World much more than vice versa. Thus, "South-South trading" may take place under the auspices of First World TNCs.

This is where the fourth and fifth phases enter the picture. Armed with capital gained in the first phase, and control gained from the much more political second phase (which is still to come), the Third World has the opportunity to start establishing itself in Center roles, as some OPEC countries tried in the 1970s. The first steps would be counter-penetration of various kinds, such as investment and buying of stock and real estate in the First World. The more basic steps then follow: control of the control positions, by conquering the World Bank, the International Monetary Fund, and related institutions, and by controlling an increasing number of transnational corporations.

The latter should not be that difficult. What was once considered the supreme instrument for Third World control by the First—because of the ease with which intracorporate maneuvers could take place given the mobility of production factors and products, of capital and personnel, and of goods and services—can now also be seen as a tool turned against the power-wielder. Precisely because of the intimate correlation between communication and economics, and the speed of both, the TNCs may prove one day to become the media through which assets can effectively be transferred from North to South, although so far they have been moving to the Fourth World (Southeast) rather than the Third (Southwest). When this process really gets started, the governments in the North will probably be inclined to intervene to try to stop the flows. By that time, however, it may already be too late.

In short, the New International Economic Order is old as an "order." But it will certainly change the world, and affect individual countries and their people alike, by changing the locations of Center and Periphery rather than the meanings of Center and Periphery. The process is quick. In a sense, it started with Japan after the Meiji Revolution (not "restoration;" what happened was a real break with the past) or with the post-1945 fights against colonialism and neocolonialism, or with Iran in 1951-1953. Or perhaps it began with UNCTAD I in Geneva in 1964. At any rate, it started much before the Sixth and Seventh Special NIEO Assemblies of the United Nations General Assembly in 1974 and 1975. The four mini- Japans/Chinas joined in the 1970s; China entered in the 1980s in its particular oscillating manner. There is more to come.

By the magic year 2000 much of this project will probably have been completed, but not for the poorest Third World countries. The present authors are among those who believe that it will lead to a capitalist world with the Center in the Japan-Korea-China Southeast Asia triangle—meaning that the expression "Third World" used everywhere above is actually a misnomer. It certainly applies to some Third World countries more than to others, and more particularly to those we refer to as the Fourth World. The process for a recolonization of most of the classical Third World may open, but this time it will emanate from the world's Southeast rather than its Northwestern corner (the Southeastern corner being the Fourth World). *Plus ca change, plus c'est la meme chose.*

THE NEW WORLD INFORMATION AND COMMUNICATION ORDER

An Order Emerges

The nonaligned movement, with deep roots in anti-colonialism and anti-imperialism, originally was created to encourage member nonalignment with any superpower. As it has evolved, the independents (Bangladesh, Burma, Cameroon, India, Iran, Jordan, Nicaragua, Nigeria, Pakistan, Panama, Peru, Sri Lanka, Sudan, Trinidad and Tobago, Yugoslavia, etc.) have tended to follow the original purpose of nonalignment. The conservatives (Argentina, Bolivia, Cyprus, Egypt, Kenya, Malaysia, Morocco, Saudi Arabia, Singapore, Zaire, etc.) lean toward the West, and the radicals (Afghanistan, Algeria, Cambodia, Congo, Cuba, Ethiopia, Iraq, Libya, North Korea, Palestine Liberation Organization, Zimbabwe, Syria, Vietnam, etc.) traditionally have been oriented toward China or the Soviet Union.[25] It was during the Algiers meeting (1973) that nonaligned nations straightforwardly noted their concern about information flow:

> Developing countries should take concerted action in the field of mass communications in order to promote a greater inter-change of ideas among themselves.
>
> a) Reorganization of existing communication channels which are the legacy of the colonial past and which have hampered free, direct and fast communication between them.
>
> b) Initiate joint action for the revision of existing multilateral agreements with a view to reviewing press cable rates and facilitating faster and cheaper inter-communication.
>
> c) Take urgent steps to expedite the process of collective ownership of communication satellite and evolve a code of conduct for directing their use.
>
> d) Promote increased contact between the mass media, universities, libraries, planning and research bodies and other institutions so as to enable developing countries to exchange experience and expertise and share ideas.[26]

Developing nations were also urged to "consider that cultural alienation and imparted civilization, imposed by imperialism and colonialism, should be countered by re-personalization and by a constant and determined recourse to the social and cultural values of the population which define them as a sovereign people." [27]

Table 1. Non-Aligned Nations, 1990

Afghanistan	Guinea	Pakistan
Algeria	Guinea-Bissau	Panama
Angola	Guyana	Peru
Argentina	India	Qatar
Bahamas	Indonesia	Rwanda
Bahrain	Iraq	Saint Lucia
Bangladesh	Ivory Coast	Sao Tome & Principe
Barbados	(Cote d'Isle)	Saudi Arabia
Benin	Jamaica	Senegal
Bhutan	Jordan	Seychelles
Bolivia	Kampuchea	Sierra Leone
Botswana	(Cambodia)	Singapore
Burkina Faso	Kenya	Somalia
Burundi	Kuwait	Sri Lania
Cambodia	Laos	Sudan
Cameroon	Lebanon	Suriname
Cape Verde	Lesotho	Swaziland
Central African Rep.	Liberia	Syria
Ceylon (Sri Lanka)	Libya	Tanzania
Chad	Madagascar	Togo
Colombia	Malawi	Trinidad & Tobago
Comoros	Malaysia	Tunisia
Congo	Maldives	Uganda
Cote d'Ivoire	Mali	United Arab Emirates
Cuba	Malta	Upper Volta
Cyprus	Mauritania	(Burkina F.)
Djibouti	Mauritius	Vanuatu
Ecuador	Morocco	Vietman
Egypt	Mozambique	Yemen
Equatorial Guinea	Nepal	Yugoslavia
Ethiopia	Nicaragua	Zaire
Gabon	Niger	Zambia
Gambia	Nigeria	Zimbabwe
Ghana	North Koria	
Grenada	Oman	

It is believed that later resolutions by UNESCO on the New International Economic Order were an outcome of this 1973 Algiers conference. This makes Algiers the actual birthplace of the New International Information Order.[28] Following the meeting it was decided that a Third World news agency should be established to help offset the Western agency dominance of information flow. This recommendation would be expanded at the UNESCO sanctioned symposium in Lima (August 1975), Tunis (Tunis Symposium on Communication Issues, March 1976), and Mexico City (May 1976). In Tunis, the meeting resolved that "(s)ince information in the world shows disequilibrium in favouring some and ignoring others, it is the duty of the non-aligned to change this situation and obtain the decolonisation of information, and initiate a new international order in information." Surfacing here was the nonaligned countries' concern that "former colonial and semi-colonial countries" were not sharing equally in the "global production of and trade in information."[29] Taking the lead was Yugoslavia, which offered its Tanjug Agency facilities as a locus for Third World news gathering operations. Its specific constitution was deferred to the Ministerial Conference of Non-Aligned Countries on the Press Agencies Pool (NANAP) held in July 1976 in New Delhi. Opening the meeting, Indian Prime Minister Indira Gandhi helped set the stage:

> In spite of political sovereignty, most of us who have emerged from a colonial or semi-colonial past continue to have a rather unequal cultural and economic relationship with our respective former overlords. They often remain the main source of industrial equipment and technological guidance. The European language we speak itself becomes a conditioning element. Inadequacy of educational materials made us dependent on the books of these dominant countries, especially at the university stage. We imbibe their prejudices. Even our image of ourselves, not to speak of the view of other countries, tends to conform to theirs. The self-depreciation and inferiority complex of some people of former colonies makes them easy prey to infiltration through forms of academic colonialism. This also contributes to the drain.
>
> I am not saying that we should not learn English or French. Nor am I for any narrow linguistic chauvinism which would only divide us. We must learn international languages to communicate and widen our horizon. But rather than unguardedly accepting versions put out by news agencies and publishing houses of the western countries, we should get to know one another directly and keep in touch to have firsthand acquaintance with our respective views.[30]

Noting severe deficiencies in global information flow, non-aligned members at this meeting further developed the concept of a news "pool" in their draft of a constitution. Due to concerns surrounding a prior Soviet Union proposal calling for strong government control,[31] the decision was made for the news "pool" to be a "self-financed activity" with "none of the pool-participating agencies (having) a dominant role." In 1976, India also merged its four national news agencies into one named Samachar, hoping to provide a leading role in the nonaligned news "pool." Mrs. Gandhi's repressive actions against journalists at the time of the "emergency" were viewed negatively, however, and helped to downplay Samachar's orchestration of a leadership role. All financing, operational, and organizational decisions were made by the 59 member states and 7 observers at the conference. The draft constitution and recommendations made at this conference were later endorsed at the Fifth Summit Meeting of Heads of State or Government of Non-Aligned Countries (Colombo, Sri Lanka, August 1976).

During the 18th UNESCO General Conference (Paris, November 1974), the First Draft of the Mass Media Declaration was presented.[32] The Draft declaration called for mass media responsibility in disseminating information and opinion, and reinforced the notion of freedom of speech and the press.[33] Along with freedom of speech, the declaration asserted that it was the public's "right to seek, receive and transmit information. . ."[34] It emphasized the two-way flow process in helping to strengthen "peace and international understanding."[35] Western pressures were already in evidence during this meeting.

Opening the 19th session of UNESCO's General Conference in Nairobi (November 1976), the Director General called attention to the global nature of information by categorizing it as the *problematique* of communication.[36] The increased attention given communication stemmed from the "the adoption of resolutions concerning the establishment of a new international economic order and, in particular, the efforts of non-aligned countries to institute regional co-operation in the field of communication and information." He concluded that "the distribution of communication media and the immense potential they represent reflects the uneven international distribution of economic power."[37]

Also during this meeting the move for strong government control initiated earlier by the Soviets surfaced in Article XII, calling for State responsibility "for the activities in the international sphere of all mass media under the jurisdiction." Western delegates argued that government supervision amounted to encroachment of freedom of speech. A lengthy debate followed. The dialogue underlined dissimilarities among Western, Communist, and Third World countries.[38] While there was general concern over Western dominance of global information flow, the differences and individual national interests were too complex and varied to be resolved in this meeting. Many Third World journalists supported the notion of press freedom. The atmosphere was nicely summarized by a Nigerian commentator speaking on Radio Lagos on November 10, 1976:

> Members of the UNESCO conference argued that government control of the Press was certainly not a cure for the ills of the mass media in the Third World countries, nor would it help the free flow of information. It was obvious that, if adopted, the draft declaration would have the effect of fettering the freedom of foreign newsmen operating across national boundaries.

> Besides, the imposition of regulations as implied in the draft declaration, restricting the dissemination of domestic news abroad or to state-controlled news services, would amount to placing curbs on the free flow of information. The Soviet-inspired draft declaration was ultimately shelved because of the view of the majority of the UNESCO conference that the correct solution to the problem of developing countries lies in measures which will give people the greatest possible diversity of opinions and to allow them to communicate easily with one another.[39]

The United States was obviously one of the principal parties threatened by such a draft declaration. The conference's position finally brought a United States threat to withdraw from UNESCO should the matter not be resolved to their satisfaction. Sussman provides a review of the events surrounding the U.S. position in 1976. The narrative also serves as a kind of precursor to the U.S.'s 1983-1984 actions regarding membership in UNESCO:

> The United States had paid $3.2 million in arrearages shortly before coming to Nairobi in order to vote there. By mid-1977, the United States, which is committed to provide 25% of UNESCO's annual budget, would owe UNESCO some $90 million in arrearages, current dues and other assessments. The only vocal U.S. opinion on the issue favored withdrawing funds until UNESCO reached satisfactory positions on critical confrontation issues. Mr. M'Bow paid a hasty visit to Secretary of State Kissinger just before the biennial opened; in turn, M'Bow was visited privately by members of the UNESCO Commission. In the hectic hours before the sessions opened, M'Bow sent a trusted aide to the United States to make certain the threats of withholding further funds, and even of withdrawing from UNESCO formally, were not empty gestures. M'Bow was assured they were not. He apparently accepted these estimates and devised the negoti-

ating group as a face-saving format for those backing the Soviet resolution.[40]

Director General M'Bow was apparently convinced that it was best to momentarily avoid a confrontation with the United States on this matter. In the end the decision was made to table the matter, but it was given a place on the 1978 meeting agenda.

Nevertheless, general concerns about the information order were not totally abandoned, and the General Conference did finally adopt Resolution 100 which underlined the important role communication plays across the globe:

22.

Stresses the importance of free and balanced circulation of information and the need vigorously to intensify the efforts to put an end to the imbalance which, as regards capacity to send out and receive information, typifies the relationship between developed and developing countries, by helping the latter to establish and strengthen their own communication and information systems, so as to promote their development, in particular their educational, scientific, technological and cultural development, and their ability to play a full part in the international dissemination of information;

23.

Considers that these efforts should be based upon deep deliberation taking into consideration all the problems of communication in society, and taking account of those things which are needful for the establishment of a new international economic order;[41]

At the same conference Resolution 4.142 called for UNESCO to help develop communication systems and liberate "developing countries from the state of dependence" on their current systems.[42] This resolution gave the Director General the charge of coordinating and implementing information programs of nonaligned countries and insuring resources for UNESCO programs related to communication and information activities.[43] It also lead to a decision by the Director General to set up an International Commission for the Study of Communication Problems (later known as the MacBride Commission after its President, the late Irish politician, Sean MacBride). The Commission was mandated to analyze the state of world communication, study problems related to the free and balanced flow of information, analyze communication problems "within the perspective of a new international economic order," and define the role communication might play as a "sensitizing" agent for public opinion. The Commission was directed to file a final report in

1979 so that it would be available for discussion at the 21st session of the General Conference (1980).[44]

As Nordenstreng has observed, this period of the 1960s and 1970s was marked by many nations accumulating political and economic power. This was expedited through the movement of nonaligned countries and, of course, OPEC.[45] During the 1976-1977 period, however, reaching agreement was not always an easy matter. The Western counter-movement was but one event unfolding. Disagreements among Third World countries added to the complexity of the situation. While solutions were being sought to remedy the global communication disorder, world politicians did not seem well prepared to offer definitive solutions.

The MacBride Commission

As mentioned above, the Commission for the Study of Communication Problems had its origins in the Nairobi meeting of the UNESCO General Conference. Its charge was to study the new communication order. Irish Ambassador, Director of Amnesty International, and Nobel Peace laureate, Sean MacBride, was named to head the Commission. Sixteen individuals were selected to sit on the Commission by Director General Amadou Mahtar M'Bow.

In late November 1978, the Commission released an interim report which proved to be highly controversial. The forum for debate was set during the 20th General Assembly meeting (Paris, 1978). Plenary sessions, along with subcommittee sessions, were held from October 24 through November 28. The Culture and Communication Committee sponsored one of the meetings (Committee IV). On November 14, MacBride held a press conference at which he reported on the Commission's progress. Considerable debate followed. Concerns centered around the nature of the Western press, particularly its wire services. The proposal for government intervention, involving the licensing of journalists, was perceived antagonistically by many in the West.[46] On November 18, COM IV began its discussion of the mass media declaration. Through some maneuvering, the West managed to engineer a compromise declaration. In a press conference following the revised declaration's approval, U.S. Ambassador Reinhardt acquiesced on the international flow issue, but noted that the current declaration was much more acceptable than earlier versions.[47]

The final report of the Commission was presented at the 21st General Conference in Belgrade (1980). The anti-Western rhetoric found in the preliminary report had been noticeably toned down in this version. Also apparent was the compromise which had been struck.

Demands had been moderated in exchange for development subsidies from industrialized countries. In addition, the concept of "a free and balanced flow" was altered. This was changed to "a free flow and a wider and better balanced dissemination of information," with the goal being to create "a new, more just and more effective world information and communication order."[48]

The report made 82 recommendations. Along with a variety of developments in the area of media economics (including tariffs) and administration procedures, technological implementation and uses, and training and research, it called for "the setting up of a new world information and communication order." The report also set out a resolution dealing with "professional integrity and standards," which underlined the notions of freedom and the responsibility of journalists, "including a concern for professional ethics." It rejected, however, the idea of a licensing system. Mr. MacBride dissented arguing "that they [journalists] should be granted a special status and protection."[49]

This final report of the Commission for the Study of Communication Problems has been criticized for being highly philosophical and taking a middle road between often controversial, markedly opposed, issues. Critics charged that it was too general and lacked practical programs for implementing change. It did not, for example, address issues of telecommunication infrastructure and effects of technology and economics, existing tariffs, and magnetic spectrum allocations.[50] Most of the reports' recommendations were not enacted by the General Conference.

It is argued that some very legitimate recommendations were made in the MacBride Report which American journalists generally chose to ignore. Yu points to two recommendations about which the "U.S. news media have not shown much interest (numbers 46 and 47)." The former deals with the ability of reporters assigned at foreign posts to have specific language training plus a knowledge of the region's history, culture, and politics. The latter calls for gatekeepers (editors, etc.) from the developed world press to have a familiarity with "cultures and conditions" in developing countries. Says Yu, "(n)o thoughtful American would expect a Third World news organization to cover the United States adequately with a correspondent who is ignorant of English and American affairs, even though the correspondent is assisted by able interpreters." While U.S. news organizations would not send correspondents to France or Germany without knowing the language, Yu observes they often fail to employ the same criterion in "China, Egypt, Greece, Iran, Korea, Saudi Arabia, Thailand, Vietnam (and) even Japan."[51]

Other Belgrade Actions

The Conference also created an International Program for the Development of Communication (IPDC), a move proposed and encouraged by the Americans. Major funding was pledged by Western countries. This organization was charged with implementing many of the objectives of the NWICO. Its mandate fell into four basic categories—to provide assistance, coordination, information, and financing regarding international communication development and the promotion of self-reliance. Just about all of its projects were tailored to cultivate information flow in the Third World. Opposition arose, however, when some of its projects centered on ideologically controversial agenda related to government-controlled media. Illustrating how U.S. sentiments were affected, Sussman notes:

> Though the nonideological nature of the IPDC was specifically agreed between the U.S. negotiators and a UNESCO attorney before the structure of the IPDC was cast in statutes, significant changes have since been made in the IPDC formula. Some projects would affect content rather than provide solely infrastructure. The director of the program will not be as independent of the director-general of UNESCO as has been promised. And decisions in the intergovernmental council may be by majority vote instead of consensus as had been agreed. To be sure, the funding of the IPDC will be on a voluntary basis. Unless the contribution system is made more flexible, enabling the donor to choose one or more projects from a list of possible proposals, some major donors — nongovernmental agencies as well as governments — may be reluctant to assist.[52]

A general criticism of the IPDC has been that it never was able to realize its true potential due to the lack of sufficient funding. The major thrust of its efforts went into programs geared toward addressing problems of underdevelopment.

Some controversial motions did surface during the Belgrade meeting. One was the adoption of the so-called Venezuelan resolution. It called for a study of elements that would be part of a New World Information Order, attempted to create a universal definition of "responsible" journalism, and sought assistance for the Palestine Liberation Organization, thus drawing the attention of one American observer, Leonard West, the secretary of the World Press Freedom Committee, who cattily referred to the resolution as "son of MacBride."[53] The U.S. delegation saw such moves as evidence of the "futility of New World Information-type rhetoric," thus confirming existing suspicions. "The time has come," said Marks, "to stop the rhetoric and go on with practicalities."[54]

After Belgrade

It has been the World Information and Communication Order Debate rather than the Economic Order Debate that seems to have generated most of the attention from international critics, and the controversies surrounding this Order helped set the stage for a showdown between UNESCO and the United States. Following the submission of the International Commission for the Study of Communication Problems's final report, other meetings were held which centered on communication issues. One of these was the World Press Freedom Committee (WPFC)-sponsored conference, "Voices of Freedom," held in Tallories, France (May 15-17, 1981). As its name implies, the gathering was devoted to the promotion of free press ideals. Delegates included representatives of some 24 countries and the four major Western news agencies. The agenda was to build a defense for Western journalism practices. According to one report on the meeting, an "explosive confrontation" occurred between guest speaker, UNESCO Director General Amadou-Mahtar M'Bow and delegates. "His interpreter was unable to keep up with the angry exchanges." When confronted with his earlier comments about the role of the press in Third World "cohesion and integration," M'Bow denied that his intentions were to muzzle the press.[55] Basically, the conference reiterated its support of the Universal Declaration of Human Rights (Article 19), and urged UNESCO to search for more practical global communication problem remedies than regulation.

> We are deeply concerned by a growing tendency in many countries and in international bodies to put government interests above those of the individual, particularly in regard to information. We believe that the state exists for the individual and has a duty to uphold individual rights. We believe that the ultimate definition of a free press lies not in the actions of governments or international bodies, but rather in the professionalism, vigor and courage of individual journalists.
>
> Press freedom is a basic human right. We pledge ourselves to concerted action to uphold this right.[56]

Coming out of the meeting, *Los Angeles Times* editorial page editor, Anthony Day, reflected the disposition of the majority of delegates: "The West does better to stay in for now and fight. It just has got to be tougher."[57] A second meeting was held in Tallories some 2 years later at which these recommendations were reiterated and a reference was developed that helped document efforts to improve world news flow.

Another interesting set of meetings were those of the International Telecommunications Union (ITU), a UN agency. The ITU oversees and coordinates technological developments and systems in the telecommunications field. These include radio spectrum allocations (AM and FM radio, television, high frequency broadcasting, land mobile radio, short wave maritime mobile, fixed and mobil satellite services, radionavigation, earth exploration, and amateur services, etc.), satellite orbits, direct broadcast satellites, and telephones, among other communications technologies. In May 1983, the ITU established the Independent Commission for World-Wide Telecommunications Development to recommend ways that telecommunications growth could be spurred on globally. The 17 member commission was led by Sir Donald Maitland of the United Kingdom. Its report, often called the Maitland Report, was submitted to the ITU in January 1985.

Traditionally, the ITU had been a meeting of engineers and other highly technically-oriented individuals. The Maitland Report helped focus the ITU's attention on the influence social considerations have on their technical decision making. As the Report noted:

> It cannot be right that in the latter part of the twentieth century a minority of the human race should enjoy the benefits of the new technology while a majority live in comparative isolation.[58]

The Commission made a variety of recommendations including industrialized country government assistance programs focused on telecommunications issues, the promotion of telecommunications resource self-reliance among developing countries (via training and research programs, pooling purchases, etc), and the encouragement of cooperation between industrialized and developing countries to promote a telecommunications system which "meets demand" as well as "generates wealth."[59] They concluded:

> There is no single remedy. A range of actions over a wide front and at different levels is required. Progress will be made only in stages. But, if the effort is sustained, the situation world wide could be brought within easy reach of a telephone by the early part of the next century and our objective achieved.[60]

The stage was thus set.

Meeting at the 1985 Space WARC (World Administrative Radio Conference) conference in Geneva, stiff criticisms were offered by members of the U.S. delegation. Ambassador Diana Lady Dougan, U.S. Coordinator and Director of the State Department's Bureau of International Communications and Information Policy, commented that the body's work "was, in effect, held hostage by a handful of delegates who seemed prepared to jeopardize the interest of the majority in pursuit of their own narrow ideological goals."[61] Exemplifying the U.S. perception of these threats is the following report in *Broadcasting*.

> . . . Developing countries arrived in Geneva seeking rigid a priori planning for bands virtually across the board. They said they needed guarantees in writing of access to the orbital arc and associated frequencies, even if they were not prepared to launch or buy a satellite for 50 years.
>
> To the developed countries, such planning is wasteful and inefficient. The U.S. had proposed turning over the expansion bands associated with 6/4 ghz for long-range planning by developing countries as well as devising a multilateral planning method. . .
>
> By the time the issue had made its way, tortuously, to the decision-making stage of the plenary session, the U.S. had given some ground. . .[62]

While the inherent political nature of this forum was noted by members of the U.S. delegation at the ITU meetings, all indications were that the U.S. wished to continue participating and even take a pioneering role "in giving new life. . .[to the] spirit of trust and compromise that has enabled ITU to tackle the world's telecommunication problems over 120 years."[63]

Despite some reservations, the U.S. delegation walked away from Geneva feeling fairly optimistic. "We feel very good about . . [the satellite situation]," commented Ambassador Dean Burch. "An allotment plan will not place a cloud over our operational bands."[64] "Considering our vital interests, we came out well."[65] David Markey, head of the National Telecommunication and Information Administration, who attended, added that only the year before there was speculation that the U.S. would be engulfed by developing country demands for conventional and expansion bands.[66] Things appeared to be heading in a positive direction, as far as the U.S. was concerned.

United States Withdraws from UNESCO

Much has been written about the way American journalists covered the free information flow issue during the Belgrade General Conference and immediately thereafter. The literature has already been reviewed in detail in Chapter 2. While the news coverage may have been accurate, it also was "unbalanced in its total effect," concluded one of the authors.[67] There also were cases where editors came out for a U.S. withdrawal of UNESCO. At Tallories, *Washington Star* editor Murray Gart proposed that members "withdraw support of and representation in UNESCO" if the perceived negative campaign on press freedom continued.[68] But nothing ever came of these threats, and it seemed that matters were cooling down after a Communication Order compromise plan was struck during the 22nd UNESCO General Assembly meeting (Paris, 1983).[69] Soon after news stories appeared suggesting that a U.S. withdrawal might indeed be forthcoming.[70] Then in a move that some considered anti-climactic, Secretary of State George Shultz, in late December 1983, sent a letter to the UNESCO Director General, Amadou-Mahlar M'Bow, informing him that the United States intended to withdraw from the organization at the end of 1984.[71] The U.S. cited trends in "the policy, ideological emphasis, budget and management of UNESCO" which were "detracting from the Organization's effectiveness." He went on to note that, in their opinion, UNESCO had wandered from "the original principles of its constitution," specifically underlining what they believed to be a situation which "served the political purposes of member states." Shultz concluded that the United States planned to apply resources otherwise devoted to UNESCO to support "other means of cooperation."[72] Speaking in a State Department briefing, Gregory Newell, Assistant Secretary, noted:

> Unesco policies for several years have served anti-U.S. political ends. The Reagan Administration has frequently advised Unesco of the limits of U.S. toleration: for its misguided policies, its tendentious programs, and its extravagant budgetary management. For nearly three years now, the Administration has applied to Unesco the same goals and priorities that guide our relations with all multilateral institutions. But Unesco alone, among the major U.N. organizations, has not responded.
>
> Now, at the conclusion of a long effort to reason with Unesco, and a careful reassessment of our relationship to it, the President has concluded that U.S. participation in Unesco, as it is currently organized, directed and focused, does not serve the interests of the United States. Our conclusion is firm. . .[73]

When asked by a reporter for examples of the United States's objections, Newell said that much time had been spent on Soviet-led peace plans, and that over three-quarters of a million dollars was approved for peace and disarmament measures "inspired from the Eastern bloc," but only $32,000 was earmarked for education of refugees, while there are 10 million refugees worldwide.[74]

The U. S. elaborated on its position in a memorandum prepared by William G. Harley, Communication Consultant to the Department of State, released in early 1984. The highly charged politics can be seen in some of the prepared answers. Also apparent is how far apart the State Department and UNESCO were:

Q. What are our complaints about UNESCO's traditional sectors of education, science and culture?

A. UNESCO has admittedly done considerable competent work in these fields in the past. But even here, there has been an unfortunate reorientation and unacceptable waste of resources:

In education, UNESCO promotes literacy, standardization of degrees, publication of valuable information, and assistance in economic development in such fields as teacher training. But it increasingly orients its educational activities toward such purposes as 'peace and disarmament,' not as they are legitimately sought after by many peoples, but as they are promoted and distorted in Soviet propaganda.

In science, UNESCO has been valuable to the United States. But politics has also begun to make itself felt here, with the injection of such concepts as 'scientists for peace' and 'scientists for disarmament.'

In culture, UNESCO has helped save important monuments and historical sites, sponsored useful international agreements in the copyright field, and promoted valuable historical and contemporary research. But its effects are diffuse. . .

Q. We understand that there was some progress — perhaps because this is where the United States has concentrated its fire power — and this movement was recognized in the review. However, the basic problems still exist, and, even in the communication area, UNESCO's program of seminars and studies still contains the potential for developments hostile to a free press. . .

Q. What specifically would UNESCO have to do to satisfy the United States to the point where we would not withdraw?

A. Major changes to address our complaints and redress across the board shortcomings of UNESCO would have to be made. Generally, they deal with program orientation, politicization, budget growth, and management. It is not expected that substantial changes could be made before the scheduled withdrawal.[75]

The repeated references to "peace" and "disarmament" make it likely that these were the very issues behind the decision to withdraw. Pulling out of UNESCO, incidentally, also meant that the United States no longer would participate in the IPDC.

Roach argues that numerous contradictions existed in the United States's position attacking the New World Information and Communication Order. Many complex issues were reduced to the simple "slogan" of "government control of the media." Among other things, she contends that: (1) ". . . the U.S. backing for privatization and deregulation at the global level" was already quite evident in many negotiations carried out at UNESCO; (2) "'the government control of media argument'" makes a bold assumption that the U.S. media are totally free of "state intervention;" and (3) it is likely that "the term 'free and balanced flow of information' can be traced back to the United States for its origins."[76]

American conservatives were already against many facets of UNESCO long before the Communication Order debate was formalized. Communication issues calling for a free international flow of information, and guaranteeing all the "right to communicate," just helped highlight many of the reservations they already had about United Nations's operations. But by addressing the licensing of journalists, "assigning them 'responsibilities,' and monitoring their output," notes Sussman, UNESCO lost esteem among "the influential American press" too.[77]

One example of the irony surrounding the debates in the U.S. press was when the *New York Times* editorialized about the licensing of journalists in Latin America. The liberal, New York-based magazine, *The Nation*, addressed the editorial:

The odd thing about the story is the unstated assumption that no such licensing system exists in the United States, similarly impairing its freedom. It exists, of course, the only difference being that in the United States the orthodox media are trusted by the government to maintain and police the system informally, thus sparing the government much time and expense.[78]

Justified or not, the defensiveness found among many U.S. newspapers allowed two unlikely partners in the American political system to join forces. In a detailed study of these events, Giffard found only a small number of U.S. newspapers regularly willing to come out on the side of UNESCO in their editorials during the withdrawal debate.[79]

The withdrawal itself does not seem to have been a well-reasoned strategy on behalf of the Reagan administration, and was a reversal of that recommended in a State Department report just prior to the action. McPhail offers compelling evidence which suggests that final actions resulted from a campaign of "selective misrepresentations" in the United States State Department, lead by Gregory Newell; Newell had been reappointed to the State Department from the White House staff only a short time earlier.[80] It was he and a core of senior administration officials who recommended withdrawal against the recommendations of the Department review.[81]

This and other administration actions during the period seem to have been heavily influenced by the politically conservative Heritage Foundation. Heritage Vice President Burton Pines publicly claimed responsibility for the withdrawal, and claimed that his group served as a "key intellectual resource for the Reagan administration."[82] At the time this organization was operating with an annual budget of nearly $10 million dollars, donated by leading figures such as Joseph Coors and Richard Mellon Scaife.

Newell is also credited with leading a campaign to manipulate the news in support of the withdrawal. This included a State Department coordinated effort to support the publication of letters to the editors and articles in major newspapers including the *New York Times* and *Washington Post*. *Washington Post* op ed editor, Meg Greenfield, responded that "the fact that they would be doing this is not a surprise: It's standard operating procedure for government these days."[83] Ironically, the first newspaper to report on the Newell plan was not American, but British. "Where was American investigative reporting when it was needed?" asks Sussman.[84] In an editorial, *Editor & Publisher* came out against these tactics.[85]

While the U.S. departure was welcomed by some UNESCO members, it did leave the organization without a major portion of its funding; the United States' annual contribution ($43 million) was about one-quarter of UNESCO's general budget, and when to this was added to the loss of revenues resulting from the United Kingdom's later withdrawal (1985), the loss was brought to 30%.[86] Some thought the U.S. would have been more influential if it had remained. Sussman is critical of the American press for the U.S. pull out. ". . .(T)he case against Unesco was won not in 1984 or 1985, but in the years from 1976 to 1983 when Unesco programs critical of news flows were vilified regularly and made to appear to be the only program of the multifaceted organization."[87]

Twenty-Third General Conference

With the United States officially absent at the 23rd General Conference of UNESCO (Sofia, Bulgaria, 1985), other Western countries carried on the crusade for improving the general organization of UNESCO and argued for a reduction in the pursuit of politically tainted activities. In one move, the Western delegation lead by Great Britain sought a transfer of funds from controversial areas into more practical programs geared to help the Third World.[88] Earlier in the year there had been indications that UNESCO would react favorably to selective cuts in activities unpopular with Western members when France agreed to offer $2 million to help offset the loss of funds created by the U.S. withdrawal.[89] Also, as a surprise move to Western representatives prior to the close of sessions, the Soviet Union agreed to go along with a declaration which defined UNESCO goals. In emphasizing UNESCO obligations, it stated that it was its "duty to promote respect for individual human rights and encourage free communications."[90]

News Agencies Since 1976

Generally, the Western news agency dominance issue is no longer a matter of loud public debate.[91] For many years, however, the question of Western dominance of information flow largely through news agencies was at the heart of the NWICO discussions. When the debate was in full swing, it was estimated that while about 120 countries and territories had news agencies, some 40 countries had none, and this included 24 countries with populations greater than one million.[92] Of great concern were the five major news agencies—Agence France-Presse (France), Associated Press (USA), Reuters (UK), TASS (USSR), and United Press International (USA)—which dominated in both size and technological strength. Four of these (all but the Soviet Union's TASS) have been typically grouped along with the leading television news agencies—Visnews and UPITN. There appears to be little question that these organizations wielded much control and dominated global news flow. They became known as the Transnational News Agencies. Collectively these agencies have bureaus or offices in more than 100 countries, and employ thousands of individuals.

As Beltran and de Cardona note, "The U.S. news agencies manage 80% of the international news in Latin America, and in many countries a significant percentage of national and regional news as well is controlled by these agencies."[93] Many other studies report similar imbalances,[94] although Atwood and Bullion challenge the often quoted figures by noting that the criticisms are not grounded in empirical evidence.[95] Attempting to address some of those limitations, their research concludes that Third World news (at least on the Asian wires which they studied) does not appear to be as negative or as abundant as "routinely suggested." They conclude that the United States, in particular, has gotten "'bad' world press" in the debate.[96] While the exact volume may be in question, and not only the United States is to blame, the point here remains that Western press has played a controlling role in global news flow.

Taking another perspective, a study by Matta found that when the Surinam Republic was established on November 25, 1975, while it dominated in both size and technological strength, no Latin American newspaper chose to send a correspondent to cover the story. Matta suggests that this case "exposes the continent's inability to look at itself, and its failure at self-interpretation. The easy option was taken, to reproduce a version of the news whose political character was obviously different from that which motivates the Third World countries." In other words, Latin American journalists did not see the importance of a regional story such as this, as they were conditioned to rely on Western news agencies.[97]

There has been considerable debate surrounding the role of transnational news agencies and their effect on global information flow. Many have argued against the TNNAs attacking them for their "for profit" orientation, comparing them to worldwide corporations such as IBM (International Business Machines) and Unilever.[98] Schiller comments:

> The decisions affecting . . . (unindustrialized state) economies are made by forces largely outside national boundaries. In this process, transnational media occupy an important position. Though profitability is their main concern, they comprise, at this time, the ideologically supportive informational infrastructure of the modern world system's core — the multinational corporations (MNC'S).[99]

He goes on to suggest that U.S. media organizations:

> . . . cover their expansionist drives for markets under the principle of the 'free flow of information,' and more recently, 'the right to communicate.'[100]

The transformation of national media structures into conduits of the corporate business system, and the heavy international traffic of commercial media products flowing from the center to the periphery, are the most prominent means by which weaker societies are absorbed culturally into the modern world system.[101]

Taking a counterview, others downplay this argument. Tatarian posits that the agencies "do not disdain profit," and profit is what "permits them to function independently from government."[102] For comparison, Richstad reminds us that the $112 million in revenues which the largest of the four largest transnational news agencies (AP) generated in 1978 were less than a major state university in one of the smaller U.S. states would spend on its annual operating budget.[103] Also, note the bankruptcy conditions under which UPI has been operating recently (circa 1991-92). The largest communication transnational (IBM), on the other hand, had $18 billion in yearly sales in the early 1980s.[104] We should point out, however, that while the news agency has long been thought to be central to global information flow problems, it never was specifically addressed by the 1978 Mass Media Declaration.[105]

As noted above, in 1986 the Movement of Non-aligned Nations set up a news service pool composed of existing regional agencies. Presently some 50 nations are participating in the news exchange, Tanjug. Basically, the Yugoslavian news agency has simply served as a clearinghouse for the channeling of news items. It does not involve itself in editorial chores. Although designed to complement rather than replace the major news agencies, Tanjug has been criticized by Western critics for acting as a propaganda exchange.[106] One other source worthy of mention is the Inter-Press Service (IPS), founded in 1964. This is actually a large news agency with bureaus in dozens of countries, offering multiple language reports. Notable are its news services concentrating on oil news, Latin American economics, agrarian and strategic issues, and its women's feature service.[107]

Future of NWICO

The New World Information and Communication order debate was faulted for its inability to sharply delineate the problem, its failure to effectively merge the NWICO with a major examination of economic concerns, and its inability to find an equitable solution to the perceived imbalance of information flow and exchange. "So far as the [New World] information order is concerned," observes Eli Abel, one of the members of the MacBride Commission, "the plain fact is that nobody knows what it would mean . . . The new world order obviously means different things to different people. It is more slogan than plan of action."[108] Without doubt, this uncertainty contributes to some confusion.

As far as the future goes, UNESCO has redirected its energies. Its agenda seems to have been designed in an effort to avoid the politically sensitive issues found in the past. In Resolution 21 C/4.19, adopted at the General Conference of UNESCO (September-October, 1980) which met in Belgrade, it was agreed that:

"The General Conference, . . .

14. *Considers* that:

(a)   This new world information and communication order could be based, among other considerations, on:

    (i)   elimination of the imbalances and inequalities which characterize the present situation;

    (ii)   elimination of the negative effects of certain monopolies,public or private, and excessive concentrations;

    (iii)   removal of the internal and external obstacles to a free flow and wider and better balanced dissemination of information and ideas;

    (iv)   plurality of sources and channels of information;

    (v)   freedom of the press and information;

    (vi)   the freedom of journalists and all professionals in the communication media, a freedom inseparable from responsibility;

    (vii)   the capacity of developing countries to achieve improvement of their own situations, notably by providing their own equipment, by training their personnel, by improving their infrastructures and by making their information and communication media suitable to their needs and aspirations;

    (vii)   the sincere will of developed countries to help them attain these objectives;

    (ix)   respect for each people's cultural identity and for the right of each nation to inform the world public about its interests, its aspirations and its social and cultural values;

(x)   respect for the right of all peoples to
        participate in international exchanges of infor-
        mation on the basis of quality, justice and
        mutual benefit;

(xi)   respect for the right of the public, of ethnic
        and social groups and of individuals to have
        access to information sources and to participate
        actively in the communication process;

(b)   this new world information and communication order
        should be based on the fundamental principles of
        international law, as laid down in the Charter of the
        United Nations;

(c)   diverse solutions to information and communication
        problems are required because social, political, cultural
        and economic problems differ from one country to
        another and, within a given country, from one group to
        another."[109]

As Dissanayake has argued, "there is a growing lack of intellectual excitement in the work of UNESCO." He goes on to note that within the communication field today, "we can seriously ask questions about the lack of a grand theory," but "UNESCO could play a central role in formulation of such a theory."[110] Perhaps conscious of such criticism, UNESCO is showing signs of promoting a more moderate stance toward the communication issue.

The consensus seems to be that UNESCO should now be building on the traditions begun during the 24th session of the General Conference with an innovative agenda that takes "the lessons of past experience to heart."[111] In setting out this new, innovative agenda, UNESCO reaffirms "its adherence to the principles of freedom of the press, pluralism and diversity," and welcomes activities aimed at "strengthening communication capabilities in developing countries." This is to be achieved through the development of infrastructures and capacities, personnel training, and media education.[112] All are designed to help ensure "a balance in regard to the flow of information . . .,"[113] and include the study of media and new communication technologies.[114] Essentially, UNESCO's goal is to try and make the program "more operational," so that the free flow of information can be attained.[115] UNESCO seems to be is responding to many of the earlier criticisms.

While UNESCO has become less central in the NWICO dialogue, debate is far from over. Other parties are providing leadership, and are proving to be effective hosts for the continuing discussions. For example, in June 1989, the Union for Democratic Communications and the National Lawyers Guild met in Los Angeles to host a symposium on "Media Accountability under International Law." The meeting brought together communication and legal experts to address the nature of cultural human rights.[116] Then, in October, the World Association for Christian Communication held its first international congress in the Philippines and adopted its "Manila Declaration," the thrust of which focused on communication, within a depoliticized environment, as an individual right. In late October, the first MacBride Round Table was convened in Harare, Zimbabwe to evaluate world communication ten years after publication of the MacBride Commission report. The Round Table was organized by the Federation of Southern African Journalists along with the International Organization of Journalists (IOJ) and the Media Foundation of the Non-Aligned (NAMEDIA). The meeting restated the original NWICO concerns and suggested that changes occurring since the publication of the MacBride Report helped to make the topic even more relevant today. The rapidly expanding communication technologies were identified as one of the primary causes for such concern. Investment to improve frail communication infrastructures in various developing countries was urged. The participants stressed that media operations principles should be set by media professionals. The notion of a free and responsible press was enunciated, and this included a public interest orientation without excessive government or commercial control. It was noted that the MacBride Report was built on the tenet that communication is a basic human right, an individual need and a social requisite. It was decided that further Round Tables would meet at regular intervals.[117]

Also during 1989, a panel chaired by former U.S. Senator Robert T. Stafford recommended that the United States reinstate its formal membership in UNESCO, emphasizing the seminal job the organization can and does perform in the promotion of free speech and unimpeded international dialogue.[118] Nonetheless, many were disappointed with the more conservative approach UNESCO chose to take with its new Medium-Term Plan.

Major outside interest in the NWICO issue continued. A number of meetings convened with the NWICO as the exclusive, or at least major, discussion topic. Among these were a World Association for Christian Communication (WACC)-sponsored colloquium in London in September 1990; a WACC and Institute for Latin America (IPAL) seminar in Lima in November 1990; the Intercontinental Journalists Conference in New Delhi in November 1990; a Gannett Foundation Media Center conference on "News and the New World Order" held in New York City in January 1991; and an International Press Service Council on Information and Communications meeting in Rome in June

1991 that centered on press treatment of the Persian Gulf War.[119] Another demonstration of interest can be found in the production of a 37 page bibliography on the NWICO by the Prague-based International Journalism Institute (IJI) in June 1991. This is the first of a series of intended resources to "serve journalists" in light of the continuing importance of the world news flow topic.[120]

Following the First Round Table, subsequent meetings were convened in Prague, Czechoslovakia (September 1990) and Istanbul, Turkey (June 1991). Coming on the heels of the Persian Gulf War, at the Third meeting it was concluded that efforts must be made "to develop a culture of non-violence, of dialogue and negotiations, practicing the art of democracy, and promoting a culture of peace." Participants called for alternate systems of peace and security and new "coalitions and constituencies" to help regain "participation in cultural policy-making," made up of media professionals, citizen activists, consumer groups, and members of women's, minority, religious, labor, and environmental groups.[121] A fourth Round Table is scheduled to convene in Guarujá (São Paulo), Brazil in August, 1992.

Continuing interest in the NWICO is evidenced by the publication of recent major works such as Mowlana's *Global Information and World Communication* (1986); Giffard's *Unesco and the Media* (1989); and Gerbner, Mowlana and Nordenstreng's *The Global Media Debate: Its Rise, Fall and Renewal* (1992) to name a few.[122] The present work adds to this list.

OBSERVATIONS ON THE NEW WORLD INFORMATION AND COMMUNICATION ORDER

In the political realm, the effect of the New World Information and Communication Order Debate has been something less than conclusive. Nonetheless, many of the criticisms levied toward the Western-dominated press seem to have been in large part merited. As U.S. State Department representative Edward Pinch observed during a department-sponsored seminar:

> Western journalists do not have to accept all Third World criticism of their coverage of events in order to recognize legitimate complaints regarding the superficiality or irrelevance of some of it. Third World officials, in turn, should be able to aspire to reducing the imbalance in their own media capabilities without seeking to inhibit the communications capacities of others.[123]

He went on to conclude that the development of a news pool by the Yugoslav agency, Tanjug, was "indeed welcome" for its potential to provide a more competitive spirit in international news distribution.

The problem, of course, came with the general inability of the UNESCO-led forum to take more than two decades of debate and translate it into any solid program for change. Stevenson suggests that it was the "hallowness of the Marxist rhetoric" that lead to the movement's failure.[124] While not all would agree with such criticism, it remains that the political arena in which this debate was staged may not have been capable of fostering radical change. Critics like Dissanayake argue that it has been the increasing politicization of UNESCO which has led to a counter-productive environment.[125] Mowlana argues, on the other hand, that politicizing could not be avoided since it was impossible to isolate the organization from "the main issues of world politics."[126] Whether an increased involvement in politics was inevitable or not, the matter remains that perhaps UNESCO was not best equipped for monitoring such a debate. But then, who else would have been qualified?

A problem with the Mass Media Declaration, as Nordenstreng points out, is that it quickly became manipulated by political extremes. "[T]he Declaration came to serve as a symbol and catalyst for conflict between the forces of the new order and its adversaries No wonder, then, that this document became controversial; it stood not only for what was written in the text, but came to symbolize the struggle between conflicting forces in the world arena as well."[127] Sussman refers to the Third World countries as "diversely-motivated."[128] In another work he provides examples of the UNESCO debate being influential where media was already controlled by governments: (1) Peru nationalized all newspapers to limit access by foreign correspondents, and (2) a 1984 Non-Aligned Ministers Conference in Jakarta was addressed by President Suharto who called for stronger state control of news media to reverse "domination" by Western news agencies.[129] Sussman observes:

> The valid critiques of Western journalism and the Third World's natural yearning for better coverage and infrastructure were lost in the eight years of Western reporting of these acrimonious debates. Emphasized instead were the objectives of those who seek to change the content of news and information by defining journalistic 'responsibility' and who would control staffing of news media through licensing devices linked to 'protecting' journalists.
>
> UNESCO, meanwhile, failed to communicate to its global audience the distinctly differing objectives of those participating in the NWICO debates. Still more self-defeating, UNESCO tried repeatedly to forge consensual statements out of principles that were regarded

as non-negotiable by many participating delegates and the citizens they represented.[130]

While some continue to debate the merits of a new communications system, we offer the following observations: political actors, be they at the state, group, or individual level, are motivated by a project, consciously or unconsciously—usually the latter. The NIEO seems to be one implementation of that general project, quite successful as long as it is seen merely as an international order. And it never pretended to be anything else. It never pretended, for instance, to be concerned with the basic needs of those most in need. NIEO becomes a confirmation of the general project, an empirical projection of something deeper. Concretely, it also produces more possibilities for implementing the communication aspects of the project because the economic resources are present. But the thesis here is that this is not done simply because of economic expediency. There is a deeper reason: a general world transformation program to be implemented in all kinds of fields, thus ultimately ushering in the New International Language Order (with Chinese and Hindi); Diplomatic Order, Airline Order, Sports Order, and so on and so forth.[131]

If this is correct, it is easy to predict what will happen in the field of NWICO, taking the lead from the five points for NIEO:

1. There will be better news ratios for the Third World—meaning more news about the Third World in the First World and less about the First World in the Third;
2. There will be increased Third World control over communication assets—control over which events news personnel from the First World are permitted to extract from the Third World and process into news, and local control over local media;
3. There will be more news about other Third World countries in all TW media and less about the First World;
4. There will be some Third World control in the First World over what events should be processed into news, and increased Third World control over local media (buying up newspapers, and television and radio stations); and
5. There will be some Third World control over world communication institutions, including U.N. agencies in the field, if established.

Again, this is a process that is already fully underway. Anyone reading the Third World press through the 1960s, 1970s, and 1980s will appreciate the tremendous increase in attention given to other Third World countries, although usually within the same region and/or within the same former colonial empire. The directions of these trends have already been confirmed by research reviewed earlier in Chapter 2. Just as significantly, this is accompanied by a decline in news about the First World, except for events at the extremes of drama or of a negative nature. A Briton who believes that the press in India or Malaysia will give an adequate account of what happens in the former "mother" country will be disappointed. The Indian press writes mainly about the "subcontinent"; the Malaysian press about itself, ASEAN, and Islamic countries. The transformation is there, but is superficial, suffering from the same emphasis on quantity (*how much* is written), not on quality (*what* is written) similar to the terms of trade approach in NIEO.

At the same time there is the effort to control the First World image of the Third World through selective access to information—that is, to the events eventually processed as news. Not that this is exactly unknown in the First and Second worlds. But under colonialism, which involved most of the countries within today's "Third World," First World media people were used to unlimited access as they themselves controlled this—except, of course, for the access to the secrets and atrocities of colonial rule itself. The access was differential to say the least, excluding even the "natives." Efforts to change this can hardly be done without Third World government action, and will, of course, be referred to as censorship. In all probability, a transition period to learn how to treat Third World countries more on their own terms is indispensable here. The classic example was the way conferences of the nonaligned movement Conferences of Heads of States of the Non-aligned Countries—Bandoeng (Indonesia) Conference, 1955; Summit I: Belgrade (Yugoslavia), 1961; Summit II: Cairo (Egypt), 1964; Summit III: Lusaka (Zambia), 1970; Summit IV: Algiers (Algeria), 1973; Summit V: Colombo (Sri Lanka), 1976; Summit VI: la Havana (Cuba), 1979; Summit VII: New Delhi (India), 1983; Summit VIII: Harare (Zimbabwe), 1986; and Summit IX: New Delhi (India), 1989 have been treated; for example, the focus on the costs and accommodations rather than on the substance of the Lusaka summit. The West is now paying with resistance and conflict for the way in which major events devoted to world transformation were reduced to some kind of teenage or nouveaux riches festival.

Along this line of reasoning, it is to be expected that Third World interests will buy into First World media to ensure better control over the images.[132] So far this has mainly taken the form of advertising for the latest pronouncements from some of the leaders (Kim Il Sung; Khomeini).[133] It is interesting to note that the countries rapidly gaining economic control in the Southeastern part of the world seem least interested in putting across political messages. Those interested in doing so are countries less important in the world economy; perhaps they are hoping that changing the information and communication order will prove easier than changing the economic order. After all, production of words is cheaper and easier than producing goods and services of sufficient quality. But control over the distribution may prove more difficult, and over the long run consumption impossible. The basic human need for identity/meaning is not that easily controlled; nor the control pattern easily changed.

This process will go further. There is no reason why the "international" wire agencies should be less susceptible, in the longer run, to sliding along the power gradients than other transnational corporations. In the first phase, Third World agencies will start competing—as they now do in the economic field—with Prensalatina, Inter-Press Service, and others. But in the next phase, takeovers might be contemplated. Western governments will likely intervene to control, and protect the control over, the TNAs. It will be interesting to see what happens with financially troubled UPI. Just as with the economy, this might lead to a breakdown in the "world" aspect of the cycles, as the West probably will prefer a breakdown to control by others. There is also the possibility that Third World papers will eventually emerge as world papers, much like the *International Herald Tribune* is published today (as of this writing it is printed in three Fourth World capitals: Tokyo, Hong Kong, and Singapore, in addition to eight places in the First World; but nowhere in the Third World, nor in the former Second World for that matter).

THE INTERFACE AND THE REACTION

As mentioned in the introduction to this chapter, not *if*, but *when* all of this happens, there is no doubt that the efficiency in conventional economic growth in terms of a tight correlation between economic and information-communication cycles will become evident. Just as part of the Third World learned something about market mechanisms from textbooks in capitalist economics and practiced this by raising the price of oil (knowing that the demand for oil was, practically speaking, inelastic within a wide range), they also learned the intimate relation between economics and communication. The latter knowledge was useful, not only for such trivialities as information about business opportunities, but also for image control, self-presentation, and transfer of ideology in the broad sense. The question is what the reaction in other parts of the world, such as in the West, will be when they are forced to live with their own medicine as patients, not as physicians.

In a sense, this may be a reason why the fight over the New World Information and Communication Order in UNESCO has been more bitter than the fight over the NIEO in the U.N., and even in the major forum of confrontation, UNCTAD (United Nations Conference on Trade and Development). Perhaps it is because NWICO goes one step deeper, at least potentially, touching culture, the very identity of the countries of the world, and not only the way they want to look to others, but also to themselves. If Third World country X starts writing with the same distance and lack of understanding about developed country Y as Y used to write about X—describing a country as a Boeing 707 not ready for takeoff (in the Rostowian sense) because this and that is wrong or missing, because the crew is untrained, and, in addition, corrupt, when X perhaps did not conceive of itself as a Boeing 707 at all—this is in itself not so bad. But if X starts having power over the mass media in Y and reports this image of Y back into Y, and this is the dominant image of Y available to Y, then it starts becoming ominous. It starts hurting. All of that is probably going to happen, for the simple reason that the two orders, the old and the new, are steered by the same logic.

It can be compared to the standard theory of the relation between *discrimination* (a pattern of behavior) and *prejudice* (a pattern of attitudes). According to one way of thinking, discrimination is enacted prejudice. But it can also be put the other way. Where there is a pre-existing structure of discrimination—for instance, toward black people, or toward black countries—the corresponding prejudice serves as a theory of justification. If we behave that badly toward them, there must be good reasons somewhere.

Correspondingly, when the countries in the former First World become objects rather than subjects of investment, when they become an external sector in the economies of other countries (particularly of the countries of the Southeast), what kind of images will then be produced and reproduced? When, for instance, the Japanese run factories in the United States using less expensive, yet productive U.S. labor combined with the advantage of being close to the market, what kind of images will the Japanese tend to develop of the United States and of North Americans? As underdeveloped people not capable of managing their resources rationally? Will they not only run factories but also send technical assistance missions to develop the North Americans, teaching them the work ethic? Or will the Japanese be content to receive Americans on study tours who are trying to understand the tricks that make the Japanese tick, convinced they will not be able to practice more than 50% of the 50% they understand anyhow? Whatever the answer, control over one's own media is a basic condition for harmony between objective position in the economic structure and the subjective image; simply by making the subjective look objective.

It will hardly be long before such imagery develops. For a fore-taste, some of the notions Brazilians have about the Portuguese and

Spanish-Americans have about Spaniards may be indicative: neither dirty nor lazy, but behind; uncomfortable with modern machinery, not quite knowing which buttons to push; dressed in quaint 19th century clothes and speaking the language of their grandparents. It is far from easy to escape from this. The configuration is already present in the form of jokes. The next step is to let it color news stories and background material. When reporting like this occurs, attitudes are elevated to the status of social theory. It means control, and that is power.[134] That is essentially what the New World Information and Communication Order is about: the old order with new centers.

Could it be that the new center(s) created through the NIEO process, and the NWICO process, will treat the old centers better than they used to treat them? The answer is that we do not know. Still, there is a certain Western arrogance so hard to beat that it might be unique to the First World. On the other hand, there may also be reasons to believe that the arrogance comes with the changes in the objective basis, neither as a cause nor as a consequence, but simply together with it. The discovery of a country's own strength may lead to the idea that the other side is weak, and that there are good reasons for the weakness. We shall see, and even relatively soon, how these factors are related.

ECONOMICS AND INFORMATION-COMMUNICATION: TWO DIFFERENT PARADIGMS

Let us now change the focus and explore another meaning of the word "communication." So far, the similarities between economics and communication have been the basis on which our argument has been built. They have been seen as two institutions concerned with the processing of raw materials, natural resources in the first case, events in the second, so as to make them fit each other and fit a new world structure in the process of formation.

Communication can also be seen in another way, and so can economics, although with more difficulty. Communication can be something different than two parties processing events into news and images, trying to push these images on each other, using the power of a communication structure. Communication can also become a *dialogue*. A dialogue is characterized by the possibility of open-ended change, not programmed by either party. Both parties enter some kind of tacit pact: "I make myself open to what you say on the condition that you do the same for me, and we both try to rethink the problem together, from the beginning, with the possibility of arriving at something different from what we would have arrived at independently." Thus, dialogue goes far beyond debate. In debates there may be winners or losers (or a "draw"). Dialogues may be successful or unsuccessful, and the criterion of success is not only the growth of the participants individually, but their growth together in the effort to construct something new. This part is relatively unproblematic. Everybody has experienced this miracle of *synergy*. Two or more parties come together to discuss something and suddenly, out of that dialogical process of communication emerges something *sui generis*, something noone had thought of in advance, because the process creates something new in all parties.

The problem is that this is not so easy in economic life. There is, of course, the concept of the positive-sum (actually increasing-sum) game. Both parties win relative to what they had before. There is not just one winner and one loser, as when economic competition comes to its more brutal conclusion and one is forced into bankruptcy. There is the idea of the expanding cake; both can win, maybe one more than the other, because their joint participation in the economic system makes that system expand.

There is no denial that it may work like this for some time. But the problem lies with the little clause above, "maybe one more than the other." When one party gets an edge over the other, the expanding system often works to increase that "edge" until the point that oligopoly/monopoly is approached. From that point on the system can be dominated by one or a few parties (typically firms) setting the prices and defining the terms of participation (collusionary tactics, etc.). It is similar to the logic of a war, only just the opposite. The argument that "there is no winner; both parties lose" is insufficient as an argument against war. Parties go to war also because they think they will "win more" in the sense of "losing less" than the other party and in order to improve their relative, not their absolute, position.

As long as there is a competitive spirit, including the idea of gaining (or at least not losing totally) at someone else's expense, and as long as the structure and even the rationalization called the "theory" of economic or strategic activity (war) point in that direction, the relation will tend to be vertical in its consequences, with winners and losers. Of course, this applies not only to the fields of business and war, but also, for instance, to schooling. To get ahead, to be better than others, to even enjoy others falling behind, to make more room at the top, are other species of the same genus. For many more examples, see the *Guiness Book of World Records*.

Then there are areas of social life where this social logic presumably does not hold. One of them is called love; another, friendship. The idea of building each other up, of not exploiting the weakness of others, but trying to remedy such weaknesses in order to make the other as strong as possible, is basic in such relations. Critics of the present period of history point to how the logic of contract and business—or even of war, for that matter—penetrate into institutions such as marriage, family, and clubs or associations, which are all presumably built around love and friendship. More constructive people with a utopian or romantic bent would try to run the relation the other way, exploring the possibility that the social logic of love and friendship might penetrate into institutions such as business and even war. In that case, business would be more a question of cooperative work. And war would, needless to say, be excluded, as its basic purpose is to destroy the other party.

The realist and the social scientist trying more dispassionately to analyze all of this would say that the two extremes, fully competitive and fully cooperative relationships, are obtained only under very special circumstances. Normally, there will be an element of cooperation in the competition, just as there will be an element of competition in the cooperation. Which element prevails certainly varies over time. But the point in this connection is the possibility of another type of communication, somehow pushing the total equation in another direction, toward cooperation and harmony.

Many would say this is already happening. There is considerable difference between the Diktat of colonialism and the seemingly endless series of North-South dialogues currently taking place (although they often sound more like debates), just as there is considerable difference between the highly exploitative relation the North had to the South before and what is now emerging (even if the poor in the South may now suffer even more). Yet the problem is clearly seen. The new rhetoric of challenge and assertiveness is a sign that at the verbal level something new has emerged. There has hardly ever been so much talk about harmony of interest, cooperation, interdependence, and partnership all over the world as today. In certain economic relations this is also to some extent put into practice—for example, by paying what the market can bear for oil, and more like what it is worth to the consumer. Since the logic of the system remains the same, however, the impact of this is limited for other relations because of the flexibilities and also the resilience of the capitalist economic system. It is a system capable of instituting a cooperative relationship where before there was none—for example, in the form of a joint venture which may unite managerial capabilities on either side, or other production factors. It is also capable of instituting a competitive relationship where formerly there was none. In either case, the pressure on the workers may increase, and so may the pressure on Third World countries.

Given this propensity of the system, the conclusion would be that it is probably easier and more productive to push forward toward a meaningful global and cooperative interdependence in the field of information-communication than to arrive at an economic exchange relation that is not exploitative one way or the other. This is not an argument against any form of economic exchange. Still, it is an argument in favor of more self-reliance economically so as to let the exchange part of the economy become a smaller portion than it is today. Concomitantly, it is an argument in favor of maximum exchange in the field of information-communication, conducted as much as possible in the form of dialogue, making the parties equal by having them exchange dialogue as equals.

CONCLUSION

The purpose of this chapter has been to show some of the complexity, at the macro level, of the relationship between economics and information-communication within the new international order. From a First World point of view, what happens is not necessarily that the two relate to each other in a new way. Whereas before they both worked unambiguously in favor of the First World, now they are more ambiguous. The debt catastrophe postpones this process, but is also so grotesque that it may serve to accelerate it. However, the struggle between the First and the Third worlds is being won by the Fourth, much like the struggle from 1914-1945 between Germany and the U.S. was won by Japan. The Fourth World with a China-Korea-Japan common market (with an United Korea) may ultimately run away with the first prize in this competition, even after the European Community (with an united Germany) gets its Single European Act together. There is evidence to support this beyond the fact that the Fourth World will have one billion more inhabitants!

So the conclusion is simply this: whereas the old international order was based on much economic exchange and exploitation, and not much communication dialogue, one relatively viable new international order might be based on much dialogue and not so much economic exchange, but much activity within the great trade block. The most likely "development" still appears to be that that the new order will be based on much rhetoric that sounds like dialogue and on the structure of the old international economic order, only located at new places.

NOTES TO CHAPTER 3

1. Stuart James Bullion, "The New World Information Order Debate:

How New?" *Gazette* 30 (1982), pp. 155-165.

2. Two major congresses of journalists were held, one in Chicago, May 1893, and another in Antwerp, in Summer 1894. Discussions continued periodically, until the First World War intervened. Later, the 1927 League of Nations meeting held in Geneva adopted several approved resolutions pertinent to both the working conditions of journalists and press freedoms. Other conferences on press matters followed in Copenhagen (1932) and Madrid (1933). In September 1936, the League-sanctioned Inter-governmental Conference, held in Geneva, proposed a number of recommendations regarding radio broadcasting, including the prohibition of broadcasts likely to be incompatible with international order or internal security and authorized the monitoring of broadcasts coming from outside territories to control radio's use in the provocation of war. These interests were later incorporated into early United Nations activities. One action came from the third session of UNESCO (Beirut, 1948) which adopted a resolution recognizing the rights of all persons to listen to broadcasts from other nations. While specifically this dealt with radio signal jamming, the implications go much further. (see *From Freedom of Information to the Free Flow of Information; From the Free Flow of Information to the Free and Balanced Flow of Information*, Preliminary paper for discussion, Paper No. 8, International Commission for the Study of Communication Problems, Paris, Unesco, 1977.)

3. For example, the 1948 Conference on Freedom of Information held in Geneva; and the *Declaration* by the United Nations Economic and Social Council, 1959-1960.

4. See, for example, Jacques Kayser, *One Week in the World* (Paris: Unesco, 1953).

5. Hilding Eek, "Principles Governing the Use of the Mass Media as Defined by the United Nations and UNESCO," in *National Sovereignty and International Communication*, eds., Kaarle Nordenstreng and Herbert I. Schiller (Norwood, N.J.: Ablex Publishing Corporation, 1979), p. 184.

6. Ibid., p.184

7. Meetings on development of news media in Asia (Bangkok, January 1960), Latin America (Santiago de Chile, February 1961), and Africa (Paris, January 1962), and on development of news agencies in Asia (Bangkok, December 1961), and Africa (Tunis, April 1961). "Symposium on Mass Media and International Understanding," Meeting of Yugoslav National Commission for Unesco and International Association for Mass Communication Research in Ljubljana, 1968. Meeting on news media and society, organized by Unesco, in Montreal, June 1969. See *Mass Media in Society*, Reports and Papers in Mass Communication, No. 59 (Paris: Unesco, 1970).

8. See *From Freedom of Information to the Free Flow of Information; From*

the Free Flow of Information to the Free and Balanced Flow of Information, Preliminary paper for discussion, Paper No. 8, International Commission for the Study of Communication Problems, (Paris: Unesco, 1977), p. 17. Discussions began with the formation of the United Nations Working Party on Direct Satellite Broadcasting in 1969, and were clarified with the issuing of The Declaration of Guiding Principles for the Use of Satellite Broadcasting for the Free Flow of Information, the Extension of Education and the Development of Cultural Exchanges in 1972.

9. The Declaration of Guiding Principles for the Use of Satellite Broadcasting for the Free Flow of Information, the Extension of Education and the Development of Cultural Exchanges, 1972.

10. Kaarle Nordenstreng, "Behind the Semantics—A Strategic Design," *Journal of Communication* 29 (Spring 1979), p.195.

11. Records of the 16th General Conference of Unesco, Paris, 1970, 16 C/4; Vol. 2, p. 109, para 1223.

12. Meeting of the International Group of Specialists in Communication Research, organized by Unesco, Paris, April 1971.

13. *Proposals for an International Programme of Communication Research* (Paris: Unesco, September 1971) (COM/MD/20).

14. Meeting of Experts on Communication Policies and Planning, *Final Report* (Paris: Unesco, July 17-28, 1972).(COM/MD/24}.

15. Resolution 4.301, Sixteenth Session of the UNESCO General Conference (Paris: Unesco, November 1970).

16. Records of the 17th General Conference of Unesco, Paris, 1972.

17. 17th General Conference of Unesco, Paris, 1972, Resolution 2916.

18. *The United States and the Debate on the World "Information Order"* (Washington, D.C.: USICA, 1979), pp. 20-21.

19. The Declaration of the Establishment of a New International Economic Order was adopted at the Sixth Special Session of the U.N. General Assembly in 1974, and followed by the adoption of the Action Program at the Seventh Special Session (Resolutions 3201 and 3202/S-VI, and Resolution 3362/S-VII). It is believed to have been an outcome of the Fourth Conference of Heads of State or Government of Nonaligned Countries, Algiers, September 5-9, 1973.

20. Fifth Conference of Heads of State or Government of the Non-Aligned Countries, Colombo, 1976, and 19th General Conference of UNESCO, Nairobi, 1976.

21. Rohan Samarajiwa, "The History of the New Information Order," *Journal of Communication* 34 (Autumn 1984), p. 111; arguments cultivated in writings by Raul Prebisch, *Economic Development of Latin America and its Principal Problems*, Lake Success, (New York: United Nations, Department of Economic Affairs, 1950); "Commercial Policy in

the Underdeveloped Countries," *American Economic Review* 49 (1959), pp. 251-273.

22. Mustrapha Masmoudi, *The New World Information Order*, International Commission for the Study of Communication Problems, Paper No. 31 (Paris: Unesco, 1978), pp. 21-22; and Mustapha Masmoudi, "The New World Information Order," *Journal of Communication* 29 (Spring, 1979), p. 185.

23. See Goran Hedebro, *Communication and Social Change in Developing Nations* (Ames, Iowa: Iowa State University Press, 1982), pp. 55-58.

24. International Commission for the Study of Communication Problems, UNESCO, *Many Voices, One World*. (Paris: UNESCO, 1980), p. 39.

25. *Newsweek*, September 17, 1979, p. 50.

26. Documents of the Fourth Conference of Non-Aligned countries, Algiers, 1973: Action Programme for Economic Cooperation; also in Vlasdislava Bulatovic, *Non-Alignment and Information* (Belgrade: Federal Committee for Information & Jugoslovenska Stvarnost, 1978), p. 71; and Breda Pavlic and Cees J. Hamelink, *The New International Economic Order: Links between Economics and Communication*, Reports and Papers on Mass Communication, No. 98 (Paris: Unesco, 1985), p. 14.

27. "Programme of Action for Economic Development," Fourth Conference of Heads of State or Government of Non-aligned Countries, Algiers, September 5-9, 1973.

28. Tran Van Dinh, "Non-Alignment and Cultural Imperialism," in *The Non-Aligned Movement in World Politics*, ed., A. W. Singham (Westport, CT: Lawrence-Hill, 1977); Anthony Smith, *The Geopolitics of Information* (New York: Oxford University Press, 1980).

29. Gunnar Garbo, *A World of Difference; The International Distribution of Information: The Media and Developing Countries*, Communication and Society Reports, No. 15 (Paris: UNESCO, 1975), p. 66.

30. From Ministerial Meeting of the Coordinating Bureau of Non-Aligned Countries, New Delhi, April 16-19, 1986.

31. A 1972 resolution calling for the drafting of "Fundamental Principles Governing the Use of News Media in Strengthening Peace and International Understanding and in Combating War Propaganda, Racism and Apartheid."

32. Presented by the Director General to the 18th session of the General Conference, Paris, October-November, 1974, UNESCO document 18C/35, July 12, 1974.

33. Ibid., Article I, paragraphs 1 and 2.

34. Ibid., Article II.

35. Ibid., Article III.

36. *Origin and Mandate*, International Commission for the Study of Communication Problems, Paper No. 2 (Paris: Unesco, 1977), p. 2.

37. 19th General Conference of UNESCO, Nairobi, 1976, 19 C/INF, 12, p. 22.

38. Colin Legum and John Cornwell, *A Free and Balanced Flow: Report of the Twentieth Century Fund Task Force on the International Flow of News: Background Paper* (Lexington, Mass: Lexington Books, 1978); Colin Legum and John Cornwell, *International Flow of News*, unpublished 1978 manuscript for Twentieth Century Trust Fund, UNESCO news flow collection, Paris.

39. Ibid.

40. Leonard R. Sussman, *Mass News Media and the Third World Challenge*, The Washington Papers, vol. 5, no. 46 (Beverly Hills, CA: Sage Publications, 1977).

41. 19th General Conference of UNESCO, Nairobi, 1976, "Resolution 100," paragraphs 22 and 23.

42. Ibid., "Resolution 4.142."

43. *Origin and Mandate*, International Commission for the Study of Communication Problems, Paper No. 2 (Paris: Unesco, 1977), p. 3.

44. Ibid., pp. 4-5.

45. Nordenstreng, "Behind the Semantics—A Strategic Design," p. 195.

46. See Thomas L. McPhail, *Electronic Colonialism*, 2d ed. (Newbury Park, CA: Sage, 1987), pp. 196-8, for observations on this meeting.

47. See observations by Thomas L. McPhail; Ibid., pp. 196-8.

48. See Hedebro, *Communication and Social Change in Developing Nations* p. 64.

49. International Commission for the Study of Communication Problems, UNESCO, *Many Voices, One World* (Paris: UNESCO, 1980), pp. 253-275.

50. See Pavlic and Hamelink, *The New International Economic Order: Links between Economics and Communication*; Meheroo Jussawalla, "The Economics of International Communication," *Third World Quarterly* 1 (3) (1979); Meheroo Jussawalla, "Economic and Information Orders: Emerging Issues for International Communication," paper presented at the World Communications Conference, "Decisions for the Eighties," Annenberg School of Communications, Philadelphia, May 1980; Meheroo Jussawalla, *Bridging Global Barriers, Two New International Orders: NIEO, NWIO*, pamphlet (Honolulu, HI: East-West Center, 1981); also see Cees Hamelink, *The New International Economic Order and the New International Information Order*. International Commission for the Study of Communication Problems, Publication No. 34 (Paris: Unesco, 1985).

51. Frederick T. C. Yu, "Improving U.S. Journalists' Understanding of the Third World," in *Third World News in American Media: Experience and Prospects*, Conference Proceedings Monograph (New York: Columbia University Graduate School of Journalism, Center for Advanced Study of Communication and Public Affairs, May 20-21, 1982; released 1983), p. 33.

52. Leonard Sussman, "Independent News Media: The People's Press Cannot Be Run by Government," *Journal of International Affairs* (Fall/Winter 1981/1982), p. 214.

53. "Split Decision over UNESCO," *Broadcasting*, November 3, 1980, p. 28.

54. Ibid.

55. "Confrontation at Tallories," *Time*, June 1, 1981, p. 82.

56. Declaration of Tallories, Voices of Freedom Conference; reprinted in *A Documentary History of a New World Information and Communication Order Seen as an Evolving and Continuing Process: 1975-1986*, "Communication and Society," Report No. 19 (Paris: UNESCO).

57. "Confrontation at Tallories," p. 82.

58. Independent Commission for World-Wide Telecommunications Development Report, *The Missing Link* (Geneva: ITU, 1985), p. 31.

59. Ibid., pp. 19, 57-69.

60. Ibid., p. 69.

61. "The Way it Was and Wasn't at WARC '85," *Broadcasting*, November 4, 1985, p. 71.

62. "Space WARC Reaches Consensus," *Broadcasting*, September 16, 1985, p. 41.

63. "The Way it Was and Wasn't at WARC '85," p. 70; The International Telegraph Union, predecessor to the ITU, was created in 1865.

64. "Space WARC Reaches Consensus," p. 40.

65. "WARC 1985: The Politics of Space," *Broadcasting*, September 23, 1985, p. 56.

66. "Space WARC Reaches Consensus," p. 40.

67. Interview with Leonard Sussman, as reported in A. H. Raskin, "U.S. News Coverage of the Belgrade UNESCO Conference," *Journal of Communication* 31 (Autumn 1981), p. 167.

68. "Confrontation at Tallories," p. 82.

69. "Unesco Approves a Compromise on World Communications Plan," *New York Times*, November 26, 1983, Sec. A, p. 6.

70. "U.S. Weighs Unesco Pullout over Budget and Policy Fight," *New York Times*, December 1983, p. 1.

71. One observer who expressed surprise since "the NWICO ha[d] substantially withered away in the face of the economic and political

realities of the 1980s," was Majid Tehranian. See Majid Tehranian, "World Forum: The U.S. Decision to Withdraw from UNESCO," *Journal of Communication* 34 (Autumn 1984), p. 141.

72. Letter from George P. Schultz, Secretary of State, United States of America, Washington, D.C., to The Honorable Amadou-Mahtar M'Bow, Director General, United Nations Educational, Scientific and Cultural Organization, Paris, December 28, 1983; letter reprinted in the *Journal of Communication* 34 (Autumn 1984), p. 82.

73. U.S. Department of State transcript, "On the Record Briefing on United States Withdrawal from UNESCO by the Hon. Gregory Newell, Assistant Secretary of State, Bureau of International Organization Affairs," December 29, 1983.

74. C. Anthony Giffard, *UNESCO and the Media* (New York: Longman, 1989), pp. 88-89.

75. Memorandum from William G. Harley, Communications Consultant, United States State Department, Washington, D.C., February 9, 1984, revised April 1984; reprinted in the *Journal of Communication* 34 (Autumn 1984), p. 89.

76. Colleen Roach, "The U.S. Position on the New World Information and Communication Order," *Journal of Communication* 37 (Autumn 1987), pp. 36-51.

77. Leonard R. Sussman, "World Forum: The U.S. Decision to Withdraw from UNESCO," *Journal of Communication* 34 (Autumn 1984), p. 159.

78. "Old World Information Order," *The Nation*, July 7-14, 1984, pp. 6-7.

79. Giffard, *UNESCO and the Media*, pp. 167-181; the *Christian Science Monitor, Hartford Courant, Cleveland Plain Dealer, Houston Post, St. Louis Post-Dispatch, Akron (Ohio) Beacon-Journal*.

80. McPhail, *Electronic Colonialism*, 2d ed., pp. 262-63; "Editorial: Pressure by State Department," *Editor & Publisher*, February 4, 1984, p. 4; "Government Wages UNESCO Campaign," *Editor & Publisher*, February 4, 1984, p. 7.

81. McPhail, *Electronic Colonialism*, 2d ed., pp. 262-63; Sussman's actions have since been well documented in C. Anthony Giffard's thorough work, *UNESCO and the Media*, pp. 55-111; see also "Editorial: Pressure by State Department," p. 4; "Government Wages UNESCO Campaign," p. 7.

82. *New York Times*, September 30, 1983.

83. "Government Wages UNESCO Campaign," p. 7.

84. Leonard R. Sussman, "Foreword:Who Did in UNESCO?" in *UNESCO and the Media*, ed. C. Anthony Giffard (New York: Longman, 1989), p. xiii.

85. "Editorial: Pressure by State Department," *Editor & Publisher*, February 4, 1984, p. 4.

86. "Unesco Opens Debate with U.S. Absent," *New York Times*, February 13, 1985, p. A5.

87. Leonard R. Sussman, "Foreword: Who Did in UNESCO?" p. xiv.

88. "Unesco Parley a Disappointment for Britain," *New York Times*, November 10, 1985, p. L12.

89. "France Is Giving $2 Million Extra to Unesco," *New York Times*, February 14, 1985, p. A16.

90. "Unesco Parley a Disappointment for Britain," p. L12.

91. See, for example, European Institute for the Media, *World Communication Report*, compiled by John L. Ecclestone and Brigitte Meyer, Final Report; UNESCO Report, World Communication Report Data Base, The University of Manchester, September 1987; p. 35.

92. International Commission for the Study of Communication Problems, *The World of News Agencies*, Report No. 11.

93. Luis Ramiro Beltrán S. and Elizabeth Fox deCardona, "Latin America and the United States: Flaws in the Free Flow of Information," in *National Sovereignty and International Communication*, eds. Kaarle Nordenstreng and Herbert I. Schiller (Norwood, N.J.: Ablex Publishing Corporation, 1979), p. 39; also Mustapha Masmoudi, "The New World Information Order," *Journal of Communication* 29 (Spring, 1979), p. 172.

94. See J. W. Marham, "Foreign News in the United States and South American Press," *Public Opinion Quarterly* 25 (1961), pp. 249-262, all foreign stories in seven Latin American dailies were found to come from AP, UPI, and Agence France-Presse.

95. L. Erwin Atwood and Stuart J. Bullion, "News Maps of the World: A View from Asia," in *International Perspectives on News*, ed., L. Erwin Atwood, Stuart J. Bullion and Sharon M. Murphy (Carbondale, Il: Southern Illinois University Press, 1982), p. 104.

96. L. Erwin Atwood and Stuart J. Bullion, "News Maps of the World: A View from Asia," p. 126.

97. Fernando Reyes Matta, "The Information Bedazzlement of Latin America," *Development Dialogue* 2 (1976), 29-42.

98. See Herbert I. Schiller, "Transnational Media and National Development," Paper presented at Fair Communication Policy for International Exchange of Information Conference, East-West Communication Institute, Honolulu, Hawaii, March 28-April 2, 1976; Herbert I. Schiller, *Communication and Cultural Domination*, (White Plains, N. Y.: International Arts and Sciences Press, Inc., 1976); Herbert I. Schiller, "Freedom from the 'Free Flow'," *Journal of Communication* 24 (Winter 1974), pp. 110-117; Juan Somavia, "The Transnational Power Structure and Informational Information: Elements of a Third World

Policy for Transnational News Agencies," *Development Dialogue* 2 (1976), pp. 15-28.

99. Herbert I. Schiller, "Transnational Media and National Development," in *National Sovereignty and International Communication*, eds., Kaarle Nordenstreng and Herbert I. Schiller (Norwood, N.J.: Ablex Publishing Corporation, 1979), p. 21.

100. Herbert I. Schiller, "Transnational Media and National Development," in *National Sovereignty and International Communication*, pp. 25-26; also in Schiller, *Communication and Cultural Domination*, pp. 24-45.

101. Herbert I. Schiller, "Transnational Media and National Development," in *National Sovereignty and International Communication*, pp. 25-26.

102. Roger Tatarian, "News Flow in the Third World," in *The Third World and Press Freedom*, ed., Philip C. Horton (New York: Praeger Publishers, 1978), p. 32.

103. He uses the University of Hawaii as an example; Jim Richstad, "Transnational News Agencies: Issues and Policies," in *Crisis in International News: Policies and Prospects*, eds., Jim Richstad and Michael H. Anderson (New York: Columbia University Press, 1981), p. 249.

104. Richstad, "Transnational News Agencies: Issues and Policies," p. 249; other major transnational electronics-information corporations are General Electric (U.S.), IT&T (U.S.), Philips (Netherlands), Siemens (Germany), Western Electric (U.S.), GTE (U.S.), Westinghouse (U.S.), AEG - Telefunken (Germany), North American Rockwell (U.S.), RCA (U.S.), Matsushita (Japan), LTV (U.S.), Xerox (U.S.), CGE (France); see: S. Adefumi Sonaike, "Communication and Third World Development: A Dead End? *Gazette*, 41(1988), pp. 85-108. Also see MacBride Report; International Commission for the Study of Communication Problems, UNESCO, *Many Voices, One World*. (Paris: UNESCO, 1980).

105. Richstad also makes this point; "Transnational News Agencies: Issues and Policies," p. 251.

106. See Hedebro, *Communication and Social Change in Developing Nations*, p. 65.

107. Karol Jakubowicz, "Third World News Cooperation Scheme in Building a New International Communication Order: Do They Stand a Chance?" *Gazette* 36 (1985), pp. 81-93.

108. Eli Abel, "Global Information: The New Battleground," *Political Communication and Persuasion* 1 (1982), pp. 347-357.

109. Resolution adopted at the Twenty-First Session of the General Conference of UNESCO, Belgrade, September-October, 1980; Section 4/19 of the Annex.

110. Wimal Dissanayake, "World Forum: The U.S. Decision to

Withdraw from UNESCO," *Journal of Communication* 34 (Autumn 1984), p. 135.

111. *Third Medium-Term Plan (1990-1995)*, Resolution 25 C/4/104 (Paris: UNESCO), p. 100, paragraph 239 (e).

112. *Third Medium-Term Plan (1990-1995)*, Resolution 25 C/4/104, p. 101, paragraph 240.

113. *Third Medium-Term Plan (1990-1995)*, Resolution 25 C/4/104, p. 101, paragraph 240.

114. *Third Medium-Term Plan (1990-1995)*, Resolution 25 C/4/104, p. 101, paragraph 241.

115. *Third Medium-Term Plan (1990-1995)*, Resolution 25 C/4/104, p. 101, paragraph 243.

116. See *Proceedings of the Symposium on "Media Accountability under International Law,"* (Berkeley, CA: The Union for Democratic Communications and the National Lawyers Guild, June 14, 1989).

117. "The Harare Statement of the MacBride Round Table on Communication," *Media Development*, Number 1 (1990), p. 13.

118. See Hamid Mowlana and Colleen Roach for further discussion of some of these events; Hamid Mowlana and Colleen Roach, "New World Information and Communication Order Since Harare: Overview of Developments and Activities," *The Democratic Journalist* 37:12 (December 1990) (Prague); Document No. IJI R 725, International Journalism Institute, 11000 Prague, Ruzová 7, Czechoslovakia

119. See Hamid Mowlana and Colleen Roach, "New World Information and Communication Order Since Prague: Overview of Developments and Activities," Paper presented at the Third MacBride Round Table on Communication, Istanbul, Turkey, June 21, 1991, for details on some of these meetings.

120. International Journalism Institute, "Selected Bibliography on WIICO," Paper presented at the Third MacBride Round Table on Communication, Prague, June 17, 1991; Istanbul, June 21, 1991.

121. "Few Voices, Many World: The Istanbul Statement of the MacBride Round Table on Communication, 1991," Third MacBride Round Table on Communication Report, Istanbul, Turkey, June 21, 1991.

122. Hamid Mowlana, *Global Information and World Communication* (New York, Longman, 1986); C. Anthony Giffard, *Unesco and the Media* (New York: Longman, 1989); George Gerbner, Hamid Mowlana and Kaarle Nordenstreng (eds.), *The Global Media Debate: Its Rise, Fall and Renewal* (Norwood, N.J.: Ablex, 1992). Also see the "New Communications for a New Century" issue of *Media Development* 39:2 (1992).

123. Edward T. Pinch, "The Third World and the Fourth Estate: A Look at the Non-aligned News Agency Pool," Senior Seminar in Foreign

Policy, U.S. Department of State, Washington, 1976-1977.

124. Robert L. Stevenson, *Communication, Development, and the Third World* (New York: Longman, 1988), p. 165.

125. Wimal Dissanayake, "World Forum: The U.S. Decision to Withdraw from UNESCO," p. 135.

126. Hamid Mowlana, "World Forum: The U.S. Decision to Withdraw from UNESCO," *Journal of Communication* 34 (Autumn 1984), p. 139.

127. Kaarle Nordenstreng, *The Mass Media Declaration of UNESCO* (Norwood, N.J.: Ablex, 1984), p. 14; emphasis in original.

128. Leonard R. Sussman, *The Washington Papers*, vol. V, The Center for Strategic and International Studies, Georgetown University, Washington, D.C. (Beverly Hills, CA: Sage Publications, 1977).

129. Leonard R. Sussman, "World Forum: The U.S. Decision to Withdraw from UNESCO," *Journal of Communication* 34 (Autumn 1984), p. 159.

130. Ibid., p. 161.

131. Figures for "language" (defined as "mother tongue") are: (1) Chinese, 950 million; (2) English, 350 million; (3) Spanish, 230 million; (4) Russian, 200 million; (5) Hindi, 160 million; (6) Arabic, 120 million. Source: *Encyclopedia Britanica*, 1986 edition.

132. This may not seem so incredible considering the First World media purchases already being made by Fourth World parties, and the considerable First World real estate properties already owned by individuals from oil-rich nations of the Middle East.

133. For perhaps the best general analysis of Japanese influence/control on the United States, see Pat Choate, *Agents of Influence* (New York: Alfred A. Knopf, 1990), particularly Chapter 4, "Washington's Revolving Door," Chapter 5, "Japan Buys Washington," and Chapter 6, "Japan Takes Television."

134. We can see these effects on domestic reporting as well. Critics note that the U.S. media often report stories in which a person of racial minority is arrested on charges of committing some crime. In these stories, race is often identified within the report (e.g., "John Doe, a black man, . . ."). Caucasians charged with crimes are rarely identified by race when the news media report their stories.

CHAPTER 4

The Media, World-Wide Security and Peace

In Korea, the soldiers were abandoning their arms, while in Washington, the senators were brandishing the sword. Senator Knowland wanted bombs dropped on Chinese territory. Senator Ferguson and others insisted upon the immediate use of the atom bomb. They were backed by Stassen, one of the leaders of the Republican Party. Senator Pepper declared that it would be stupid to be too fastidious. Mr. Dewey, Governor of New York, shouted that America was waging a desperate fight, and could not afford to be over-scrupulous. Finally, Senator Morse jumped up and demanded petulantly for the Soviet Union to be atom-bombed without delay. The people who have not lost their reason will ask, "What's the matter? Why are the American rulers, losing a small war, striving to unleash a big one? It is difficult to answer this question. Here, there is no logic — only signs of mental disorder.
— Radio excerpt from North American Service talk on Cold War tensions, written by Soviet author, Ilya Ehrenberg, January 3, 1951. [1]

ON DATA, THEORIES AND VALUES

What the media do when they process events and what researchers do are not that different. Both of them relate to empirical reality; both are interested in getting data. The media are particularly concerned with highly contemporary events; getting fresh data about something defined as news. Researchers may also be satisfied with "olds", that is, old events, but preferably in the light of new data. Both are concerned with *theories*, with efforts to understand the data within some coherent cognitive framework—usually put into the commentary section of newspapers, such as editorials; and in the theory section of a scientific article or book. And both of them are highly motivated by *values*, only the media are usually more honest, making their values more explicit. Researchers have a tendency to hide their values even to themselves, pretending that as individuals and as a group they are "value-free" and objective—uninfluenced by anything but data; the effort to interpret them; the formulation of theories; and the correspondence between the two.

Since they are so similar, researchers and media people should understand each other. Researchers may prefer research very rich in theory, with new interpretations inspired by new data, even if such data are not about news, but new data about "olds." We might sometimes prefer the researcher, particularly the medical researcher, to be value-explicit and to try to relate theories to values, posing such counter-factual questions as: "What would have happened if?" "How could this be changed?" "What could be done in order to come closer to a reality where the following values are realized?" When empirical reality is contrasted with this potential reality, the researcher puts his theory to the test, at least on paper;[2] as when an architect looks at drawings through "but will it work in practice" eyes.

It is not clear that we should use the same criteria for the press. Newspapers in the now classical Soviet Union were longer on theory and value, and shorter on data, mainly devoting themselves to ideologically inspired commentary, with very little news to offer. However, this also applies elsewhere, and is why so few stories can be found in daily newspapers and broadcast news programs. For example, in a half hour U.S. network newscast, as little as 10 minutes may be devoted to events that took place that day; the remaining stories tend to be less time-specific and many can be inserted at almost any time over several days or weeks. The same happens with newspapers. In addition, even with events occurring on the same day as the report, most stories have evolved, and are reported, over a period of several days or longer. The redundancy quickly becomes apparent, therefore, in daily news reports. Little new information tends to be presented. In locales where there is more than one daily print or television news source, a great deal of similarity is typically seen from one media outlet to another. The same opinion leaders are often interviewed and the same wire/news film services are utilized.

Since the world changes more quickly than the commentary (including the magazine *Commentary*), such "newspapers" (or magazines and other media) tend to become reproductions of themselves from one day, week, or month to another. This is what made the Soviet bloc press as absurd before *glasnost'* as it became fascinating after. It is not that easy to write anything new and interesting every day, especially little Sunday sermons based on theories and values only. This is one more reason why reliable news is needed to make a daily paper worth reading. Hence it would be preferable for news to have front page prominence and theories and values to be buried in the back pages, in editorials and commentaries. In other words, the components are the same as for research; but the priority could and should be different.

But we might also demand of the press that same precious quality of intellectuals in general, and researchers in particular: *the ability to insert question marks.* That is, not only the ability to question theories and values in the light of new data, but also to question the data in the light of their own specific theories and values, asking the basic question: "Is that necessarily so?" No autonomous person would necessarily accept as news everything reported as such, even if the distortions and misunderstandings presented as data were compatible with values we ourselves might hold.

The editor of the *Japan Times*, Mr. Kiyoaki Murata, gives two interesting examples of such distortions.[3] One of them refers to President Kennedy's famous speech in West Berlin, June 26, 1963, 5 months before he was murdered by Lee Harvey Oswald in Dallas, Texas (November 22), in which Kennedy was reported to have said *"Ich bin ein Berliner."* He said this. However, what Kennedy actually meant, according to Murata: was "Today, in the world of freedom, the proudest boast is *"Ich bin ein Berliner."* In other words, he was not saying that he himself was "ein Berliner," only that it was a proud person who was able to boast that he was one.[4] The German audience mainly understood the four words spoken in German, ignored the rest, and Kennedy and his advisers very quickly understood how successful the semantic misunderstanding had been and did not go out of their way to clarify it. By not doing so, they certainly improved German-American relations.

The second of Murata's examples is the famous statement attributed to Nikita Khrushchev in Moscow, quoted as having said to a group of American businessmen: "We shall bury you." What Khrushchev said in Russian was *My vas pokhoronim,* which can be translated as "We shall bury you." But there are two interpretations: "bury" in the sense of first being killed and then having a funeral; and "bury" in the sense of "when you are dead, we will be present at your funeral," meaning that socialism will outlive capitalism (the opposite was pretty much what happened in Fall, 1989). In the spirit of the Cold War the first interpretation was picked up, with no effort on the Soviet side to insist on the second interpretation. References to the statement quoted in the aggressive sense of "We shall destroy you" can still be encountered. This contributes great harm to U.S.-Soviet relations.

The two examples can be used to illustrate one simple point: data alone, even when reported with great intra- and intersubjective reliability in the tradition of the best newspapers, do not necessarily contribute to better or worse relations. Accuracy in the sense of a correct interpretation, would not improve relations in the first case above, but would in the second. The situation dictates not only the way data are presented in the context of theories and values, but the whole world context. If relations are really bad, almost any statement of fact can be seen in a negative light; if there is a desire for good relations the opposite will be the case. It is against that background that the following ten proposals should be understood. Peace is a highly desirable value—interpreted not only as survival, but as peace with economic justice, political freedom, and cultural meaning. How can the media be faithful to reality, yet serve to promote peace in their reporting?

TEN PROPOSALS FOR A PEACE-ORIENTED NEWS MEDIA

First, whenever there is a conflict, one of the basic tasks, indeed duties, of the media is to give a voice to both or all parties in the conflict. It may involve world military powers in an international conflict, and the nations and people who are affected in secondary and tertiary ways; the white ruling class and the black oppressed class of South Africa with its many individual interest groups, some seeking violent solutions to apartheid, some advocating peaceful means; or right-wing and peace groups arguing over the scope of renovations to be carried out at the Hiroshima Peace Memorial Monument—the "right" wants Japan to stop apologizing for its behavior in the war and stress its aggressive activities, the peace group wants the ghastly horror, anguish, and eradicative powers of the bomb to be the only focus.[5] No view, no aspiration, should be suppressed. This presupposes that one knows who the parties are, which is not always so simple. In the East-West conflict this was relatively easy: any good newspaper in the East, the West, or the neutral/nonaligned countries could get the views of all three parties—the East, the West, and the neutral/nonaligned. The task would be to report how all sides look at, for instance, a new disarmament proposal, or at some new move up or down the armament spiral, or perhaps at some other draws in the big and dangerous game of the Cold War.

If only one side is given a voice, for instance, in the U.S-Japan or UN-Iraq/U.S.-Iraq conflicts, it is certainly likely to be that side with which one sympathizes. We will offer some examples of one-sided reporting in a later section dealing with media bias (often that bias has its basis in nationalism). In doing so the media themselves contribute, in a major way, to the conflict. To read in extenso what the other side says, might exacerbate the negative attitudes and behavior; but it may also have a sobering impact.[6] Thus, it becomes clear that the other side is also an actor with goals and strategies who acts and reacts, that the whole system is interactive, that is, it is a game of chess rather than a game of golf. This gives a more realistic image of the situation than the image of the opposing side as a thing, as some kind of natural phenomenon like an earthquake or a hurricane, with sudden bursts of evil activity. At any rate, knowledge of the parties' position is necessary to understand the issue, and knowledge of the issue is necessary to come to a solution — even if it hurts.

---

1. **Report all sides.**

2. **Clarify the frame of reference.**

3. **Media ownership should not matter.**

4. **Don't overemphasize certain views.**

5. **Enhance educational side of news.**

6. **Understand reality of arms issue.**

7. **Attend to arms race inner dynamism.**

8. **Realize weaknesses of media.**

9. **Consider North-South dynamics.**

10. **Clearly portray peace benefits.**

Figure 1. Ten proposals for a peace-oriented news media.

A threat is perceived, for instance, in the form of a "missile gap" or some other weapons gap, or a trade deficit. There are efforts to "catch up." But statements of how the other side will react, catching up with the efforts to "catch up," are ignored, or discounted as "something they will do anyhow," or as "efforts to scare us." When the other side does what is expected this is seen as a new threat, not as a draw in a possibly infinite actio-reactio chain. This view of the other side is particularly prevalent in the United States. The United States may be seen as a nation of golf-players ("there is the goal/hole; go hit it/get it") whereas the Russians are more a nation of chess-players (if I do this, he will think I am going to that, however he knows that I know that, so he'll probably think that. . . and so on), and the Japanese a nation of go-players (like chess, only more so). *Action mode* versus *interaction mode*. The action mode probably relates to a process of dehumanization of the adversary to the point where the "Other" is seen either as a thing or as totally autistic, incapable of interaction, locked into a standard stereotyped reaction to anything coming out of "Self" (our side). Good media will try to break through this distortion even when it is painful.

Included in this would be the power of the media to make peace dialogues public. The potential effect of this may be to raise the level of public concern, and promote a faster and fairer peace resolution. As CBS news broadcaster, Eric Sevareid has observed, "Mass-media coverage of the summit and similar events is a force for peace . . . [it] keeps pressure on governments."[7]

This positive effect applies to more than summit meetings, and other high-level diplomatic gatherings, however. Government personnel, policy makers, community leaders, and individuals can engage in media-produced and promoted dialogues. The American television network, ABC, has sponsored a series of live television dialogues on its program *Nightline* in recent years. The shows have been based in many trouble spots, including South Africa and the Middle East.The precedent for U.S. network television's involvement in Middle Eastern diplomacy dates back to 1977 when Egyptian President Anwar Sadat told CBS anchor Walter Cronkite in a televised interview that he was ready to go to Jerusalem to talk peace.[8] With *Nightline* the purpose has been to bring together individuals with opposing points of view in an effort to get people talking. While some have been critical of such television colloquies suggesting that it is too little too late, it seems that there is a place for this "television diplomacy" when handled properly.[9] As program anchor Ted Koppel noted following the South African program:

> What was significant about *Nightline*'s week in South Africa was not that blacks and whites of such diverse points of view agreed to appear together on TV, but their reasons for doing so. Forget (if indeed you can even remember) what was said by the various voices competing for attention during our week in South Africa. Ask only why they bothered . . .[10]

In Jerusalem, a "town meeting" featured Israeli and Palestinian representatives. At the insistence of the Arab participants, the two groups were divided on stage by a small, symbolic wooden fence. Koppel moderated a 3-hour "exhaustive public dialogue." While the rhetoric was "familiar,"it did not "diminish the salutary impact of watching both sides coming together on live television, an effect enhanced by the presence of a Jewish-Arab audience (including 150 Palestinians bused in from the occupied territories)."[11] Related to the educational responsibility of the news media (a point elaborated later), and providing the intellectual reference suggested in our next section, the report was peppered with pieces designed to enhance audience outlook and provide context. These included an overview of the complex history of the region and clips of children vocalizing their dreams for peace.[12]

Second, the media should try to make explicit some theories, the intellectual frame of reference, and the "discourse" or "paradigm" within which a conflict is to be understood. How did the conflict start? Is it obvious that it started with one spectacular event or could it have deeper cultural, historical, and structural roots as is often the case? Is it really due to someone's fault, usually (of course) on "the other side?" Or could the conflict be more like a congenital defect, something that is carried and has been with the system for a long time? Is it like the Korean conflict of 1950-53, the inevitable result of the division of a country fighting for its liberation for generations (1910-1945) only to come under two masters instead of one—rather than a question of one side attacking the other. In other words, a conflict begs the question of some theory (or preferably theories), some understanding—not only of value, on whose side you are, or how bad the conflict is or may be in its consequences. Some of this can be made explicit. But it is difficult, even painful. It is not a question of probing the mood of others. The mind to be probed is your own, including its deeper recesses. For example, consider the Christian mind when Islam and Muslims are involved, or the European mind when Arabs are involved. Or the mind of the oil consumer when oil producers are involved, as an example of an aspect of the "Gulf Crisis."

If the media feel incapable of providing an intellectual frame of reference for conflict understanding (and they usually are), then it may be wise to turn to experts. Since experts usually have at least one different opinion each (that is what makes them experts), one should ask more than one expert for their views of the matter. The best method would be to use experts from either side of the conflict divide. Good newspapers do this; only the bad ones immediately engage in solid value judgments with no effort whatsoever to explore the theoretical foundations, hiring only native male mainstream experts, for instance, as syndicated columnists. Example: How is a "terrorist attack" seen? As the only weapon of the weak? Or as the front of the strong, concealing their participation? Or as both? Or as the cranky act of a criminal, a not very mature view of terrorism. For each view, what is the evidence, what are the consequences?

In short, do not confuse the conflict with its manifestations in terms of hostile attitudes and behavior. Beneath the sound and fury there are (almost) always some hard, intractable issues, such as two nations wanting states on the same small territory such as Israel and Palestine.

Third, and this is a difficult one: the two foregoing demands should also be directed to media that are owned by big governmental or corporate interests. In East and West Europe, Asia, and Africa (but not in the U.S.-influenced Western hemisphere), major TV channels and radio stations are government-owned or -controlled. They are subject to some of the same pressures as public schools to be the unquestioning carriers of national myths and governmental messages and the purveyors of "national interests," meaning the interests of the country as interpreted by the powers that be. Such controls can be publicly seen even in the textbook selection process found in some U.S. communities where titles are chosen to comply with certain community "standards" and various historical points of view. In the Western hemisphere, but also in the rest of the world, strong commercial interests may have power over TV channels and radio stations—directly or indirectly through advertising—and over newspapers and news magazines. These commercial interests are usually private or corporate rather than state capitalist. Many of the conflicts in the world today are centered around capitalism as a way of organizing the economy, and even more so after the demise of Soviet style socialism, perhaps best referred to as "Stalinism." Hence it is even more urgent that media develop a sufficient level of understanding, even of self-criticism, to be able to reflect these conflicts adequately. In general they have not, not only because they protect themselves and their owners, but also because they don't know/understand their own ideological basis and bias.

Exemplifying how the political disposition of a media organization can become a factor is a review by Cockburn on the *New York Times'* handling of the Guatemala (or Arias) accords, signed on August 7, 1987. He considers the *Times*, in particular, to be a good example of the mainstream U.S. press's "performance . . . as accomplice and handservant of the state . . . "[13]

Cockburn believes the *Times* reporting became "increasingly attuned to the interests of the Administration and its *contras*." While the peace accord was supposed to be a simultaneous implementation of reconciliation provisions by five countries, Cockburn found a severe imbalance in the coverage the *Times* gave to accord compliances; in searching *Times* files he was able to locate only six stories on El Salvador, two on Honduras, none on Guatemala, but some 100 on Nicaragua within a 5-month period following the signing of the agreement. He concludes that "This ignoring of simultaneity and the corresponding stress on Nicaragua was congenial to the Administration, since it suggested that everything depended on unilateral actions by Nicaragua."[14]

Cockburn backs up this claim by citing *Times* stories during the period. These included a Stephen Kinzer article which noted that "Pressure is building on Nicaragua's Sandinista leaders to take 'key steps' in order to comply" with the accord regarding the release of prisoners, and to open cease-fire dialogue with the contras.[15] He notes another day where stories by both James LeMoyne and Stephen Kinzer view Nicaraguan concessions "cynically," and unilateral actions are portrayed as mere "compliance."

> On January 18, after Nicaragua had submitted to those two key demands [prisoners and cease-fire talks], LeMoyne wrote, "Mr. Ortega responded with a shrewd tactical move by making what were probably the minimum concessions he could offer." That same day Kinzer had a story remarking that "Mr. Ortega took the new steps toward compliance less than three weeks before Congress is scheduled to vote on new aid for the contras."[16]

Cockburn credits Peter Ford, reporting in *The Christian Science Monitor*, as being just about the only exception to the "mainstream press." He provides an example in which the International Commission on Verification and Follow-up (C.I.V.S.), the organization which was responsible for monitoring accord compliance, released a unanimously approved report responsive to the sensitive situation just before the Costa Rican summit. One of Ford's commission sources confirmed that the "conclusions are vague because the Central Americans were involved in drawing them up, and Honduras, El Salvador, and Guatemala were watering them down all the way." In an earlier draft of the report, amnesties in these three countries were said to be ineffective due to each country's practice of killing prisoners. The language was eventually changed at the insistence of these three countries to suggest that these prisoner executions were the practice of "previous governments."[17]

Ford reported one decisive commission conclusion which was also noted in a separate story by Julia Preston in *The Washington Post*:

> In spite of the exhortations of the Central American presidents the government of the United States of America maintains its policy and practice of providing assistance, military in particular, to the irregular forces operating against the government of Nicaragua. The definitive cessation of this assistance continues to be an indispensable requirement for the success of the peace efforts and of this pocedure as a whole.[18]

LeMoyne mentioned none of this. According to Cockburn, LeMoyne's suggestion that there was "little agreement" in the C.I.V.S. report is "an incredible lie." He also considers it "reprehensible" that LeMoyne failed to make any mention of the candid statement on U.S. aid.[19] This certainly serves as a good example of how different reporters (and media) might selectively perceive peace initiative events.

We know perfectly well that governmental/party and corporate interests usually prevail, and that often truths and possibly deeper understanding are given second priority in news coverage. Nevertheless, the public should educate itself to persist in this demand. The most effective way of bringing about a change is to make one-sided efforts at conflict understanding unacceptable, as something not to be taken seriously. Decent people are looking for such profoundly understood facts also to understand where possible solutions to conflicts might be. How can this be done without knowing the views and thinking of all parties regardless of how abominable they may appear to us?

If the media do not offer this insight, so much the worse for the media in a demand-supply society. At least this holds in principle. Market pressures can be exercised on the media in a country where the public has a choice in demand and supply. Yet in practice the public may decide in favor of the least sophisticated and least peace-building media, as it is intellectually less demanding and emotionally more satisfying. In a country where the media are streamlined by governmental and/or corporate monopolies, not even this choice is available. Of course, in such countries, newspapers and radio stations may have formally independent editorial staffs, only they are trained to perceive, think, and interpret exactly the same way so that the result is the same regardless of the diversity of the channels. Diversity of channels is neither a sufficient, nor a necessary condition for diversity in communication.

Fourth, flowing from the news paradigm, *media should be less the victim of the four key tendencies in news reporting; over-emphasis on elite countries, over-emphasis on elite persons, over-emphasis on personalization and over-emphasis on negative events.*[20] These are common charges in international journalism and have been touched on earlier in this book. Media should become better at reporting what other countries do; what people other than top people do; at reporting the slow workings of structures rather than the quick, sometimes spectacular, but also ephemeral events; and also at reporting something positive such as acts of cooperation, within and between power blocs, positive indicators of human and social development, and so forth. As argued in Chapters 1 and 2, even in countries governed by the "idea of progress," what catches the ear and the eye seems to be negative events, perhaps exactly because they are unexpected, and hence newsworthy, from the point of view of the idea of progress. In basically pessimistic cultures, perhaps any positive event would constitute news.

It would be useful for journalists and editors to be more conscious of their own inclination to report and edit according to the four types of bias mentioned, and to pin on their walls the admonition to exercise some restraint. More particularly, it might be useful to play down somewhat their view of the world as some kind of sports arena or court tribunal, where key "players" or actors are competing, fighting, accused, or even convicted; zooming in on the obvious question like a not-very-good mystery novel: Who wins? Who loses? Whodunit? Khomeini or Carter? Carter or Reagan? Reagan or Gorbachev? Gorbachev or Bush? Bush or Hussein? What was the prize? What was the verdict? There are historical and geographical, cultural and structural factors behind any drama; the drama is only the famous tip of the iceberg. It is like lava relative to the volcano, or the earthquake relative to the tectonic plates. Perhaps the "mystery" should be written more in the style of a Graham Greene novel.

One possible alternate method to reporting on peace issues would be to be more analytic in news writing. Take the following case from a *Washington Post* editorial that looked at rising ethnic and regional friction, an increasing concern in portions of Europe and the Middle East. With enormous costs, "the Cold War enforced peace and maintained stable boundaries . . . [they] have not yet begun to devise a new instrument capable of doing law and adjudication what the Cold War did by brute force." The question is: how does the world stop such civil wars before they start? Looking to Yugoslavia, we see mounting ethnic tensions between the province of Croatia, and its larger neighbor, the Serbian province. Ethnic Serbs make up a major portion of the Croatian population, and Serbian nationalism is resurrecting many old grievances. How will it end? Should anyone intervene?[21] The West has shown great reluctance to do so.

Another illustration of a surrogate approach is suggested by an op ed column written by John C. Danforth, the U.S. senator from Missouri, that appeared in *The Washington Post* some 3 months before the start of the Persian Gulf War. Danforth also is an ordained Episcopal priest. He takes the opportunity to question the role of religion as a sanction in world conflicts:

> In Northern Ireland, Catholic and Protestant Christians bomb each other as they have for decades. Hindu India and Moslem Pakistan face off against each other, offering the prospect of nuclear weapons if necessary to prove their points. And within India, the Hindus fight the Sikhs. In East Timor, Moslems slaughter Catholics. In Sudan, Christians, Moslems and animists kill each other.

> All of this killing is done with the absolute certainty that God wants it so. If thine enemy offends thee, rub him out. Indeed, it is believed that to lose one's life in God's cause is to die a martyr's death and win a reward in heaven . . .

Where are the voices of interfaith reconciliation in all this turmoil? For Christians, the concept of the Prince of Peace is largely a Christmas card slogan. The loudest voices are those of religious crackpots, while church councils debate who should be ordained and what should be deleted from hymnals and what resolutions should be dispatched to members of Congress.

It is well and good that religious bodies express their views on a variety of political subjects. But it is not well and good that the various faiths remain mute in the face of religiously inspired calamity. As a matter of urgent world necessity, religious leaders must speak loudly and clearly on what their faith demands and what it condemns. One would hope that the most insistent demands from all faiths would be for humanity and reconciliation and love. One would hope that the strongest condemnations from all faiths would be for intolerance and hatred and holy wars.[22]

Too often the people of the world engage in "holy wars." They kill in the name of God. The press can demonstrate the insanity of building wars and international conflicts on such a premise. Calling attention to this dilemma is one way in which journalists can promote peace.

Fifth, the media should pay attention to enhancing the retention elements of news reporting, and not talk down to its audience and readers. In this sense, journalists could be more interested in maximizing audience "learning" of news. Not only could stories be reported in greater detail, but journalists could give some thought to how increased viewer/reader comprehension and recall could be accomplished. Social scientists have demonstrated the limitations in recall associated with current news reporting practices. Much of this empirical news research is anchored in information processing theories from cognitive psychology. It is believed that certain news story structures can be more effective in inducing learning. Learning is thought to be passive, for example, and may be influenced by factors such as social context, viewer/reader prior experience, and current interest level.[23] In his analysis of news research, Woodall concludes that news learning can be less affected by a variety of circumstances. Among these are clashing visual and verbal content; inadequate repetition of main story points; incomplete details on context and causation; poor labeling and summaries; brevity; confusing arrangement of similar stories; inadequate or distracting visual content; and content that is too abstract.[24] Greater attention should therefore be given to the news production process. News might prove more comprehensible if attention were given to more informative and more carefully written copy, with less staccato and out-of-control tidbits.

There is often depth to the understanding so-called common people have of what goes on in the world. Many, if not most, people like more interpretation and deeper understanding, and are not at all afraid of conflicting types of information. To the contrary, they are used to that from everyday conflicts in family, school, and work situations. People are not merely passive depositories for an endless stream of news. They process the facts themselves; they have their own frames of reference, more or less explicit, and would like to have their frames of reference not only deepened, but also challenged. If words are not understood, it may be because they are meaningless for lack of context; just words fired at them, unrelated to each other. If people do not believe in the media anyhow and think someone is trying to cheat them, why bother to search for the meaning of something meaningless inside the even more meaningless?

The problem may actually be the journalists. If they are so caught up in the flow of news, acting as gatekeepers, they themselves may not have full comprehension of the stories they are reporting. A Norwegian journalist, former Rector of the Norwegian Academy of Journalism, has coined the expression "The Tyranny of the Sources (Kildenes tyranni)." The "source"—a government or corporate official, for instance—feeds information to the journalist, promising more if the journalist "behaves." The bargain can be struck at a high or low level, but remains a bargain. If the journalist breaks one of the "rules," the source no longer exists.

As noted in Chapter 3, journalists have often been faulted for writing stories about people they have flown in and met only hours earlier. Sometimes correspondents do not even speak the language of the land as they are covering remote areas of the globe, based at a desk in one of the major news capitals. Free lance news "stringers" are also often employed to write international stories; here the danger is that an individual will write what the media organization wants so that s/he will collect payment and get future assignments. Stringers obviously cannot have the same clout in developing institutional newswriting policies as a seasoned staff reporter would enjoy. The latter may, however, easily become a victim of excessive cynicism.

Somehow we have not been good at creating media as popular as second-rate newspapers, yet with the intellectual depth of first-rate newspapers. If the media are popular they tend to be shallow, and if they have depth they tend to be boring (one among many exceptions is *Der Spiegel*, but it is a magazine, not a newspaper). There may be obvious reasons for this having something to do with the way people are trained in university journalism/ broadcast journalism/ communication programs, equating depth with boredom and whatever is popular with shallowness. Efforts to remedy the situation may easily lead to media that combine the worst of both scenarios, the boring with the shallow.

This seems to be the trademark of the media in most repressive countries; the antidote is the political joke, subtle and enormously popular. People know how to defend themselves.

Sixth, when deep international conflicts are not solved there is a tendency to seek recourse to armament. Armament in one party tends to induce armament in the other, and the result is an arms race legitimized by both parties as a struggle to obtain balance of power. At this point, it should be the duty of media to make some major distinctions.

The first distinction is *between defensive and offensive arms,* not according to the party's intentions—there are usually pious declarations of defensive, non-aggressive intent accompanying most armament—but according to what the arms are capable of doing. And that is basically a question of the range of the weapons system, including the means of transportation. If the Swiss build one more tunnel or gallery in their Alps, and put some heavy guns inside, they may add to their own military expenditure per capita and possibly add to their own security, but they will not reduce anyone else's security. Alps do not move; the guns may be effective in case of an attack, but they do not provoke anybody. In short, there are arms and arms—as is the case for most other things in the world. It is the duty of the media not to mask such key distinctions by only reporting quantities of soldiers, arms, and money spent.[25]

The second distinction is *between deterrence by retaliation and deterrence by defense.* Arms are often said to deter an attack and probably do in some cases, but not in others. But deterrence by means of retaliation can only be done with long-range offensive arms capable of considerable destructive impact. The trouble with such arms is that they can also be used for attack. How does the other side know that these arms are only for retaliation, not for any first strike?

One television program which offered an excellent examination of the nuclear arms race is the 13 part U.S. public television documentary series, *War and Peace in the Nuclear Age.* It aired initially in the United States in early 1989. Weaving interviews with historical film footage, viewers were provided with a stunning look at events surrounding the development and uses of nuclear weapons. In one episode on the Cuban missile crisis, there are interviews with participants, including an aide to Nikita Khrushchev, and the former Soviet ambassador to Cuba. Thanks to secretly recorded audiotapes, we hear excerpts of John F. Kennedy conferring with key advisors. There is the hawkish Secretary of Defense, Robert Kennedy, and the more moderate Secretary of State, Robert McNamara. McNamara argues that nuclear weapons should not be thought of as weapons per se; rather they become political tools, and through their very being they help impede deployment and avert war. Also revealing in the series is a 1946 U.N. conference on disarmament. The United States attempts to maneuver regulations which would deter the Soviets from developing their own nuclear weapons. The proposal was killed by votes from the Polish and Soviet delegates. As Talbott of *Time* magazine observed, the "tone of the superpower rivalry [was thus] set for nearly 40 years to come."[26] In another episode, "On the Brink," the Eisenhower years are the topic. The program paints Eisenhower as a realist who warned of "our military-industrial complex" that needed a enemy of some kind. Producers Zvi-Dor Ner and Liz Deane intimate that the missile build-up of the 1960s might have been avoided if Eisenhower's early warnings had not been ignored. An attempt of the program is to demonstrate how U.S. and Soviet leaders had been trapped for many years. They both dreaded war but they also worried about being on the losing side of a war.[27] This series is admirable in its effort to pose some tough questions. Unfortunately, there are many other questions that journalists must still address; this program tends to be an exception rather than the rule.

The whole crux of the matter lies in the inability to find a clear answer to the rather important questions outlined above; a basic key to the dynamism of arms races as well as espionage races. One simply has to find out what the intention is, and particularly what the capabilities are. Quite the opposite is the case when dealing with arms intended to deter by putting up an effective defense. That is a question of the *military doctrine* of the country concerned—a matter that belongs to the intellectual frame-of-reference, the discourse, the paradigm within which understanding is communicated of what goes on in this important field. In general, such matters are totally neglected by the media. Once again we make the same point, trivial to the researcher: data about conflict, conflict attitudes, and conflict behavior are meaningless unless cultural and structural contexts are taken into account. The worst mistake is to limit all the reporting to attitudes and behavior.

Seventh, when it comes to the arms races that usually accompany any effort to acquire offensive arms, and armed conflicts in general, *the media should pay more attention to the inner dynamism of the arms races and armed conflicts*. It is not only a question of what the military-industrial complex gets in terms of contracts and profits, be they private or state corporations, whether West or East, or North or South. It is also a question of workers and trade unions securing their employment; of ministries getting control over a larger share of the public expenses; of researchers, and other intellectuals engaged in the research and development of armament hardware and software, getting more power and privilege. In short, there is a complex web of factors involved, well worth reporting for investigative journalism. But at no point should one be led to believe that such internal factors, necessary as they are in understanding what goes on, are sufficient to come to grips with the arms races. The arms race is a complex product of both internal and external dynamics, and both aspects should certainly be areas of focus.

Eighth, when it comes to disarmament in general, *disarmament negotiations and conferences* in particular, *and summit meetings* even more particularly, *media should pay much more attention to their own weaknesses when reporting such phenomena.* In a sense these are ideal media events: elite nations and elite people—and lurking behind all the big negative possibility, the breakdown of the conference, even wars for that matter. The drama metaphor is only too perfectly realized: top actors, a stage (usually in a beautiful setting with lots of intricate embroidery such as Geneva), lots of backstage gossip, select performances for highly select audiences. Media have a tendency to over-report the opening or closing of such conferences and summit meetings, to attribute undue significance to them, and to under-report all the small facts on the sidelines, not to mention the deeper problems and the hard work that goes into solving them or not solving them. The Costa Rican summit situation depicted earlier in our third proposal serves as an wonderful example of some of these media weaknesses which can interfere with the reporting of peace initiatives.[28] There are, of course, numerous other ways in which disarmament talks are misreported.

Among those "small facts" of disarmament conferences is whether the emphasis is on highly offensive weaponry or on weaponry in general. In the latter case the conference might be less interesting. The participants will not try to come to grips with the real problems, but conceal them inside a too vast and unmanageable agenda. Also, is there then any discussion of military doctrine, or only of the surface manifestations of such doctrines, the concrete hardware? Does the conference only focus on deployment of weapons, or does it also include maneuvers, production and stocking, testing, and research and development? Does it try to touch the military-bureaucratic-corporate-intelligentsia complex at all, or are they left untouched, and treated as sacred? What are the chances of non-superpowers not only being consulted afterwards and/or beforehand but observing, even participating? What are the chances for non-aligned countries to participate actively, including acting as presidents or conveners of the conference? What are the chances of non-governmental forces being heard, or even taken seriously?

While it is no way guarantee that things will be better if the answers to such questions are yes, the questions should at least be put by media trying to probe more deeply into matters. In no sense should this imply an uncritical attitude to the peace movement. Like governments, the peace movements also have their dogmas and their unchanging, single-minded beliefs no matter what comes their way. They may also be the carriers of deep-seated emotions, general peace approaches (such as people's diplomacy), or even highly practical ideas such as *transarmament* (from offensive towards defensive weapons) rather than *disarmament* (doing away with all weapons)—the former a more realistic position, the latter highly idealistic and moreover unnecessary. Above all genuine peace movements are people's movements, not governmental constructions. Of course, under dictatorships everything will be done to crush, ridicule, or suppress information about popular movements against governmental policies. In democracies there should be respect for people's movements. After all, is that not the essence of democracy? Should the media not reflect this?

Ninth, in this connection *one should certainly also look at the North-South conflict formations relating peace and war to development and not only to the problems of peace and war among industrialized countries.* As we know, they are interrelated, particularly with hunger and other forms of misery being used in the name of war in the political south. From this it does not necessarily follow that one can kill two birds with one stone; disarm, release resources, and put such resources into a gigantic development effort through a "massive transfer" is often argued by the Third World press as well as some people in the West.

First, it may very well be that with less capital available, the military sector will only become more research-intensive and at least equally dangerous, only less expensive and wasteful. The highly inflated military budgets of very conservative governments is also their way of exercising state control over the economy in an almost Keynesian manner, even when this is strictly speaking against their ideology. In short, these budgets may be trimmed considerably without endangering the offensive capability; and huge budgets do not necessarily spell danger (although they usually may). The savings might also serve other functions, such as economic growth and even economic distributions.

Second, more money for development will not necessarily produce satisfaction of basic human needs. More money means more available to buy expensive goods, and these are generally for the non-essential needs of the elite rather than for the basic needs of the non-elite. Some structural change within and between countries is what is needed, at least initially. While reporting what military budgets cost in lost opportunities (one fighter-bomber is the equivalent of so and so many clinics in the countryside in a poor country), one should not lead readers to believe that the question is simply one of money transfer. Seeds thrown on asphalt do produce a harvest.

A *Washington Post* article by James D. Robinson III provides an interesting twist on the arms disarmament issue. He suggests that "commercial disarmament" is just as pressing a world issue as disarmament

of the military. He points to a Uruguay meeting of the General
Agreement of Tariffs and Trade (GATT) midterm review negotiations.
The implications are many for developing nations. As he observes:

> . . . [T]here is growing consensus that if we can defuse the trade
> weapons that encourage trade conflict, this in itself will create a bet-
> ter environment for peace and prosperity based on economic growth
> in the developed and developing nations. After all, protectionist
> policies such as export subsidies carry price tags just as tanks and
> fighter planes do. These and other trade-distorting programs, while
> nonviolent, can have a crippling effect on the economic vitality of
> many nations and create adversarial relationships even with allies.
> Witness the "hormone beef" dispute that has just flared between the
> United States and the European Community.[29]

He points to the need for an agriculture compromise between the United
States and the European Community. "As members, with several developed countries, of the so-called 'Cairns Group' of agricultural producers,
the developing countries may well end up in the unprecedented role of
acting as mediators between the United States and the European
Community."[30] The possibilities are certainly intriguing.

Tenth, it should be the task of the media to *portray more clearly the
benefits of peace*. Peace is not merely the absence of war, or absence of the
threat of war. The latter should certainly be included; we do not have
peace even when there is no belligerent action in the world as long as
the terrible threat of nuclear, or other types of annihilation, hang over us
all. Peace is the opportunity for everyone to unfold themselves more
than ever before, unhampered by massive destruction and the fear of it.
"Everyone" means exactly that: common men and women, everywhere.
"Unfolding" means all the nice things that people can do alone and with
each other in love, friendship, and work; together, in solidarity with others, and with nature.

Since the media have a tendency to under-report such "small"
but indeed important things, the image of peace tends to become bland
and hence less compelling. From the way media portray the world, people might be led to believe that peace is a rather dull state of affairs.
Some might think of peace as a kind of nonentity really suited for good,
but rather weak and passive individuals—perhaps very old people or
mainly women—similar to paradise in the christian metaphor. It may
seem to be an interlude between wars, or a phase in historic time
marked "Waiting Room." War looks more real and exciting; evil, yes,
but intended for the strong and the active—mainly men. The period
prior to a war is certainly more newsworthy than a dull period of non-

events with nothing on the horizon. In this way the media may become a negative factor, contributing to worldwide insecurity rather than the opposite, slanting public opinion, training people to see violence as normal, even teaching them the techniques. How difficult it is to portray something positive, when all interest is focused on bad news.

CONCLUSION

Of course, noone would assume that the media are the major causes of war and peace. The deeper causes are located elsewhere, in our structures and culture; in people, in us. But the media, as that very word indicates, mediate between deep structures and cultures, between the reality of events and the images of news. They become interspersed between the deeper aspects of reality and people as actors, be they elite or non-elite. The media shape their images, and as people act on the basis of media-mediated images rather than reality, the way the media mediate becomes a major factor. This seems to become increasingly true the closer they come to real time, as with the U.S. Cable News Network's (CNN's) continuous flow of news during the Persian Gulf Crisis, making that war the most Real of Realities.

Consequently, the media have the power to shape images, and however skeptical people may be of media, they are generally more influenced by them than they themselves would care to admit. This becomes particularly evident when encountering people, for instance Americans and Soviets, who proclaim their independence from newspapers, TV channels, and radio stations, yet are unable to understand how the all-over national character of reporting has nevertheless left an indelible imprint on them. Hence, our final point: more pressure must be placed on the media so that they can better live up to our demands and expectations—such as the ten fairly concrete proposals for peace-oriented news outlined here.[31]

NOTES TO CHAPTER 4

1. North American Service broadcast talk, written by Soviet author, Ilya Ehrenberg, January 3, 1951; from the collection of broadcasts monitored by Professor William Howell, Department of Speech-Communication, University of Minnesota, cited in Donald R. Browne,

International Radio Broadcasting (New York: Praeger, 1982), pp. 227-228.

2. For an exploration of the general relation between data, theories, and values, see Johan Galtung, "Empiricism, Criticism, Constructivism: Three Aspects of Scientific Activity," in *Methodology and Ideology* (Ejlers, Copenhagen, 1977)

3. See Kiyoaki Murata, "Problems in International Communication," address to the International House of Japan, Tokyo, October 28, 1981; abstracted in the *House Bulletin.*

4. At the end of the speech Kennedy says: "All free men, wherever they may live are citizens of Berlin, and, therefore, as a free man, I take pride in the words: *"Ich bin ein Berliner."* [See *Public Papers of the Presidents of the United States: John F. Kennedy, 1963* (Washington, D.C.: U.S. Government Printing Office, 1964), pp. 524.]. In 1964, after the assassination, his brother, Senator Robert F. Kennedy, played on the prevailing interpretation: "I know what he meant when he said, *"Ich bin ein Berliner."* [From Alex J. Goldman, *John Fitzgerald Kennedy: The World Remembers* (New York: Fleet Press, 1968), p. 97.].

5. For the latter story, see Steven R. Weisman, "At Atomic Shrine, All the Horror, Nothing of Guilt," *New York Times*, April 19, 1990, p. A4.

6. For example, the U.S. media ran relatively few stories that attempted to explore the Iraqi motives for its invasion of Kuwait on August 2, 1990. Little effort was made to help readers/viewers understand the cultural nuances of the Iraqis, and the effect they had on subsequent negotiations. Americans might have gotten a more balanced view of events if this had been done. And when Saddam Hussein gave his lengthy television presentation on the devaluation of the Iranian dinar, the war debt, the oil fields, and other topics, it was referred to as public relations.

7. Eric Sevareid, "News Coverage 'Is a Force for Peace'," *U.S. News & World Report*, December 2, 1985, p. 33.

8. "Television Diplomacy," *Mac Leans*, October 31, 1988, p. 29.

9. See "Washington Diarist: Black and White in Color," *The New Republic*, April 15, 1985, p. 42, for a negative reaction.

10. Ted Koppel, "TV Diplomacy in South Africa," *Newsweek*, April 8, 1985, p. 14.

11. Harry F. Waters, "ABC's Mideast Peace Talks," *Newsweek*, May 9, 1988, p. 68.

12. Ibid., p. 68.

13. Alexander Cockburn, "Beat the Devil," *The Nation*, January 30, 1988, p. 116.

14. Ibid., p. 116.

15. Ibid., p. 116.

16. Ibid., p. 116.

17. Ibid., p. 117.

18. Quoted in Cockburn, "Beat the Devil," p. 117.

19. Cockburn, "Beat the Devil," p. 117.

20. Tapio Varis reports in one of his many studies ("Global Traffic in Television—Cultural Exchange, or Invasion?", *Journal of Communication*, 24 (1) (1974), pp. 102-109) that only the United States, the Soviet Union, France, England, China, and Japan had 12% or less of imported television programming, by hours, in 1970-71. Not quite incidentally, five of them are the official nuclear powers. Rolf Scheller, in *News Flow in Asia: A Study of 10 Asian Countries* (Singapore: Asian Mass Communication Research and Information Centre, 1983), reported (December 1982) that "more than 80% (of very qualified respondents, my comment) hold negative views of Western coverage of Asian countries, complaining about the prejudicial, distorted and culturally biased presentation, the inadequacy in quantitative terms as well as in qualitative terms such as stressing only sensational contents." Herbert G. Kariel and Lynn A. Rosenvall, "United States News Flows to Canadian Papers," *American Review of Canadian Studies* 1983 13 (1) (1983), report that U.S. news may account for from one- to two-thirds of foreign news, and point out that 70% of Canadian imports came from the U.S. (1973), and that 67.4% went there (as opposed to 4.3 and 6.3% for the U.K.). *Der Spiegel*, No.45/1978, reports that AFP and Reuter had a bias of 88:12 and 87:12 in favor of the First World in their UNCTAD IV reporting.

21. "Who Keeps Peace in Europe?" *The Washington Post*, September 26, 1990, p. A24.

22. John C. Danforth, "Killing in the Name of God," *The Washington Post*, October 16, 1990, p. A25.

23. Richard C. Vincent and Dennis K. Davis, "Trends in World News Research and the Implications for Comparative Studies," Paper presented at the 39th annual conference of the International Communication Association San Francisco, May 26, 1989. See also Dennis K. Davis and John P. Robinson, "News Flow and Democratic Society in the Age of Electronic Media" in *Public Communication and Behavior*, ed., George Comstock (New York, Academic Press, 1989); and Doris Graber, *Processing the News* (New York, Longman, 1984).

24. Gill Woodall, "Information Processing," in *The Main Source: Learning from Television News*, ed., John P. Robinson and Mark Levy (Beverly Hills, CA: Sage, 1986).

25. For an elaboration of this see Johan Galtung, *There Are Alternatives!* (Nottingham, England: Spokesman, 1984), particularly section 5.2.

26. Strobe Talbott, "The History of the Bomb," *Time*, January 30, 1989, p. 59.

27. "War & Peace for Viewers & Scholars," *Commonweal*, January 27, 1989, p. 48.

28. Alexander Cockburn, "Beat the Devil," *The Nation*, January 30, 1988, pp. 116-117.

29. James D. Robinson III, "Progress Toward Commercial Disarmament," *The Washington Post*, January 5, 1989, p. A25.

30. Ibid.

31. For an examination of peace and media from a legal perspective, see *The Guild Practitioner*, 36 (Winter 1989), with articles by Peter Franck, Kaarle Nordenstreng and Herbert Schiller, Howard H. Frederick, Ann Fagan Ginger, and Wolfgang Kleineachter; for a look at the Canadian media experience during the Cold War, see Robert A. Hackett, "Hot News, Cold War," *Canadian Journal of Communication* 14 (1), pp. 76-81.

CHAPTER 5

The Media, World-Wide Well-Being and Development

. . . [T]he coverage of development news both on the wires and in the newspapers raises questions about how well newsmen are prepared to cover the stories of development. They are trained to cover politics and to report striking events and feature material. Are they prepared with the economic and social understanding needed to interpret development news in meaningful terms?—Wilbur Schramm [1]

The world today is much more complex. Before the days of mass media, radio and television, the poor were more resigned to their fate. Without television, they didn't have any possibility for comparison. That's why today's poverty is more dangerous and could provoke terrible social upheavals. . .
— Carlos Andres Perez, President of Venezuela [2]

BUT WELL BEING IS SO POSITIVE

Yes, well being is positive, so how can it ever make news? But, then, the opposite of well-being, misery, is very frequent, and very far from positive, and does not make news either. It spells death, but not in any dramatic way that would justify headlines; it is only the "silent holocaust" (the title of a book by political scientist George Kent of the University of Hawaii). Over 14 million children annually are dying from hunger; 40,000 per day. Yet they are not big news; just malnutrition, some infection, diarrhea in a little body unable to retain water, dehydration, a general weakening of the body, and then the final kick from one germ or another. Certainly not the kind of thing to make the headlines, like well-being does.

Well-being simply means to feel well—physically, psychologically, and socially—which should be the normal state of affairs for humankind. Measured by the criteria of newsworthiness, nothing of this

145

is newsworthy. Misery is mainly found in non-elite countries among non-elite people. It is not even an event, if anything it can be referred to as a "permanent," a perpetual state of affairs, as argued so often above. It is certainly negative, but that is also its only newsworthy aspect. Even though it happens to people, it does not fulfill the S, P, O condition of having a subject, a predicate, and an object. Dehydration of a little human body is not something someone does to someone else, or at least it is not seen that way. There is certainly an object, but neither a subject nor a transitive verb. To make headlines under such adverse media conditions, mega-deaths are needed.

Well-being in an elite country is neither negative nor personalized even if it involves elite persons in elite countries. In order to make headlines it has to concern exceptional people, of royal or film star status, of billionaire dimensions, or of maharajah magnitude. Even so this would not hit the headlines too often.

Hence, the question is how this can be made newsworthy at all. In general, there is probably only one way it can be done: to see development, democracy, and participation as a drama. There is enough suffering in the world, and more than enough threat of suffering, to satisfy the condition that the "event" must be negative. And there is a way in which the S, P, O condition can almost be satisfied: by portraying development as a relation between subjects and objects, even if the subjects and the objects remain somewhat depersonalized and "structural."

The approach recommended here is clearly what development theory, organized around the dimension of exploitation, is all about. It is not only that "I am poor and you are rich;" but "I am poor because you are rich;" "You are rich because I am poor." The moment those words are spoken, the drama of development becomes a game played by parties with highly unequal assets. It becomes a game of chess in which one side has all the officers, and the other all the pawns; and with the board tilted so that the officers advance automatically and the pawns have to work against the forces of gravity in order not to slide down with the same automaticity.[3]

The development drama takes place both in the Center and in the Periphery, spanning the gaps between rich and poor countries and rich and poor people. They are all involved, creating a web of relationships. The task of the journalist is to unravel the threads, pick them out of that intricate web, hold them up in the sunlight, and demonstrate the connections to readers, listeners, and viewers.

In a sense, this is what Inter-Press Service (IPS) headquartered in Rome is doing or tries to do. A number of IPS clippings from one Norwegian newspaper (*Klassekampen*) will make the structure of the world as reported through IPS very clear. They are used here as a basis for discussion (translations have been made from Norwegian).

Item 1: *Radioactive tea* (from Ankara and Oslo)

> As a direct consequence of the accident in Chernobyl the tea harvest from 1986 has been polluted with radioactivity. This applies also to one of the most frequently sold brands from England, available both in Norway and in Turkey. The Turkish Atomic Energy Bureau has investigated the radioactivity in the brands on the Turkish market and it varied from 1,000 to 20,000 becquerel per kilo. The head of the bureau is of the opinion that all tea containing more than 3,000 becquerel should be withdrawn from the market for health reasons.

Comment: The story relates the Soviet Union as the subject to Norway and Turkey as the objects, via the radioactive tea linkage. No concrete persons are mentioned. Apart from the dramatic composition, the story is clear. There is a sub-script underlying the major script which mentions various spokesmen from Ministries of Health and other Bureaus who draw the limit or line between safety and danger zones where tea is concerned. The reader is left wondering whether the health authorities are on the side of the consumers or producers.

Item 2: *Foreign capital to Tanzania* (from Dar-es-Salaam)

> Tanzania has now opened the door for foreign capital. The country has for several years been closed practically speaking to private foreign investors. A number of delegations of private investors are now invited to the country. The first twelve businessmen have arrived from Hong Kong and Thailand. They will meet with leading government members for an orientation about investment possibilities in industry, tourism and the hotel industry. Tanzania nationalized most of these industries in 1967 when the country declared that it will pursue a socialist path to development. As a consequence a number of foreign firms withdrew. Last year the Tanzanian government negotiated an adjustment agreement with the International Monetary Fund. The assumption is that the country is going to liberalize the economic policy.

Comment: Again, the drama between rich and poor is apparent. On the one hand is something anonymous, but obviously very strong and rich: the International Monetary Fund, and rich countries in general. Concretely, front-stage are 12 businessmen from Hong Kong and (even) Thailand—the Fourth World at work. The presence of stronger forces backstage is felt in the article. And the object to which these forces are now being applied is Tanzania, changing its economic policy dramatically from socialism to capitalism. In doing this, Tanzania appears partly as a subject, opening the door for foreign capital; partly as an object that has to sign adjustment agreements in order for investment to take place. The reader is left wondering what the impact on Tanzania will be?

Item 3: *FAO focuses on women* (from Rome)

> Agriculture is typically a female profession in most developing countries. Women are sewing, cultivating, harvesting and processing the products. What men do is limited to plowing and threshing. This is going to be one of the major themes of the 24th FAO conference taking place right now in Rome. Stronger than ever the focus is on the role of women in the development of the Third World, and particularly on the role of women in the production of food. Two resolutions point clearly to the integration of the significance of women in development planning. It is also pointed out that the number of women has to be increased at all levels in the FAO. A number of delegates have pointed to the gap existing between the legal rights of women in many developing countries and the practical demands placed on them. Women are now demanding the right to have property, income, resources and credit. But in spite of the unanimous support for the idea of strengthening the role of women in agriculture, only few countries were inclined to economically support this part of FAO's program.

Comment: Still another drama is enacted, again not explicitly, but clearly having to do with the relationship between men and women. A new subject is being born/an old subject is made more visible: women in economic development. Reading the item conjures up in the inner eye of the reader a big conference room with lots of male delegates, who are enthusiastic that women do much to produce food, but who are disinclined to support women the moment they demand equal rights. The stage is provided by FAO, the major actors are the genders, FAO is profoundly gender biased. The reader is left wondering what s/he should think about the impact on women?

Item 4: *Coalition of leftist parties in Mexico* (from Mexico City)

> Six Mexican parties have joined forces to form the Mexican Socialist Party (PMS). The new party is aiming to become the second largest political party in the country and to have their own presidential candidate for the elections next year. The fusion process started late last year when five of the six parties were negotiating a common politi-

cal platform. Only two of the five are registered for participation in
the elections. The biggest party in Mexico, the Institutionalized
Revolutionary Party (PRI) has had power since 1929. The
Conservative National Action Party (PAN) is the second biggest
party and got 18.4% of the vote at the election in 1982 when PRI got
67.4%.

Comment: Here the drama is located inside Mexico, between the big
party that has monopolized the political scene and the small parties trying to challenge the big (or at least the second biggest). Clearly the item
is less about economic development and more about political development, democracy, and participation. The challenge to monopolistic control, offering a larger spectrum of political options at the elections, constitutes the major theme around which this particular drama is acted
out. What makes the story dramatic is the David vs. Goliath theme and
the possibility that the two may one day change roles after the new actor
has successfully entered the arena.

Item 5: *Food or coffee in Honduras* (from Tegucigalpa)

"If I grow coffee then I can make enough money for food and have
something extra for other items, other things. But if I should cultivate corn on this particular land then I would hardly be able to sur-
vive." Elaya Santos, a 48 year old farmer with about 1 acre of land
says this. As like many of the other extremely poor *campesinos* in
Honduras, her food consists of beans and corn. Nevertheless she
does not want to make use of credit from the government through
the integrated development program PRODERO to cultivate and
grow her own food. The corn-coffee dilemma is frequent for the
many small farmers in the provinces in the most mountainous
regions of the country. Only 3% of that region is in the fertile valley
belonging to rich land owners and this has forced the small farmers
to cultivate the soil ever higher up in the 45° steep mountain sides.

Comment: Not only do we learn of poverty and the struggle for food,
but we also get an insight into the strategic options of small farmers. On
the one hand, farmers obviously need food which they can grow, but in
that case there is no surplus for other things. Food plus that surplus are
made available by growing coffee. But, and that is the underlying story,
who is then going to grow the food? Could it be that the dilemma
becomes not only a drama this particular 48-year-old small farmer, but
for the country, or for that matter, the world as a whole: a choice
between beans and coffee beans? The latter fetch more money partly
because foreign markets are involved, but do not contribute to nutrition
and basic needs; on the other hand, what satisfies basic needs does not

fetch much money. In this case, the subject is not emerging as a direct actor, but is portrayed as an actor with one of the actor's trademarks— the dilemma, a choice to be made.

Item 6: *Referendum on U.S. bases in the Philippines* (from Manila)

> Next month negotiations will start on the future of the 16 military installations the Americans have in the Philippines. A special Commission from the Senate in Manila has for some time prepared the negotiations. A local population has had occasion to inform the president, Corazon Aquino, that critics of the American bases characterize them with such expressions as "colonialism" and "threats to national sovereignty." They are also seen as evident targets for a nuclear attack in case of a war, and questions are raised about the socio-economic effects for society and the possibility of the spread of AIDS.

Comment: This time the drama is in military terms, as a topic under the heading of political development. As usual, the key subject is removed from the script, but is there in the background: "the Americans," "Washington, D.C." The people to whom this is done are seen as small people, exploited under colonialism, having their sovereignty taken away from them, and possibly becoming the victims of nuclear attacks in addition to AIDS. A rather important part of contemporary reality is then explored further by discussing whether a referendum will change this, pointing out that there are also immediate economic advantages flowing from the bases. The weak actor struggling to stand up against the strong, and the strong actor throwing its tremendous resources into the conflict to influence the outcome: that is drama.

The above will suffice as examples of the basic point: development, democracy, and participation are dramas. The problem, however, is that when this drama is written out the underlying text tends to be about the same in all cases: imperialism, exploitation, and other "leftist" themes. It should be noted that the drama character, the S, P, O structure, is not brought about by focusing on evil, strong actors. They are in the background, depersonalized as structures. Rather, the focus is on the object turning into the subject, the weak and/or emerging actor, standing up against the structure, projecting not only drama but also hope.

A surface presentation of the drama, as so often presented by mainstream media to small or big actors in the world, without even a mention or hint at the deeper connections, immediately makes it sound less leftist. Thus, the responsibility of the Soviet Union (government) for what happens to tea drinkers in other countries is not made clear when only radioactivity is mentioned, not where it comes from; the IMF does not have to be mentioned in the item from Tanzania; the difficulty women encounter in achieving equal rights may not be mentioned, only their contribution to agriculture; the monopoly position of the biggest party in Mexico since 1929 may remain obscure, highlighting only small parties trying to make a coalition. De-emphasizing the inner connections makes it all less left wing, and more palatable from a mainstream point of view, but also less dramatic, and certainly less honest. In other words, we find ourselves with an agonizing dilemma. How do we solve it? The media do not have to answer such questions. Still, to pose them is already a good half of the way toward problem solving.

TEN PROPOSALS FOR A DEVELOPMENT-ORIENTED NEWS MEDIA

First, whenever there is a reference to development try to make it concrete, in terms of concrete human beings. One approach here is definitely in terms of *basic human needs* however they are conceived, and more particularly basic human needs for *the most needy.* Human needs can be seen in terms of the need for *survival, well-being, identity* and *freedom;* others might have other schemes. In the economistic approach to development that still dominates the development discourse, the category "well-being" would receive the most attention, focusing on such items as food, clothing, shelter, access to medical services, access to schooling, transportation/communication, and energy conversion.

1. Relate development to "people".
2. Focus on more than economics.
3. Dispersion data is needed.
4. Cover differences and relations.
5. Focus on concrete life situations.
6. Never forget democracy dimension.
7. Report constructively.
8. Allow the "people" to talk.
9. Give "people" some media control.
10. Let "people" run/report on society.

Figure 1. Ten proposals for a development-oriented news media.

These will always remain important, and the general focus should be on those most in need. This, in turn, can be discussed in terms of the five big dividers of humankind—age, gender, race, class, and nation.

So, instead of just saying "the population of country X is poor," one should say "the small farmers in country X are poor because of the tightening of the credit conditions," and then, if possible, be specific. One reason for this might be that most of the small farmers are women who in country X are not considered "credit-worthy." The next step in the article or news item would be to transform human beings from objects/victims with "needs deficits" to human beings as subjects, actors, and agents. The focus, for instance, could be on concrete women farmers and their particular plight including their testimony. There is also the possibility of bringing in other people involved, such as bankers. Good journalists would interview both, even if they do not relate personally. In short, focus on basic needs, the most needy, the categories most hit, the exact problem, and the transformation from structure to action. General statements will not contribute sufficient specificity to lead to development-oriented action. What is needed is the ability to report from many angles and niches in the structure, and to report about concrete people. This is the univeral human drama of conflicting interests. The good journalist gives us the script.

Having said this, the second big pillar of sustainable development should also be mentioned: *ecological balance*. There is something absolute about human needs and ecological balance: if it deteriorates, what sense does it make to talk about development at all? The rest, all the constructions we make in social space and world space, capitalism/socialism, free-trade areas, self-reliance, or active peaceful coexistence ultimately exist to serve human beings, to satisfy basic human needs. If they do not take into account the limits of nature/space, defined by ecological balance, then we are lost in both the short and long run. The task of a development-oriented news media is to define problems and solutions as clearly as possible, including pursuing the development drama into the deeper aspects of nature, as ecological drama. It is only bad that we are so poor at portraying nature as an actor. The Gaia metaphor may help us here.

Some examples of the press exploring basic human issues related to Third World existence can be seen in Africa. Our first is the acclaimed television magazine program, *South Africa Now*. This privately funded half-hour program began began with a budget of only $10,000 per week. In less than 1 year, it aired on some 45 U.S. broadcast and cable stations. Rockefeller Foundation and Carnegie Corporation grants enabled the show to secure a satellite slot thereby increasing its availability to the nation's 334 PBS stations. The weekly show offered original and imaginative spot news, background narratives, and cultural spotlights. Material was gathered from freelance journalists, independent video agencies, and documentary film and video makers. "Journalists who work for us are willing to take incredible risks to get their stories out because they know we are willing to put them on the air," noted senior producer and co-anchor Carolyn Craven. The show frequently addressed anti-apartheid themes. It portrayed the detention and apparent torture of black children, explored reasons for black-on-black violence, surveyed activities of the ring-wing terrorist "White Wolves" group, and ran footage of the Angolan war. Whereas television had defined "the South Africa story in terms of violent conflict," said one reviewer, "*South Africa Now* tries to offer a broader perspective."[4]

Next, we turn to a controversial nine-week documentary series, *The Africans*, written and produced by Kenyan academic and University of Michigan professor, Ali Mazrui. The program aired on British television and PBS in the United States, and was heavily funded by the National Endowment for the Humanities. While some (particularly Lynn V. Cheney, chairperson of the NEH) believed the program was marred by a certain one-sidedness, and an anti-Western perspective, *London Standard* columnist Wheatcroft pointed out that it is difficult to write about the slave trade or later "exploits of European imperialism in a glowingly 'pro Western' way." Other footage shows heavy earthmoving equipment made in the West molesting pristine African mineral lands. Wheatcroft then comments on a particular segment of the series, one devoted to the Colonial Khadafi/PLO-President Reagan conflict: "painful as it is, may not do us any harm to be reminded that a large part of the world simply doesn't see the conflict . . . as a conflict between light and darkness." The program also reminds us of the historical and cultural heritage of Africa.[5]

Finally, we see that television can also serve as a forum for debate and community discussion of Third World issues. Such was the case when ABC's *Nightline* broadcasted from Johannesburg in early 1985. Featured, via satellite from Lusaka, Zambia, was Oliver Tambo, president of the African National Congress (he would have been arrested had be returned to South Africa). Other guests were repressionist Connie Mulder, the white newspaperman Otto Kraus, black editor Percy Qoboza, and clergyist Desmond Tutu. While reactions were mixed on the utility of the venture, some undoubtedly benefitted. As anchor, Ted Koppel concluded, "They were talking to you New York City and Columbia University and everyone else who threatens to divest and disinvest. . . They were talking to you Coca-Cola and GM. . . And they were talking to you, Chester Crocker. Your theory of constructive engagement, set against the backdrop of an increasingly aroused public, is the right one. It permits the calibration of pressure, rather than the stark alternatives of abandonment (which would be self-destructive) or superpower bullying (which is almost always counterproductive)."[6]

All of these programs touch on concrete issues involving concrete human beings and concrete human needs—freedom, identity, well-being, and survival. We have moved beyond the economistic approach and in so doing have opened a discourse that has humanistic implications and consequences. Many problems of Third World nations can only be addressed at such a level.

Second, a development-oriented media should *focus not only on the economics of development, but also on military, political, and cultural aspects.* At this point, there is a correspondence between the needs categories mentioned above and the power categories just mentioned. Military power acting positively or negatively impacts on the needs category of survival. For the needs category of well-being, there is economic power, again with positive or negative consequences. For the needs category of identity, there is cultural power and for the needs category of freedom there is political power. All of them have to do with development in one way or another, and political with power for democracy and participation.

In a *Time* interview with Venezuelan President Carlos Perez, room is given for some of these non-economic issues. While he acknowledges that debt is one of the major problems affecting North-South equality, he also calls attention to problems such as drug trafficking ("We must attack this crime without borders with a policy without borders. Otherwise, we will never be able to eliminate it."), and environmental issues ("The great depredator of the environment is misery and poverty. If we don't correct the problem in countries that still have great ecological resources, then humanity will see itself in the long term confronting a tragedy of survival.")[7] And even on the debt, he points out that the Bush administration's so-called Brady Plan has merit for it recognizes that debt is, in actuality, a political problem:

> The economic growth of Latin America is now zero. Our countries have had to commit more than 50% of the value of our exports to debt service. That's intolerable. No country in the world can do this. . .
>
> In order for the Brady Plan to be more than just an idea, in order for it to work, the decision of the banks [to reduce debt] must not be voluntary. The U.S. Government should modify certain banking regulations to facilitate the concessions that the debt—or countries are asking for.[8]

Or consider other analyses that look at the Third World from different perspectives. *Toronto Globe and Mail* reporter Cruickshank notes that it is "the larcenous and tyrannical character of the elites of many Third World countries" that must be addressed. "The flight of capital out of the Third World to the First World has contributed to the debt crisis."[9] Still other journalists explore the problems in Western misperceptions of a people and their culture. Writing in the *Christian Science Monitor*, al-Marayati and Ibrahim observe that "Western perceptions are often shaped by the actions of dictators in Muslim nations." The assumption the West makes is that "these dictators adhere to Islamic principles and that Islam itself is an oppressive belief system."

> Ironically, Western leaders also fear changes in leadership. If the current despots are somehow replaced by Islamic leaders, the West often feels its interests in the Muslim world will be harmed. This argument is often used to justify the continued support of oppressive regimes.

> . . . [An] FBI report illustrates a double standard. Islamic opposition groups are heavily prosecuted in Iraq and Libya, the nations cited in the report. Yet, terrorist groups sponsored by these dictatorships are referred to as "Islamic extremists." Many regimes exploit Islam to maintain their own power. In other parts of the world, such as Haiti, where a charismatic former Roman Catholic priest was elected president, no one talks of Christian extremism.[10]

Again, this is an alternate, and perhaps more revealing, way to look at underdevelopment.

The point made here is only this: journalists should try not to limit the discourse to economic factors alone. Humanity certainly lives from bread, but not by bread exclusively. As a matter of fact, bread is a good example since different types and shapes of bread have deep cultural significance, particularly in a religious context. It would be perfectly legitimate for a journalist to ask people around the world strange questions such as "What according to you is the meaning of life?" "Do you feel life is worth living?" "Would you live it again?" These are not questions that should be posed by social scientists alone. To have people reveal their inner agenda, not only their striving for material benefits, or at least for a minimum material basis, is already drama. Doing so journalistically, newspapers, television, and radio would become more similar to literature. There would be more truth, more realism, and less superficiality. Development must ultimately be human development. And human development is, of course, not just economic development which caters to the outer person, not to the inner self.

A focus on the inner agenda should in no way exclude the equally legitimate focus on the outer, material agenda of persons, groups, countries, regions, or the world as a whole for that matter. Since human beings pursue both, so should the media so as to reflect, and reflect on, the human condition. By doing so the development discourse might also become more attractive to the "value-conservative" right wing of the political spectrum, since they, at least in principle, are more concerned with such items as identity and freedom and their deeper meanings, and tend to become upset when only the intricacies of the causal relationships in the economy between and within countries are exposed. There should be space for both in any development discourse.

Third, mere economic growth data will never do; dispersion data are also needed. When someone says that "country X is doing fine," and all we are told about country X are some percentages of economic growth, then there is every reason to doubt not only the intellectual, but also the moral quality of the reporter. We must look at the income of the bottom 50%, or 10%; at the income of the top 5% or 1%. If we look at the difference between the two, we immediately know so much more about the development situation in that country. Between those two poles averages may move up and down. That should be reported, but always with the warning that an upward move might conceal stagnation for the majority and a dramatic improvement in the living conditions of the upper 10% or so. On the other hand, a downward move is not necessarily deterioration for the bottom 50%. Again, there must be room for both in a development discourse.

For instance, the conclusion: "The [development] efforts were not a complete failure. Taken as a whole the third world achieved the 5 percent growth rate set for the 1960's and narrowly missed the 6 percent target adopted for the second decade." in-and-of-itself could be very misleading. The author qualifies it, however, by adding that growth was primarily urban-based, and "was spectacular in a few East Asian countries." While an Indian's average annual income rose from $150 to $250 between 1950 and 1980, a South Korean's climbed from $350 to $2,900."[11] Yet it is so easy to not provide such frames of reference.

Fourth, focus on relations, not only differences; and *do so not only within countries, but also between countries.* We are back to the basic point that makes development a drama: the relational aspect. To say that someone is poor *because* someone is rich is a dramatic statement in its own right and likely to be resented, even rejected, by the rich for obvious reasons. Consequently, the statement will have to be substantiated, indicating how, for instance, wages may be frozen but not prices so that those who live from moveable prices for their goods and/or services benefit whereas people on constant wages do not. The only remaining question would then be: who made that decision? Was it by chance those who would benefit most from it, or their biological or social relatives?

The same holds true between countries: why are prices of manufactured goods moving upward when the prices of raw materials and commodities remain the same or go down so that the terms of exchange in most fields are deteriorating for the raw materials exporting countries? Could it be that unnecessary frills are added to the manufactured goods? Could it be that fields, mines, quarries, and ocean resources are controlled by the manufacturers? If s/he looks into it, the journalist will always find something. But s/he will also be in the danger zone politically, and even culturally, by making visible what is supposed to remain invisible. Such explorations are indispensable to understand the structure of (mal)development.

One form of inter-nation relations definitely is the political realm mentioned above. Still, as this is so important, we raise the issue again. We are talking here of a "one-sided" press that takes on bias because of national politics in the press's home country. Illustrations abound in Central American reporting, where contrary to Reagan administration contentions, it has been observed that reporting was largely skewed in favor of Administration policies for the region. Millman cites a January 12, 1981 story in which U.S. Ambassador to El Salvador Robert White made an announcement that rebel commandos, presumably from Nicaragua, landed off the Gulf of Fonseca but were repelled by heavy fighting with Salvadoran troops. Since the supposed landing site was a full day's travel from San Salvador, *Washington Post* reporter Christopher Dickey chose to downplay the claim until independent confirmation could be made. The implication of going with the full story was to confirm a long-standing U.S. charge that Nicaragua was directly involved in the El Salvador civil war.[12]

The *Post* took Dickey's "'soft' dispatch and hardened it" with an interview from the Nicaraguan foreign minister denying that such an invasion took place. "The denial doesn't necessarily imply that it never happened," noted the reporter, "but it [did] create a situation where you [could] write a hard lead, and a headline like U.S. CHARGES NICARAGUAN INVASION, or words to that effect." Over the next couple of weeks the story was discredited by journalists who had an opportunity to visit the site, but no retraction was ever made. Says Millman, "Almost invariably, such episodes serve to reinforce Washington's official position. The media do the Pentagon's spadework, conditioning the American public to accept an aggressive U.S. military role in the region."[13] This "conditioning" appears to also apply to other areas of Third World life when the United States decides it has an interest in that nation or region.

Media critic Edward Herman provides an illustration from the 1982 El Salvador election where in 21 of 22 articles run by the *New York Times*, the only quoted sources were government officials. "Although the majority of Salvadorans are peasants, only two of 263 identifiable sources used by *The Times*—under 1 percent of the total—were peasants." "The Salvadoran rebels were cited twenty-seven times, 10 percent of the source total."[14] In marked contrast was the coverage of Nicaraguan elections. Only a fraction of the reporters that covered the Salvadoran elections wrote about the Nicaraguan balloting, and then they tended to focus on parties *not participating* in the elections, rather than those actually running.

> "The coverage of Nicaragua also stressed that press censorship and a state of emergency which restricted political activity were in effect. Stories about the Salvadoran election rarely, if ever, noted that there is no opposition press in that country, that opposition editors and reporters have been murdered and their plants bombed. . .
>
> A major theme in reports on the Salvadoran elections was news of guerilla attacks aimed at disrupting the voting. In contrast, *contra* raids in Nicaragua were rarely reported, although at least two election officials were killed while registering voters, another was kidnapped and seven soldiers were killed while transporting election-day materials.[15]

According to former *New York Times* reporter Bonner, "reporters routinely label Nicaragua as 'communist' or 'Marxist-Leninist.' Those terms trigger negative responses among readers and oversimplify the complex debate going on within the Sandinista leadership about the future political and economic structure of Nicaragua. . . [Western] journalists, like politicians, don't want to be labeled as leftists, or as being 'soft on communism.'"[16]

While at the *Times*, Bonner came under attack from the highly conservative "Accuracy in Media" group as well as *Wall Street Journal* editorial writers for his series on the Salvadoran Army massacre of some 1,000 peasants near El Mozote. This brought Bonner in conflict with the White House which was claiming that improved human rights conditions were prevailing in El Salvador. Ambassador Deane Hinton and his senior military advisor, Lt. Colonel John Waghelstein, were said to have spearheaded a campaign to deny Bonner access to the U.S. embassy in San Salvador. Bonner admits he began to "pull back a little bit" in his writing. "It does make you think twice." Despite the reservations he showed, the embassy continued his persona non grata status. The principal *Times* reporter in El Salvador was eventually removed from the Latin

American capital. His replacement, Lydia Chavez, has been criticized for filing extremely positive stories on questionable Salvadoran army officers and activities. Bonner later resigned from the *Times*.[17] It takes courage to buck the system and "tell it as you see it." Yet while the biases of a national press may make it difficult, they should not be a deterrent. Some will always try to exploit the weaknesses of institutions. The press can only be exploited by its own choice. The "watchdog" function of media is a widely recognized role of the press in democratic societies. How else can we correct the misconceptions we may have about the Third World and its people?

Fifth, a development-oriented press would do well to *focus on the totality of concrete life situations.* Some years ago British television had a long program on the development problematique. The unit of analysis was not a country, a region, a group of people, or an individual, but a family. The world was divided into five groups: the well-to-do, the middle class, the working class, the poor, and the dirt poor. The program devoted enough time on a family from each group to make it possible for the viewer to identify and fully understand the drama of their problems and possible solutions. What was shown were the everyday strategic choices. At the top was a family in Austria discussing such problems as where the best college education for their children could be obtained; at the bottom an incredibly poor non-family trying to scrape together a minimum for survival that very day, even by begging. And in the middle was most of humankind.

The families were concrete and their total life situation was taken into consideration. Economic aspects were not used as the sole vehicle of analysis. The journalist doing this would come closer to being an author; the media would have sections reading more like short stories. But, then, why not? Who said that what is printed in a newspaper necessarily has to be so terse, so economistic, so segmented from the totality of human life, and so fragmented from the context as is often the case? Who said that respecting concreteness and totality, or holism, would not also constitute news? New ground may be broken and new challenges addressed. Journalism would be more, not less attractive, as in the style of the best British journalism [*The (Weekly) Guardian, The European, Sunday Times*], or an American publication such as *The Christian Science Monitor.*

One recent *Christian Science Monitor* article provides a revealing look at hardships found in rural settings of Zaire. "Some sections of the country have practically been cut off from overland travel because the government has neglected road maintenance for years," observes writer Robert M Press. He depicts the hardships rural people face due to poor government transportation services. He paints a moving scene:

"Without a good road there's no development," says one vil-
lager. Farmers grow groundnuts, beans, bananas, oranges, sweet
potatoes, tomatoes, and onions. But many products spoil during the
rainy season when few trucks can reach here.

"We work too hard," says Kia Luamzai Kitomba, a former local
government official. A road, electricity, and even tractors would
help the farmers, he says.

Veronique Mameni, a farmer, typically works 11 hours a day in
the fields, six days a week. "I'm tired," she says, laughing and smil-
ing, and shaking her head, all at the same time. On Sundays, only
the men rest: The women do all the cooking, dishwashing, and other
chores, she says.

Some men rest too much—developing alcoholic problems,
according to Dokula Makambu, a nurse who runs a local medical
clinic.

The clinic serves an important role, but is underequipped. The
nearest hospital is several hours away by road—during the dry season.[18]

Such a story is potent and declarative. It has so much more power than
most stories. The reader is allowed to meet the subjects and share in
their lives. Yet very few editors believe that such stories are worth the
investment. It, unfortunately, is often a matter of journalism economics.

Sixth, a development oriented journalism *would never forget the
dimension of democracy.* The reader should conceive of democracy as a
system where people send messages to the power machinery's legislature, executive, and judiciary branches or to some other division such as
the party, military, or police. The system then talks back, acts, or does
both. The task of the media is to report what the system is doing.
Democracy can only function where there is a free flow of information
between people, the system, and the media. Using the media to *make the
people visible,* both as objects and as subjects, becomes one task. Using
them to *expose the system* through investigative reporting is the second
task. Using media to expose media that fail to do their job is the third.
All three will serve democracy and development. The latter can be done
in a development context the same way it is done in any political context; by asking what happened to some decision. Why is this and that
not being done and why is something else being done instead?

Often journalists fall victim to the manipulations of government
leaders. These leaders, of course, may stress democratic principles, but
then behave in just the opposite way. In the case of the United States,

while operating under the pretext of defending regions from Communism, the government has often supported highly oppressive military dictatorships. We have seen this in Panama, El Salvador, Chile, the Philippines, Syria, Iraq, Kuwait, and many other countries in recent times. And all too frequently the press has been coerced into supporting the decision to back repressive governments. We have already noted such manipulation in El Salvador and Nicaragua. We saw it again when the U.S. refused to come to the aid of Shiites and Kurds in Iraq following the Persian Gulf War. As an unidentified Pentagon official observed in a *Los Angeles Times* News Service report:

> Not to diminish in any way the repugnance of what's going on but some of these people are very anti-democratic themselves and very anti-American. They are not freedom fighters; they are not friends of America. There may be some who are, but we don't know enough about them.[19]

The news media often finds itself at the center of campaigns to help promote anti-democratic movements. As Millman observed after Chavez replaced Bonner in San Salvador, the *New York Times* referred to the former National Guard head Vides Casanova, who had close links to Salvadoran "death squads," "as a 'committed reformer'," and made these observations in a front page article: "There are signs that the arrogant and often insensitive army that ruled El Salvador for more than forty years has progressed. . . Colonel [Domingo] Monterrosa [commander of counterinsurgency operations—his troops were the ones which massacred the El Mozote laborers] has been a pace-setter in the military in showing the new style to foreign reporters."[20] The depiction of President Jose Napoleon Duarte as a "moderate" by Chavez and others was criticized when *Washington Post*'s Christopher Dickey observed: "If you deal with the 1984 elections as if the massacre of 1980 [during Duarte's earlier term] never happened, then the elections look pretty good." "But ask yourself what the elections represent if the military agreed to have them only after it eliminated ten thousand people."[21]

It is not so easy to promote democratic dimensions of development in news, particularly not within the context of a new world information and communication order. In the present phase, given the poor record of the private international wire agencies trying to come to grips with the development problematique, governments have sometimes stepped in trying to improve the situation. In so doing governments may, of course, be self-serving. A news agency such as IPS trying to participate on the side of development, democracy, and participation may easily run into difficulties. As an alternative news agency, they depend on governmental sources; on the other hand, good reporting on development practice would demand exposure of governmental activity. Hence, the prediction would be that investigative reporting focusing on the system would tend to be limited. And this is, of course, precisely what the critics of the new world information and communication order suspected.

Consequently, ways and means have to be found to forge ahead. One formula is very simple: contrast government statements, some of them obtained in interviews, with development reality without necessarily implying that there is a link between the two. The relation may be more complicated. If the rhetoric is good and the situation is bad, the rhetoric may not necessarily be a way of covering up. If the rhetoric is good and the situation is also good, the latter may not necessarily be because of government rhetoric or government action. If both are bad it does not necessarily mean that the government is honest.[22] Conclusions can best be left to the reader provided that the journalists have done a sufficiently good job of putting rich, diverse information into the media.[23]

Seventh, there is always the possibility of *reporting about development, not critically in terms of problems, but constructively in terms of positive programs.* In that case it should be done as concretely as possible, almost like a "how-to" book. Any story showing how things were successfully done, and telling where to get more information will be useful for someone else in the same or similar situation. Moreover, success stories may contribute to a general sense of optimism that might generate more momentum for democracy and development. More particularly, the "system" should not enter the media only as culprits, with the suspicion that something always goes wrong because of the system. They should certainly also have a right to be in the media when something is successful, letting everyone benefit pedagogically and politically from the experience.

Let us look at one effort where Spain, France, Italy, and Portugal helped to organize an initiative to spur political stability and economic development in the Mediterranean. The movement includes a "global approach to the region's problems," according to one Spanish official. It encompasses a concern for population growth, urban concentration, Islamic fundamentalism, unemployment, and immigration. Drawing parallels to the 1975 Helsinki accords, the Mediterranean Conference might eventually include a common conduct code that would have bearing on political and human rights and could establish democracy as a central goal.[24] Another case comes from a report by Sampie Terreblanche, economics professor at Stellenbosch University, printed in

the *Johannesburg Sunday Times*. Terreblanche addresses the black population shifts projected for South African urban areas by the next century.
He notes that "black urbanization will only bring a shift in poverty from
the homelands to the urban areas," and argues that the government
must develop:

> a new economic policy in the white urban areas . . . Actually, we
> must develop two completely different economies: one for the mod-
> ern or formal sector, and another for the marginal or informal sector
> . . .

> Existing First World regulations operate as a form of structural
> apartheid. They keep some people "in" and protected, and others
> "out" and unprotected. To abolish these regulations will not be easy.
> Moreover, measures to create a proper environment for the informal
> sector will be opposed if the slightest danger exists that they may
> harm economic growth . . .

> Will the government go the full length toward the creation of
> two economies? I am not optimistic. White South Africans are too
> bourgeois to appreciate the opportunities and the welfare that can
> be created by blacks in their own informal sector.[25]

Eighth, let the people talk. In addition to exposing the system, and
praising the system when praise is due, the media should also give a
voice to the people.

Development dialogues, simply sitting down with people from
high to low discussing the meaning of development, can be a very useful approach. It immediately becomes clear what an enormous range of
visions there is in this world and how differently people perceive development problems. At the same time, it also becomes clear that there is a
wealth of information and "how to" insight available from people in
general. The media often make the mistake of focusing too much on
popular opinions—"are you for this and that"—and too little on popular
knowledge—"how do you think we should do this and that." The general tendency is to assume that for knowledge there are always experts
and that the input from people in general will be opinionated, in terms
of values, and sometimes exotic as well. The opposite profile, "expert
opinion versus people's knowledge," should be equally prominent.[26]

The tragedy of the matter is that people also have, by and large,
internalized the "expert knowledge versus people's opinion" syndrome,
and so have the media. In the columns found in most newspapers (and
"teaser" interviews on television and radio), with photos of "ordinary
people" and some quick statement obtained from them over the tele-

phone or on the street, the focus is almost always on whether they are for or against something. The stronger the views, the better. No analysis needed. True *glasnost* would also give people a voice *as experts*, and not only about themselves, and their own situation, but through talented interviewing, in line with the seven preceding ideas for a development-oriented press. Some "community" channels on U.S. cable television systems demonstrate how this can also be enacted in the broadcast media.

Ninth, go one step further, *let the people to some extent run the media*. One way of doing this is via the Letter to the Editor or the op ed page. However, this input tends to be opinionated and hence insufficient as a mirror of what development resources are available in the population at large. In addition, the space/time available is much too limited.

The next stage is to let people write/produce much of the newspaper/program; by contributing articles and volunteering their own knowledge, experience, and expertise. This is also very possible with the "community access" cable television formats noted above; the ethnic and minority owned/issue-oriented radio, and low power television stations found in the United States; the many "community" newspapers that exist in parts of the world, including South Africa—despite the oppression they have endured in recent years; and the "underground" newspapers we have seen in the United States, most notably those published in and around the Haight Ashbury District of San Francisco during the 1960s, and the labor-oriented publications still circulated today. One might even go so far as to say that the quality of the newspapers and broadcast journalism of a country could, up to a point, be measured by how much is written/produced by the readers/viewers, not by the editorial staff. Needless to say there is a problem with wide-scale adoption of this approach since any employed graduate from a school of journalism or broadcast journalism, and they are increasing in number, would be then entitled to have his or her stuff out at least once a week. A high level of popular participation would make a lesser number of inches, or minutes, available for media staff members. It would be a clear case of a competitive game between producers and consumers-turning-producers.

The *tenth*, and final point: *let people run more of society*, in other words true participation, *and then report on what happens!* Democracy puts people into the legislature; the jury system puts them into the judiciary. People's movements and organizations (non-governmental movements as they often are called by governments) do precisely this. In terms of broadcast media in the United States, the United Church of Christ (UCC) and Action for Children's Television (ACT) campaigns have already proven that this is possible, and appropriate, when discussing media issues.[27] These groups can find a niche in society where they can enact some of their programs, empower other people, and devise strategies pursuing the distant goals, profit or non-profit. A major objection to socialist societies would be that they do not provide people with these types of experimental niches. Everything tends to become governmentally coordinated. All resources are already "collective," meaning that they cannot be put to private, non-governmental, unauthorized uses.

The remedy would be to report more on what popular movements are doing; not only their successes, but their failures too. The "system" is not the only part of society to be exposed. This also holds for the "anti-system." Accountability should apply to the people as actors. However, there is one major consideration. Even if a popularly based project is a failure, it usually serves a function an expert project never can serve: people get training through participation, including learning from mistakes. Is that not rather important in a democracy? Communication flows best in the people-system-media triad. It is absolutely essential for the health of a democratic society. Thus, people have to have access both to the system and the media.

CONCLUSION

Of course, no-one would assume that the media are the causes of development, underdevelopment, or overdevelopment. The deeper causes are located elsewhere in our structures and cultures. As pointed out in the preceding chapter, however: the media mediate between deep structure and culture, between the reality of the events and the images of the news. More than that, being the closest most people ever come to the real world beyond the horizon, the media start constituting a reality for most of us. A media event is an event as defined by the media. Who would care to check, or have the opportunity to check, the relationship between the media event and the real world? Who can travel to the Persian Gulf area or the Soviet provinces or to Beijing or Washington? Who has access to the deeper layers of decision-making?

In the standard news outlet where these ten rules are not respected, there are never people in development, but only issues, problems, and large aggregates such as countries. The focus is always economic to the point of being economistic. No attention is paid to the tremendous variation between rich and poor within and between countries; the focus is on average growth or decline. Contemplating these average differences between rich and poor would be one way out, and that would give some idea about dispersion. Since this is not done at the level of people, only at the level of nations, the total picture does not emerge. Moreover, all this deficient reporting takes place at the expense of exploring the reasons for these differences. To a large extent, these differences exist in the relations between countries and groups of people, yet the connection is not easily seen by the untrained eye.

The perspective is never concrete. The single human being or single family is almost never in focus except if it is a very special family such as the "Royal family" or the "Presidential family." Investigative reporting is rarely engaged lest sources deep inside the system (people who give information, often scandalous, about the relations among the people of the system) should withdraw or seek revenge. No concrete information about how people could do things better is given, only news about what went wrong. People are made invisible by never giving them voice because all interviews are focused on elites. At most, the "people" appear in statistical tables, having been exposed to polls, or as exotic condiments in a "human interest" story.

News media like this seems professional, and may be run by certified journalists and editors. If people should appear, more likely than not they would be elites writing sharp, concentrated letters to the editor on the op ed page. They are usually not common people; the tiny space allotted to them will not give them a chance to really voice their agonies.

Finally, society will not offer much space for the amateur, private project; and if it does will not pay much attention to it. "Non-governmental" is often interpreted as "market," even "capitalist," as if capitalism were the same as democracy or a free society. People doing their own thing are left unreported in times of peace; particularly women. That this "own thing" in reality might be an alternative way of handling the whole development problematique often does not occur to the journalist. His development agenda is prepared by the system itself, at the national and international levels.

The ten negations of the ten proposals look familiar. They are more or less identical with the mainstream development menu we have already seen. It is not only poor journalism suffering from lack of vitamins; it is positively dangerous to our developmental health, strongly anti-democratic, and antithetical to Western humanism. Only rarely will it stimulate people into action, whether out of agony, pain, or anger, or because something has moved them (bad conscience, compassion, constructive ideas badly in need of enactment).

In short, standard conservative development reporting serves humankind badly. Alternative reporting may do a better job, inspire people into action, and make them not only more conscious of their goals, but also of the complicated relation between them. Such reporting not only stimulates development, democracy, and participation, it is these three qualities rolled into one.

NOTES TO CHAPTER 5

1. Wilbur Schramm, "Circulation of News in the Third World: A Study of Asia," in *Mass Communication Review Yearbook*, vol. 1, eds., G. Cleveland Wilhoit and Harold de Bock (Beverly Hills, CA: Sage Publications, 1980), pp. 605-607.

2. John Moody and Strobe Talbott, "On Drugs, Debt and Poverty," *Time*, November 27, 1989, p. 14.

3. For an interesting discussion of communication and development, see Majid Tehranian, "Communication, Peace and Development: A Communitarian Perspective," in *Communicating for Peace: Diplomacy and Negotiation*, eds., Felipe Korzenny and Stella Ting-Toomey (Newbury Park, CA: Sage, 1990), pp. 157-175.

4. Naushad S. Mehta, "Filling the South Africa Void," *Time*, March 6, 1989, p. 58.

5. Geoffrey Wheatcroft, "Tout of Africa," *New Republic*, October 27, 1986, pp. 25-27; Gerard Alexander, "Africa Skewed," *National Review*, October 24, 1986, pp. 56-57.

6. Ted Koppel, "TV Diplomacy in South Africa," *Newsweek*, 105, April 8, 1985, p. 14; "Black and White in Color," *The New Republic*, 192, April 15, 1985, p. 42.

7. Ibid., p. 13.

8. John Moody and Strobe Talbott, "Interview: On Drugs, Debt and Poverty," *Time*, November 27, 1989, p. 12.

9. John Cruickshank, "The Rise and Fall of the Third World," *World Press Review*, February 1991, p. 29.

10. Salam al-Marayati and Riad Ibrahim, "The West's Misperception of Islam," *The Christian Science Monitor*, January 17, 1991, p. 19.

11. Paul Lewis, "For the U.N., New Thinking on the New World," *New York Times*, November 5, 1989, p. E 2.

12. Joel Millman, "Reagan's Reporters: How the Press Distorts the News from Central America," *The Progressive*, October 1984, p. 20.

13. Ibid., p. 20.

14. Ibid., p. 20.

15. Raymond Bonner, "A One-Sided Press," *The Nation*, December 8, 1984, pp. 604-605.

16. Ibid., p. 605.

17. Millman, "Reagan's Reporters: How the Press Distorts the News from Central America," p. 22.

18. Robert M. Press, "Despite Hard Times, Zaire's Rhythm of Life

Goes on in Hard-to-Reach Villages," *Christian Science Monitor*, January 31, 1991, p. 10.

19. Norman Kempster, "Bush Holds Back Forces Despite Plea from Kurds," *Honolulu Advertiser*, March 30, 1991, p. D1.

20. Millman, "Reagan's Reporters: How the Press Distorts the News from Central America," p. 22.

21. Quoted in Millman, "Reagan's Reporters: How the Press Distorts the News from Central America," p. 23.

22. For a very practical, as opposed to theatrical, exploration of some of these themes, particularly the relationship between the investigative reporter and what is we call the "system," see The Thomson Foundation Editorial Study Centre, *Eight Ways to Improve Development Reporting* (Cardiff, Summer 1974); presented as the conclusions of a specialist course.

23. However, should all demands be placed on the media people, or should we also request some inputs, some work, so to speak, from the readers/viewers/listeners? Findings on poor news comprehension are demonstrated by Doris Graber in *Processing the News* (New York: Longman, 1984); Dennis K. Davis and John P. Robinson, "News Flow and Democratic Society in the Age of Electronic Media" in *Public Communication and Behavior*, ed., George Comstock (New York: Academic Press, 1989); and Richard C. Vincent and Dennis K. Davis, "Trends in World News Research and the Implications for Comparative Studies," Paper presented at the 39th annual conference of the International Communication Association, San Francisco, May 26, 1989. Of course, communication is active work also on the receiver side, otherwise it is brainwashing/filling. The receivers have a right to demand to be challenged. But do they also have a right to demand not to be challenged, to be spoon fed with superficial and distorted news all the time?

24. Alan Riding, "4 European Nations Planning a New Focus on North Africa," *New York Times*, July 30, 1990, p. A6.

25. Sampie Terreblanche, "The 'Quality of Poverty'," *World Press Review*, June 1985, pp. 40-41.

26. See "The People Were Right (at Least So Far)," Johan Galtung, *Methodology and Development* (Copenhagen: Ejlers, 1988), pp. 93-106.

27. ACT is a consumer interest group that has been quite effective in lobbying for less commercial time on children's television, encouraging prosocial programming, and engaging in other activities to promote the interests of children within the TV industry. The United Church of Christ has been engaged in various activities to help individuals increase their awareness of TV and its effects, and was instrumental in promoting minority and free speech interests in some Federal Communication Commission (FCC) licensing and rule making activities over the years.

CHAPTER 6

The Media and Ecological Survival

LONDON—Will U.S. consumers do without air conditioners in new cars?

Will China deny citizens the chance to own a refrigerator?

Will Brazil go deeper in debt by cutting back logging of its lush rain forests?

Will Britons pay billions of dollars more for electricity to reduce their reliance on polluting coal-powered generating plants?

In short, will the nations of the world—rich and poor alike—make huge sacrifices in an effort to spare the global environment from further destruction?

Such tough questions are coming to the fore as world political leaders try as never before to cooperate and confront as a group the problems of a planet in distress.

— Larry B. Stammer, Los Angeles Times Environmental Writer[1]

Just about everyone would agree that the key ecological problems—global warming, the ozone hole, deforestation, desertification, decreasing bio-diversity, and toxic pollution to name some—singly, and particularly in combination, constitute major threats to life in general and human life in particular. The consciousness-raising initiated by the Stockholm UN conference in 1972, celebrated constructively, in Brazil in 1992 (despite the embarrassing performance of the Bush administration as reelection campaign pressures mounted for the President), has been successful. People seem to recognize the severity of the problem; and that goes not only for the consumers, but also for the producers of the pollution and of the multiple forms of depletion.

Yet consciousness has to be followed by action, and that action has so far been deficient. The following is an effort, in five points, to indicate how that action could become more effective.

THE PRINCIPLE OF MULTIPLE COLLECTIVE ACTION

Ultimately human-made environmental degradation hits individual human beings, through scarcity and/or toxic pollution, and is responsible with other factors for cardiovascular diseases and malignant tumors, for damage done to the respiratory system, and more subtly through damage done via sight, noise, and smell pollution. The sense of utter well-being when we experience undestroyed, pristine nature is indicative of what we are missing and how far the damage has actually gone.

The social structures and processes producing the degradation are strong; however single individuals are weak. To change the structures to generate more benign processes, collective action is indispensable; by informal movements and/or formal institutions, at the local (e.g., municipal), national, regional, and global levels. In combination, this yields eight possibilities, and we need all eight. We should not think of only movements, or only institutions as being useful. Similarly it would be restrictive to think exclusively in terms of just local levels, or national levels, or regional levels, or even global levels. The problem, of course, is how these actors can become more than the mere sum of their parts.

The ecology will undoubtedly always be threatened by human economic action, whether from private or public sectors motivated by a search for profit, power, or both. Eastern Europe is a clear example that the public sector does not possess any built-in ecological wisdom superior to the private sector; and shows how helpless a system becomes without the corrective forces of democracy. Destructive forces are also organized at the same levels: from the individual hunter-gatherers via small/local and medium/national enterprises to regional and global transnational corporations. Their ecopolitical power, for good and for bad, becomes the major factor in ecopolitics.

THE PRINCIPLE OF SUBSIDIARITY

The principle, as such, is simple enough: solve the problem at the "lowest," meaning closest to local, level possible. Every human individual is responsible for his/her own action, for handling garbage, and for wise, non-depleting, protective approaches to nature in general. This is a tremendous educational task in which not only schools of all kinds, but also parents, elder siblings, and others are playing a major role. The same goes for municipalities—what can be handled locally should be handled locally—and for nations—what can be handled nationally should be handled nationally. The same pattern applies to regions, and the world as a whole.

Still, there are problems with these five levels, and they are contained in three types of actors—economic, institutional and movement worlds. The economic actors are, perhaps, particularly strong at the lowest and highest levels. There is the consumer in all of us longing for attractive products regardless of the ecological impact of their production, distribution, and/or consumption. There is the strength of the transnational movements and transnational institutions, such as the United Nations Environment Program (UNEP), with headquarters in Nairobi. The system leaks.

In general, the world level, through the UN system and other institutions, produce norms for the regions and the nations, and they, in turn, for the local levels which try to regulate the ecological behavior of individuals and enterprises. This process has been operating, prescribing and controlling downwards, punishing or at least exposing and admonishing those who break the rules, with the usual competition, as to who should be the ultimate non-sender: the United Nations, regional bodies like the European Community, ad hoc conferences, or single governments.

But the real problem is still more complicated. Imagine that lower levels, for instance local movements, municipalities, or districts of municipalities, such as those in the northern part of Northern countries, want stricter rules. Also imagine that rules from above have come about as a compromise between economic and institutional actors, which is what generally happens at the global, regional, and national levels. Further imagine that the movements are strongest locally and nationally, which is also what generally happens. The stage is then set for a clash between the small who want to remain beautiful or regain beauty, and the big who want to remain or become productive, profitable and growing, and, above all, powerful.

Should a municipality have ecological autonomy? Should or could the municipality enforce rules that are stricter than the rules from higher levels? The individual is free to do so, as do those who are ecologically very conscious. What about nations that want stricter rules than the region; a well-known problematique from the debate over Nordic membership in the European Community. Will the economic actors, and particularly the manufacturers, not complain to the national government about ecologically superconscious municipalities? Of course they will. This conflict formation is already taking shape.

THE PRINCIPLE OF ACTIVE DEMOCRACY

Eastern Europe and the ex-Soviet Union are, as mentioned, not only examples of how the public sector in socialist economies can be every bit as destructive to the environment as the private sector in a capitalist economy; but also of the enormous costs to society when democratic mechanisms—and particularly people's movements—are weak or absent. In other countries, those mechanisms should also be strengthened. The question is how.

There is, of course, the role of ecological issues in the political platforms of political parties and their ability to implement those positions at the four levels of collective actions. Thus, in the last elections in Norway (September 1989) there were no less than six parties with clearly green platforms: the Christian greens, the Farming greens, the Marxist-Leninist greens, the Socialist left greens, Labor party greens and the Green greens, together effectively placing the ecological issue at the top of any political debate.

This is only indirect democracy, via parties and governmental institutions. There is direct democracy via direct, nonviolent action by movements and action groups of which we would like to mention three.

First, independent monitoring of the environmental situation by the movements, and by the people in general. People should learn how to assess the quality of the air they breathe, the water they drink and the food they eat, the clothes they wear, and the houses they live in. This is also a tremendous way to teach natural science in schools, with great pedagogical advantages because of concreteness and relevance. Students may even be motivated for pure self-defense reasons.

Second, demonstrations, confrontations, and spectacular action against destructive economic actors or dormant institutions. Noone has done this more productively than Greenpeace.

The third possibility is perhaps the most important and still largely untapped: conscious economic behavior. Consumers are already trained to be choosey in market-oriented societies, to prefer higher to lower quality and lower to higher prices, and more particularly higher to lower quality to price ratios. So why not let the environment enter the quality concept fully as the *Shopping for a Better World* movement and booklets do? [New York: Council on Economic Priorities, 1990]

Yet we need information, not only about the environmental impact of the product, but also about the production process leading to the product. This information also should be about the product, in easily understandable form. The ultimate economic decision maker is the end user, and the end user has a right to get all relevant information. Democracy has at its basis respect for the individual, including the individual joint capacity to make what in the long run will be a wiser decision. Yet the individual depends on the media for much of his/her information. Hence absolutely crucial in the whole fight for environmental survival is the ability of the media to give accurate pictures of the situation, including possible remedies.

THE PRINCIPLE OF IMPACT STATEMENTS

If each municipality demanded an environmental impact statement from each economic actor, including itself, as mentioned above, not only for the product but also for the process, then we would have a tremendously effective tool for sound environmental management. Statements should be publicly available, be exposed to scrutiny not only by institutions but also by movements, and be subjected to dialogues in hearings. Ultimately, the economic actor should be held accountable to the words of the statement. In addition, the customers/clients/consumers should make their choices on the basis of these statements. An unsatisfactory statement would be sufficient reason for refusing use of municipal resources, including grounds. This is where the problem of how much municipal ecological autonomy there is enters once again.

THE PRINCIPLE OF CYCLICITY

Ultimately, the problem of ecological balance, essential to the idea of sustainable development, is the problem of restoring nature to nature. Just as the Native American does, we should have high respect for nature. We take from nature and we should give back what we can both use, together. Ideally, we should neither deplete, nor pollute. After our economic activity, we should still enjoy our lives, not just move on to destroy someplace else instead.

The best way to realize this is probably through a simple test: can we suffer the consequences of our own economic action? The products we rather like, otherwise we would not buy them. However, can the chief executive officer of a company drink the water downstream or breathe the air "up-air" from his/her factory? Could he/she tolerate a pipe from that water into his/her drinking water, or that air into his/her air conditioning? If not, what right does he/she have to send it on to others? Or the manufacturer of highly dubious food to push it onto customers, even whole nations of customers as is now being done with fast foods and hormone treated meat?

Perhaps one day such linkages between cause and effect will be routine, standard parts of our ecological self-defense. This should also apply to municipal boards that delay action. Maybe we will realize one day how much of this is actually class politics, with people high up, and decision-makers in particular, living in clean and protected environments, leaving the suffering to others in poorer classes in poorer districts in poorer countries.

Take all of these principles together and we have a dense grid of protection measures against eco-threats to our existence. Use only one and we have probably lost.

TEN PROPOSALS FOR ENVIRONMENT-ORIENTED NEWS MEDIA

While most agree that ecological threats are a key concern, there is less agreement on the solutions to be employed or the timetable that should be followed to "clean" the environment and remove such hazards to human health and safety. When discussions enter the domain of the politician, other issues surface: who will bear the costs of clean-up and reform? and how much inconvenience is a society willing to bear in order for changes to actually be implemented in a timely fashion?

This is where the journalist can play a vital role, for it is this tool of communication that can not only disseminate information, but can also serve as an agent of investigation—a "watchdog" over the community.

1. Be aware of cycles.
2. Identify all cyclular nodes.
3. Demand impact statements.
4. Identify long-term impact.
5. Identify environmental supporters.
6. Name the abusers.
7. How can citizens get information?
8. What can citizens do?
9. Identify rules broken.
10. Do follow-ups.

Figure 1. Ten proposals for environmental journalism.

An effort will now be made to convert the five principles outlined above into ten proposals. There will be two for each principle, starting from the end with the more basic themes.

First, beware of the cyclical nature of environmental problems. Thus, it is not sufficient to say about a product that it is harmless, for instance biodegradable, or has been made biodegradable. What about the process producing that product? A solar energy converter may be both depletion and pollution free, standing on the roof, absorbing heat from the sun, imparting that heat to water for heating and cleaning. What about the process producing that converter? What happens to the converter after it has served its term? What happens to all the paper collected and bundled by eager hands after it has been collected? If it is shipped from New York to Japan for recycling, what about the eco-impact of the transportation relative to local Japanese production? In other words, environmentally investigative journalism does not stop at the product only.

One of these concerns involves newspaper recycling, something that affects the newspaper industry directly. Newspaper recycling is so popular that a major oversupply of old newspapers now exists in areas such as the U.S. Northeast. Some fear that the industry will simply discard millions of tons of aged newspapers into the environment. The problem is the low demand for recycled newspapers, and some environmentalists charge that newspaper publishers are shirking their responsibilities by failing to use paper they helped to originally create.[2] In one analysis of the problem, Knight, writing in the *Washington Post*, provides these revealing insights on the problem:

> Ecologists accuse the publishers of trying to wrap their trash in the First Amendment, raising freedom of the press issues when what they really want is freedom from responsibility for the cost of disposing of waste they create.

> Environmental groups aren't the only ones offended by the newspaper industry's stand on recycling issues. Petrochemical industry lobbyists have been passing around a transcript of a radio broadcast in which an executive of The Washington Post Co. said that while newspapers share responsibility for the problem, it isn't fair to expect them to solve it by having to take back old newspapers. "The general philosophy here in this country is that when you sell something to someone, it's their property."

> That's not the philosophy that has applied to government regulation of pesticides or chlorofluorocarbons, plastic packaging, aluminum cans and glass bottles, one industry executive pointed out . .

> Industries that have been labeled as polluters by newspapers

are understandably unsympathetic to what they regard as the hypocrisy of newspapers on recycling regulation. Our businesses have been forced—often at the urging of newspaper editorials—to spend billions to meet environmental standards, they say, so why shouldn't newspapers pay their share of environmental costs?

Ecology groups as well argue that newspapers' reporting and editorializing on environmental issues are often at odds with the newspaper industry's stand on the same issues. If newspapers really believe in preserving the environment, the recycling advocates say, then newspapers ought to set up their own recycling plants just as the plastic packaging industry is doing.[3]

For another example of journalistic exploration of "process," we turn to a review of American corporations where public relations efforts are confusing the issues of environmental safety. They sometimes make changes in product packaging where the new material may actually be more harmful to the environment than the old. As Holusha observes, companies often implement changes "because of unrelenting public pressure rather than as a result of conclusive environmental analysis."[4] Such appears to have been the case when the McDonald's Corporation chose to abandon its heavily criticized plastic-foam hamburger containers in favor of a slimmer plastic coated paper wrap. Some environmentalists reportedly feel that the new packaging material is theoretically less recyclable than the abandoned one. As National Audubon Society scientist Jan Beyers noted, though, "'McDonald's decision was actually neutral' because both types of packaging go directly into the trash after use. . . Only by going to re-usable packaging, like washable plates, would the company have substantially improved its environmental performance."[5] Another product faulted by Holusha are the Procter & Gamble Company's Pampers and Luvs disposable diapers where a heavily funded advertising campaign is strongly pushing composting as a way to discard them. The fear here surrounds "neglecting to mention that 20 percent of the diaper is non-compostable plastic."[6] Still other concerns surround the environmental-friendly messages found on many product labels. Gillette Foamy shave cream advertizes "no CFC's" and S.C. Johnson & Son's Lemon Pledge boasts that it "contains no propellant alleged to damage ozone." Yet chlorofluorocarbons have been outlawed by United States law since 1978. "It would be equally true to put a label on the cans saying they have no radioactive ingredients or pesticides."[7] In another case, the plastic bottles used for Lever Brothers's cleaning products Wisk and All declare on the back label that the company is "now using technology that can include recycled plastic in our bottles at levels between 25 percent and 35 percent." As Holusha observes, "nowhere does it say whether recycled plastic is actually in the bottle. Indeed, company officials say the bottles may or may not contain recycled plastic."[8] As he concludes, these actions "may do little more than inappropriately raise the hope of consumers who want to do the right thing for the environment."[9] The improper promotion of consumer trust is at issue here.

Particularly important is the span of the cycle of causes and consequences. Is the whole nature-production-distribution-consumption-nature span contained within the local community? Or is the span national, regional, or global? If so, is it recognized as such, or are only "lower" level problems seen clearly? Are there similar local, national, and regional problems elsewhere? Is there any compensation in exchange for lost direct, local association between environmental causes and effects?

Second, give identity and voice to all nodes on the cycle. A company may be located in solar heated houses even made of biodegradable material, and still make decisions to deplete nonrenewable resources, feeding them into highly polluting production processes and production by-products. A transnational corporation has that power, derived from its unique capacity to coordinate capital, technology, and management, handling nature and labor in the process. The nodes on the cycle may then be easily identified as local branches or daughter companies (why "daughter," they usually look more like "son" companies?). In other cases, the identification is less direct. Questions have to be asked to identify the concrete individuals in concrete firms in concrete countries whose outputs serve as inputs to the next line, with or without environmental consequences.

Yet identification is indispensable for voices in a dialogue with the journalist. They should explain their angle, why they act the way they do, how they react to alternatives, and so forth. There are human beings hiding behind the abstractions of structures and cycles. The weakness of the media is that it does not often bring those abstractions to our attention; the strength of the media is that it shows us the people whose myriad acts constitute the social tissue of those structures and cycles. In giving them voice it is usually more interesting to focus on how they rationalize or legitimize environmentally dangerous action than on "whodunit" types of journalism. With the latter you may catch one bad polluter, with the former you may understand why the whole problem arises. For example, consider the twist on the rain forest destruction issue found in comments made by Kilaparti Ramakrishna, a senior research associate at the Massachusetts-based Woods Hole Research Center: "Are you prepared to lower your standard of living? You won't drive less miles in your car, but you tell the Third World not to cut trees."[10]

But the names and addresses remain important in all cases, and not just for the eco-actors (where "eco" stands for both "economic" and "ecological," after all, there is the common root of household, oikos). Equally important are the victims, as in the thalidomide, itai-itai, and minamata eco-scandals. They are usually more anonymous. For media to make them mutually visible is a major condition for social action, and hence a political act. So is silence.

Third, demand impact statements from everyone concerned. As mentioned above, impact statements are probably among the more powerful instruments to prevent further eco-degradation. Yet as anyone in the field rapidly discovers, they depend on who makes the statement, which depends on whom the society authorizes to make such statements (which, in turn, may depend on what kind of statements are wanted). Hence, the function of the media as the watchdog, not the lapdog, of society is not terminated with impact statements.

First of all, there may not be consensus. Do others, particularly, those who live down-stream, down-wind, or more generally "down-cycle" from the eco-activity contemplated agree? Do the colleagues of those who drafted the statement agree? Do those who know of similar conditions in other places agree?

Next, does the statement only focus on how to avoid damage—laudable in itself—or also on the more positive approach; how to improve existing conditions by building eco-stability instead of eroding it? Let's consider the "debt-for nature swap," promoted by certain U.S. legislators including Tim Worth, Albert Gore, and the late John Heinz. What they proposed was that governments, such as Brazil, would be allowed to reduce their foreign bank debt in exchange for a promise to save the Amazon rain forests. Scandinavian banks already raised a similar idea with Poland in exchange for industrial air pollution curbs.

Rowen, writing in the *Washington Post*, helped showcase the rain forest idea. Outside donors would retire some debt and the equivalent local money (from bonds) would be earmarked for Amazon region preservation and to support projects such as biological prospecting. As Rowen concludes, such swaps would not be the principal solution to Third World debt, but a very nice start. "It's time for Brazil, the World Bank and rich industrialized nations to wake up to this reality: In the Third or First World, it's no longer a matter of economic development versus environmental protectionism. We can't have one without the other."[11]

In all we must ask: what activities are contemplated to leave the human being/environment interface better off than before, not defining the present as an acceptable baseline just because it exists, here and now?

Finally, is this a single-shot statement, an entrance test for some new activity, an exam or an election program soon to be forgotten, or is it to be repeated, like passing a driver's test every 5 years or so? In other words, what about the follow-up, not only in terms of promises that may be broken, but in terms of new statements, in light of new designs and new knowledge in the rapidly changing field of environmental sciences? The moral for economic actors and for media actors is: get back to the statements. Don't forget them.

Fourth, reflect on long term impact. In retrospect, after a crisis, it is easy to see how little we knew, and more importantly, how little we knew that we knew so little. Who are the people who could be helpful in that regard? Usually, not the "experts," if we define an "expert" as a person who knows more answers than questions. The intuitions of a probing philosopher, or some other generalist; of a person in deep contact with nature (nature people, nature lovers); or of women often in possession of both dimensions, are perhaps who we should pay attention to before we venture into the ecological unknown. When the CFCs were invented at the end of the 1920s, there seems to have been no warnings about their possible impact on the air cover protecting us. What about the many space ships/ferries burning their way into outer space—what kind of holes do they leave behind?[12] What does the entrance ticket cost for that kind of problem to enter the public discourse? What is the long term impact on human beings, not to mention on the human species, of so often being exposed to electromagnetic fields?[13] Another question is the possible relation between radioactivity and AIDS.[14] We should be sufficiently trained by now not to take expert silence or "no problem" as an answer. But there is a deeper problem that has to do with the position of intellectuals in postmodern societies. By definition, intellectuals are supposed to have never-resting, inquisitive minds, never ceasing to ask questions, but equipped with some tools to get at least the beginning of answers. Thus, "intellectual" is a state of mind rather than a profession (the profession is better referred to as "intelligentsia").

As an example of a long-term ecological problem, consider a review of the problems afflicting U.S. national parks by Egan.[15] At danger is the very preservation of the U.S. national park system as it is known. "From the saw grass marshes of the Everglades in Florida to the glaciers of Denali in Alaska, the national parks are faced with threats from within, as the clutter of concessions has turned wild domains into comfortable playgrounds, and threats from without, as urban frontiers and a tide of pollutants advance."[16] Los Angeles smog is slowly killing trees in Kings Canyon and Sequoia National Parks in California, and is even contributing to impaired views at the Grand Canyon in northern Arizona. Acadia National Park in Maine is one of the worst areas with polluted air drifting in from Boston, and from as far away as Ohio. In Zion Canyon, Utah, nearby residénts in the community of St. George want to dam the Virgin River, the major stream that formed the canyon, to help support its quickly growing population. Acid rain is destroying high altitude trees in the Great Smoky Mountains of Tennessee and North Carolina, and the Florida Everglades hosts only 10% of the marine birds it protected 6 decades earlier.[17] In sum, things are at crisis levels.

In 1991 the visitor count at the nation's "357 monuments, seashores, historic homes and recreation areas" (representing more than 80 million acres) was expected to be almost 300 million. Within 15 years that annual number is projected to double.[18] The parks are literally in danger of being trampled to death. The larger concern is what effect these trends will have on other national park systems. Some 100 countries now have developed national park programs of their own. The United States was the first thanks to legislation passed in 1916. As Egan puts it, "there is soul searching among park officials about their mission: Are they running theme parks, the best of Disney and geology, or zoos without cages?"[19]

The problem is not one with which only Americans must struggle. There is a similar situation in the Alps. Writing in *Stern*, Doinet satirically observes: "The most violent avalanches long ago overcame the law of gravity. . . These avalanches consist of thousands of cars carrying thousands of people calling themselves *Bergfreunde* (friends of the mountains) . . . One billion tourists are expected between 1990 and the turn of the millennium."[20] The flood of visitors has led to inexcusable acts. In Austria, the Stuiben Falls operate only between 8 a.m. and 7 p.m. for the tourists. During the night the water is diverted to operate electric turbines to meet demands which are undoubtedly brought on, in part, by the deluge of tourists. "These streams used to carry excess water and rock out to sea. Now the debris stays put, until it makes its way to the valleys in the form of avalanches."[21] Other signs of wide-scale disaster include the fact that some 80% of the Bavarian Alps trees are classified as ailing, 50% in the Austrian-Yugoslav Alps, and 40-60% in Switzerland. And "whole meadows of the Alpine flower edelweiss are being trampled flat under the ski slopes. To save the flower, one tourist manager wants to move a couple of specimens of it to New Zealand."[22]

Similar problems can be found in the southern Argentinean Andes: ". . . [O]nce well forested, [they] are covered only by crippled trees and trunks rotting in the soil. Genetically debilitated by 100 years of harvest of its healthiest trees, besieged by 500 species of fungus that eat the wood, the Rio Percey area is more a green cemetery than a forest."[23] Argentina's woodlands have dwindled from 140,000 square miles in 1905 to 40,000 today. "In addition, these woods are of dubious quality; for many years loggers cut down the best trees, the straightest and the healthiest, so that new seeds came from the worst specimens: those trees most vulnerable to pests and disease.[24]

To combat the problem of humans literally loving natural resources to death, the U.S. National Park Service has begun to eliminate concessionaires who lend an air of commercialism to the parks, and to set quotas for daily visitor counts at certain heavily visited locations such as Yosemite.

> Yosemite, in many ways, may be the park of the future. Its quota system for controlling automobiles inside the valley was instituted in 1985, after a Memorial Day throng produced the first case of gridlock in a national park. For several hours, on a hot holiday afternoon, nothing moved inside the valley where Muir, Theodore Roosevelt and Ansel Adams once found their greatest source of inspiration.[25]

> Reservations, though a central ticketing agency in Chicago, are already required for camping in the most popular national parks. Now many park officials are calling for restricted entry. The crowds have taken a particularly harsh toll on some national historic sites.

> "When you pass 10,000 people a week through a door of a house that was built for a family of four, that monument is not going to be around very long," . . .[26]

But present national park leadership is not yet willing to agree to broader system-wide restrictions. Such policy appears necessary, however, and does not necessarily run counter to democratic ideals of freedom and access. Such freedoms do not give us carte blanche to squander our natural resources as we please. The needs of future generations also must be protected, and visionary policy-setting is an obligation of any thinking civilization. Journalists can do much to help promote such an agenda, through reports that educate the population, and editorials which help direct public opinion to positive action.

Each society has its intellectuals, with or without university degrees; the problem is how they are unpredictable. They ask questions and thus will always be a problem for the powers that be. Yet intellectuals are capable of posing such interesting questions.

One opportunity involves the continuing debate on global warming. While there is wide acceptance of the problem and its various causes, many still dispute the projected timetable of destruction. By going to the intellectual community, the press can find ample views, most likely quite different than those found in political capitols. For example, in covering a meeting of the Pacific Science Congress, many potential interviewees could be found. *Honolulu Star-Bulletin* reporter Altonn caught up with Washington University botany professor Peter Raven. Raven, a leading advocate for preservation, warns that "the next 20 to 30 years are going to be the most crushing, threatening and debilitating for the productive ecosystem that the human race is ever likely to encounter." He warns of potential plant and animal extinction as a result of global warming. "It's faster-moving, much more threatening and totally irreversible," but is downplayed because of its complexity. "For most of us, the solution is to engage in wishful thinking, to hope it'll go away."[27] "By 2020, about 77 percent of the [world's] population will be in developing countries, living on only 15 percent of the world's wealth and with only 6 percent of the world's scientists." Raven calls for industrialized countries to help others with "agri-forest systems" and knowledge of crop production, but adds that we also "must understand people instead of telling them what to do."[28] In another report, *Honolulu Advertiser* reporter TenBruggencate interviewed meteorologist William W. Kellogg. Kellogg proposed two methods in which global warming might be addressed: reduced dependence on fossil fuels, and slowing the world's population growth. In a straightforward comment on global warming, Kellogg put it bluntly: "The theory of the greenhouse effect is one of the best established in the field of meteorology, and it has been tested on our planet as well as on Venus and Mars. On our sister planet Venus this effect results in a surface temperature hot enough to melt lead."[29]

Such observations are indeed eye opening. As Kellogg notes, the skepticism surrounding the introduction of the global warming theory in the scientific community some 2 decades ago has now passed.[30] Now the general public must be made aware of the stark realities the greenhouse effect will bring. Journalists can help by providing these opportunities. Governments will act more quickly if citizens demand such action.

Rulers cannot be intellectuals only; they have to have more questions than answers. One reaction is obvious: repression to the point of persecution, even including banishment and extermination. Another reaction is banishment to those modern ghettos for intellectuals, the university campus, where there is overheated intellectual life at the expense of undercooling the rest of society. And a third is escape from that marginalization on the condition that participation in society at large, in Habermas's *Öffentlichkeit*, is within the narrow confines of the expert, with few questions and predictable answers. The result is obvious: short term impact statements, not long term reflection. That makes it even more important that the media raise these disagreeable questions by giving intellectuals the voice they are denied by the system, and not only in the form of short, frustrated op ed statements.

Fifth, active democracy I: who cares for the environment? Of course, there are obvious answers. Victims of environmental degradation care most, particularly those (and that means almost everyone "in the developed countries") hit by the modernization diseases (cardiovascular diseases, malignant tumors, and mental disorders), to the extent they can be attributed to environmental causes.

Still, in practice it is not that simple. The case of tobacco shows us very clearly the long and tortuous road from the first suspicion to real protection against active and passive smoking. In retrospect, we may talk about false consciousness or no consciousness at all. Yet it is rather arrogant to issue such certificates, in the old Marxist tradition, to people who do not share one's own views. Those who "should be" conscious, even actively confronting environmental hazards, may refuse to believe reports, even to believe what their senses tell them. Others may have no such problem even if not affected at all.

One way the press can help is by concentrating on people who do care about the environment and have made special efforts to work for ecological issues. Such was the case in a *New York Times* article that looked at "a new breed of young environmentalists" — MBAs who are bringing their degrees and putting them to good use on the front lines of the eco-campaign.[31]

> ... [F]rom Washington to San Francisco, environmental and conservation groups are reporting that their offices are awash in job applications, despite the fact that the pay they offer is much less than what for-profit fields offer.
>
> "Young executives and new M.B.A.'s are seeking environmental services as the blue-sky growth industry for the 90's," said Eric Lombardi, who is 35 years old and is the executive director of Eco-Cycle in Boulder, Colo., a nonprofit organization that has a city contract to collect residential curbside waste. "They see an exciting chance to use their entrepreneurial drive to make money while helping the environment."[32]

These young people are moving into jobs with large companies "taking environmental records much more seriously," and nonprofit corporations and agencies traditionally involved in the environmental protection business. In the latter group there is Greenpeace, which received 7,000 applications for 250 available jobs in the United States in 1989. The World Wildlife Fund had 6,000 applications for 40 Washington positions. Some applicants have "Wall Street experience and law degrees." "'We're seeing a huge wave of very high-quality applicants who normally would have chosen careers in the for-profit world,'" commented the World Wildlife Fund conservation finance director. The tide has changed from that which was experienced just a few years earlier. "'You're seeing a lot more people in the legal community who are willing to give up the big bucks and do something more important socially,'" commented one University of Maryland law student.[33] It is significant when journalists take the opportunity to home in on stories such as these. Undoubtedly, it takes more work than covering a traditional assignment, but it also may be more personally rewarding, both for the journalist and the reader/viewer.

Finally, there seems to be a strange factor at work making us more willing to accept matter as a health hazard in its liquid (alcohol) and gaseous (smoke) than its solid form (salt, sugar, fat, animal protein, non-fibrous food). Melt or evaporate the latter and there would probably be a public outcry. Consequently the good environment journalist would have to think not only in terms of what people do identify as environmental hazards, but also in terms of what they probably will identify as such in the not too remote future, regardless of the "experts." Media could lead, not lag, keeping an open discourse that includes agendas for tomorrow.

Sixth, active democracy II: who does not care for the environment? Again, the obvious answer: those who can profit money-wise and/or power-wise from environmental degradation may be a good point of departure, but this is far from sufficient. It would serve to identify not only major public or private depleters and polluters but also the many who derive their livelihood from working in such industries. As for the arms industry, it would expose not only the factory owners, but also the factory workers; the poor and low class as well as the rich and upper class.

When identifying abusers of the environment, we first turn to political leaders, nations or municipalities, and companies and corporations. There are many examples of each of these as eco-violators. The press can carry stories which call attention to these violations, and can offer commentaries and editorials to help promote community discussion of issues. The following is an example:

> Reagan, who not entirely in jest blamed air pollution on trees, established what is probably the worst environmental record of any President in history. Bush, by contrast, ran for President as a self-proclaimed "environmentalist." But he's done so poorly that a senior civil servant despaired to me last week that "It's not as bad as when Ronald Reagan was the President. It's worse."[34]

The author goes on to elaborate the Bush record, addressing the Exxon oil spill when he first "vacillated," then adopted an entirely inadequate "let-Exxon-do-it cleanup policy;" global warming and the famous 'White House effect' speech; and the zero additional money allocated to clean up Boston Harbor, an issue that Bush made a target when lashing out at Michael Dukakis's record. This Washington-based environmental writer posits a summary question: "Will he be able to see the all-important forest despite the killer trees?"[35] Similar finger pointing can be found in good investigative journalism in those stories that expose U.S. executive branch opposition to proposed clean air legislation,[36] national efforts to squelch international carbon dioxide accords (in this case the culprits were the United States, Japan, and the Soviet Union),[37] or Mexican destruction of tropical rain forests.[38]

Then comes the problem that those who benefit from eco-damages also have to pay the same costs of pollution as the rest of us. We all have to pay the costs of resource depletion. This makes the lines more blurred. The problem of priority of values, not only economic and political interests, comes to the forefront. The struggle for the mind starts, beyond a simple line-up according to the class interests of the polluters and the polluted. Actually, the most "exploited classes" here are animals, plants, and future generations and they cannot stand up and be counted on for participation in a democratic decision process. One reason why the environmental issue is a good one for liberal democracy is that it tests our ability to mobilize on the basis of ideas.[39]

To demonstrate the links between ecology and other social issues, one *New York Times* story proved particularly interesting for it targeted world poverty as one of the largest culprits endangering the ecosystem. In the Sudan, farmers clear trees of the Nile headwaters, affecting the watershed and resulting in floods; throughout Latin America landless peasants cut down rain forests.

> "For centuries there has been moral outrage about disparities in standards of living," said Alan Durning, a staff member of the World-watch Institute, an environmental research organization. "Today we find poverty is not just a moral issue, because we now have a situation where poor people endanger the well-being of the better-off."
>
> . . . To subsist, the poor must consume or shatter the very resources that give them life . . .[40]

The article goes on to elaborate the threat to rain forests by landless, deculturated tribes. When they are "'people whose lands have already been developed throughout the world, . . . [t]hey are the ones who are moving up the sides of hills,'" says Sheldon Annis, a member of the Overseas Development Council, an economic research group.[41]

It is painfully clear that industrialists afraid of the costs of recycling and cleaning up, much like workers in heavily polluting/depleting
industries afraid of losing jobs, will look for others (in the same branch,
the government, the customers) to share the costs. The big problem is
whether such formulas will work or if a deeper restructuring is necessary. [42]

Seventh, local action I: how do ordinary citizens get information? The
answer, "through the media," is of course not sufficient. Knowing this,
many media today add information about where to find more information. This is a very commendable practice. This will have to be done on a
nonpartisan basis, at least in society as a whole, so that all groups have a
fair chance of being known and heard. It may be hard for politically par-
tisan media to advertise their adversaries. Such was the case when a special National Audubon Society program was scheduled to air on the U.S.
cable television Turner Broadcasting System network. The 1-hour special examined ancient evergreen lear cutting practices on government
land in Oregon and Washington. Stroh Breweries were informed that
loggers would boycott their beer, and Stroh withdrew its sponsorship
from the series ($600,000). Automaker Ford, and oil company Exxon
were among other companies which withdrew as advertisers. The program was shown anyway, but without the advertising. As show co-pro-
ducer James Lipscomb observed, "No one objects if you do a story about
the Brazilians burning up their forests. . . But if you produce a program
where a Forest Service scientist says we are cutting down our virgin forest at a faster rate than Brazil, the funding dries up."[43] Not all stations or
networks would go ahead and run such a controversial program, and
few, if any, would find it possible to support such a decision over a period of time. When this happens, "local public-oriented" radio and cable
television access channels may be the only outlets capable of giving a
voice to everyone.

An issue such as the environment, involving so many so deeply,
is also an excellent occasion to talk about where information ought to be
available, even if it is not. An environment journalist might even include
as a routine question: "Can we say/write that interested people may
come to you for further information about this issue?" The basic links in
a democracy are between the rulers and the ruled, not between either or
both and the media. The task of the media are precisely that, to mediate.
A modern society can be seen as having two rulers, state and capital,
ruling in different ways over the civil society, people and their organizations. But as Plutarch asked, "Who then shall rule the ruler?"[44] The task
of the media is not to be an information society, but to help bring it
about by making all three more knowledgeable of, and accountable to,
the other. All three may then decide that the other two operate on the

basis of wrong information or no information at all. That is in itself information, and very important as such. Plus, the media can help in increasing not only the level of information, but also the level of awareness of non-information where there should be even an abundance of information.

Eighth, local action II: what can ordinary citizens do? This brings us to the heart of politics "who shall do what for whom and against whom, when and where," referring both to the rulers and to the ruled. The media will certainly report on the former. However, the question, "what can ordinary people do?" is also a good candidate for the routine repertory of an environment journalist. That only answers within the bonds of the law should be communicated goes without saying. We are talking about eco-politics, not eco-terrorism. Yet a large number of acts of terrorism come from the rulers, from state and/or capital, and should be exposed, denounced, counteracted, and transformed irrespective of origin.

To make information about environmentally correct behavior generally available, down to the trivia of various categories of garbage disposal, would probably meet with few objections, again showing how good the issue is for democracy. Unlike the peace issue, there is something for everyone to do. On the other hand, how about counteracting environmentally incorrect behavior? This smacks of power-over-others and can generally be done in three ways: through appeal to values, through rewards, and through punishment. Praising a clean, bountiful environment, and those who build such environments, is unobjectionable. But demonstrations, even noncooperation, civil disobedience against the real evil-doers, not to mention the possibly most effective instrument of them all, the boycott of firms engaging in environmentally harmful activity by spreading consumer information and labeling the products?[45]

Journalistic attention can be directed to efforts to increase awareness through school curricula. Such was the case in one article that showcased activities at the eastern Connecticut Porter School. In this town of 4,000, children are learning about the environment through a creative program of "assemblies, songs, and posters" all designed to help "reinforce the message that pupils must conserve, recycle and save the earth by [starting with] saving their own back-yards.[46] "You see the message sinking in as they sing 'recycle, recycle, recycle'" said Mr. Callinan, an environmentalist, folk singer and former teacher who came here with his wife, Ann Shapiro, to perform for the pupils. His songs and patter, he said, are directed at young, impressionable minds. "It's not very subtle," he said. "But it works."[47]

Ninth, multiple action I: whose rules have been broken? The whole point about multiple collective action is the ability both to think and to act on several levels that do not exclude each other. Four such levels of action have been mentioned above: local, national, regional, and global. The frequently mentioned injunction to the effect that we should "think locally, and act globally" is not good enough, covering only two of the eight. This is a lot to keep together, both for individuals as well as the media.

The power struggle between these levels will loom high on the political agenda for the future. In principle the "higher," more inclusive level should have priority. Thus, a European Community rule might carry more weight in a member country than national and local rules. That does not mean, though, that the UN carries more weight than the EC in this field; it has authority but little or no power. Additionally, a firm might be more sensitive to local boycotts, not to mention to local demands on the managers to consume down-stream and up-air effluents, than to any directive regardless of origin.

Two conflict types are becoming increasingly clear: the "lower" level as less restrictive, and the "lower" level as more restrictive. If it is "less restrictive," we have the classical case of the state, state-community, or super-state imposing its will locally or nationally. If it is "more restrictive," the state may interfere against the will of local authorities or groups, imposing less strict norms, for instance, in the name of universal standards of fair competition. The latter type will be important for journalists to identify; this is where democracy will really be tested, and contested.

Tenth, multiple action II: what is the follow-up story? Yes, what is the follow-up story? We have had ecological consciousness for 2 decades now, at least officially; and a lot of eco-positive action. Yet the combination of topic pollution, global warming, ozone depletion, desertification, and deforestation, not to mention loss of bio-diversity, seems to weigh heavier than ever on us all. On top of that comes the increasing population pressure on decreasing resources, at least in some fields. Evidently something has gone wrong.

One place where things may have gone wrong is probably in the media. An environmental scandal appears (Torrey Canyon, Exxon Valdez, the oil fires in Kuwait). It is reported, action is taken, the damage gets worse. But sooner or later action comes as a result of at least the visual damage and the issue exits from the media scene with a bang or with a whimper, usually the latter. To reopen a dead story is not easy. Stories have their birth and death, but not much life after natural death. Even issues come and go; new issues then generate new types of stories. We usually do not get to know the true extent of an eco-catastrophe, such as Bhopal, for example, as it became focused on economic damage assessment to the victims. Or, take for example, the follow-up to the Exxon Valdez spill. Some 7 months after the spill, Exxon U.S.A. was still demonstrating highly defensive behavior regarding the contentions of the National Wildlife Federation, a 15 member panel of top executives from General Motors Corporation, the Monsanto Company, Dow Chemical, DuPont, Arco, Tenneco Inc., and the Miller Brewing Company. An Associated Press story dated October 28, 1989 reported that Exxon's environmental coordinator Raymond Campion criticized the Federation for "not meeting our expectations" regarding solutions to environmental problems. He went on to question their alleged objectivity and fairness toward the Valdez spill; they had been among the plaintiffs who sued Exxon in quest of total payment for the cleanup.[48] Federation president Jay Hair wrote a stinging reply:

> I regret we did not meet your "expectations," but did you really think your membership on our Corporate Conservation Council would buy Exxon immunity from the National Wildlife Federation's response to such a massive and poorly managed environmental disaster? . . . The fact that Exxon has been judged a corporate parish in the court of public opinion has little or nothing to do with the National Wildlife Federation. That distinction has been clearly earned by Exxon's leadership.[49]

After making the interchange public, Hair later commented that this "typifies the insularity of Exxon management. . . Instead of engaging in constructive dialogue with the environmental community over this tragedy [they] apparently would rather complain about how unfairly we have treated them."[50]

The moral is clear: journalists should return not only to the general issues, but also to the concrete stories. Some of the stories may even have happy endings, and this may be the real reason why there is no follow-up. If so, this is even more tragic since we probably learn more from happy, inspiring endings than from having our brains polluted and depleted every day by disaster stories about pollution and depletion.

CONCLUSION

The argument for adequate environment reporting is exactly the same as for peace and development: to get at the truth, *plus* promote such consensus goals as peace, development, and environmental balance. There are two obvious problems, however, with this. The consensus may not be very deep, and there may be other values which have higher priority. The truth may not necessarily support some of the points espoused by those who advocate peace, development, and environmental balance. So there is no final answer. It is exactly for this reason that the guidelines above are suggested for discussion and for testing and practice. They are slanted in favor of environmental balance as a matter of human survival, just as peace and development. Again, there are some basic principles: give a voice to all concerned; tell what the effects are, what is going on, where to get more information; who support what, and who are against. Get the politics of it all. The last thing to conceal in a democracy are the politics; and politics have a surface level and a deeper level. The concerned citizen needs both. The task of the media is to address the concerns of concerned citizens.

NOTES TO CHAPTER 6

1. Larry B. Stammer, "Saving the Earth: Who Sacrifices?" *Los Angeles Times*, March 13, 1989, Sect. I, p. 1.

2. Jerry Night, "Newspaper Industry on Collision Course With Environmental Groups Over Recycling," *The Washington Post*, September 26, 1989, p. C3.

3. Ibid., p. C3.

4. John Holusha, "Coming Clean on Products: Ecological Claims Faulted," *New York Times*, March 12, 1991, p. C1.

5. Ibid., p. C1

6. Holusha, pp. C1, C6.

7. Holusha, p. C6.

8. Ibid., p. C6.

9. Ibid., p. C6.

10. Larry B. Stammer, "Saving the Earth: Who Sacrifices?" *Los Angeles Times*, March 13, 1989, Sect. I, pp. 1, 16.

11. Hobart Rowen, "Help for Amazon: `Debt-for-Nature' Swaps," *Washington Post*, April 2, 1989, pp. H1, H10.

12. See M. Mendillo, et al., "Space-lab-2 Plasma Depletion Experiments for Ionospheric and Radio Astronomical Studies," *Science*, 27 (November 1987), pp. 1260-1264. "The space shuttle Challenger—releasing large amounts of exhaust molecules—creating so-called 'ionospheric hole,'" p. 1270. According to Lenny Siegel, "No Free Lunch," *Mother Jones*, September/October 1990, pp. 24-25, solid rocket fuel burns puncture the ozone layer and produce acid rain, whereas "NASA's own ozone-depletion specialist, Michael Prather, admits that solid rocket could harm the ozone layer, but he argues that, at the current launch rate, the effect is negligible compared to the combined global impact of

industrial uses of CFCs, methyl chloroform and other chemicals," p. 24. Follow-up!

13. For an early warning, not in the sense of before the giant production of man-made electromagnetic fields, but in the sense of before real warnings (if they come), see "Electromagnetic Fields: A Link to Cancer?" *International Herald Tribune*, April 4, 1991.

14. We are indebted to Dr. Rosalie Bertell, President of the International Institute for Concerns of Public Health, Toronto, for sensitization to this possibility.

15. Timothy Egan, "National Parks: An Endangered Species," *New York Times*, May 27, 1991, pp. 1, 7.

16. Ibid., p. 1.

17. Egan, p. 7; also see Seth Mydans, "Plant Owners Fighting Plan to Clean Canyon Air," *New York Times*, October 15, 1989, p. 24.

18. Egan, p. 1.

19. Ibid., p. 1.

20. Rupp Doinet, "The Alps Are Dying," *Stern*, reprinted in *World Press Review*, March 1991, p. 54-55.

21. Doinet, p. 54.

22. Ibid., p. 54.

23. Daniel Arias, "Killing 'Eternal' Forests," *Clarin* (Buenos Aires), reprinted in *World Press Review*, April 1991, p. 46.

24. Ibid., p. 46.

25. John Muir, founder of the conservation movement, is sometimes called the father of Yosemite National Park although *New York Tribune* editor, Horace Greeley, was the first to champion the cause of preservation for Yosemite.

26. Egan, p. 7.

27. Helen Altonn, "Earth Courting Ecodisaster, Expert Warns," *Honolulu Star-Bulletin*, May 29, 1991, pp. 1, 10.

28. Altonn, p. 10.

29. Jan TenBruggencate, "Global Warming Is Concern at Meet: Scientist Says Governments Must Face Up to It," *Honolulu Advertiser*, May 29, 1991, p. A11.

30. Ibid.

31. "Earth Issues Lure a New Breed of Young Worker," *New York Times*, July 29, 1990, p. A 41.

32. Ibid., p. A41.

33. Ibid., p. A41.

34. Curtis Moore, "Is Bush Another `Killer Trees' President?" *Los Angeles Times*, June 7, 1989, Sec. II, p. 7.

35. Ibid., Sec. II, p. 7.

36. Matthew W. L. Wald, "White House Objects to Bills on Cleaner

Fuel," *New York Times*, September 25, 1990, p. A24

37. Paul L. Montgomery, "U.S., Japan and Soviets Prevent Accord to Limit Carbon Dioxide," *New York Times*, November 8, 1989, p. A8.

38. Larry Rohter, "Tropical Rain Forest in Mexico Is Facing Destruction in Decade," *New York Times*, July 10, 1990, p. C4.

39. See, for example, "Disease and Destruction of Habitat Are Killing Off Koalas," *New York Times*, November 28, 1989, p. C4.

40. "Land Is Losing to the Poor's Fight for Short-Term Survival," *New York Times*, November 28, 1989, p. C4.

41. Ibid., p. C4.

42. The difference between more expensive gasoline, making it possible for the rich to drive more quickly because the poor can no longer afford to drive at all, and closing inner cities partially (Florence, Italy) or completely (Dubrovnick, Yugoslavia) to car traffic is hardly lost on anyone.

43. Anthony Lewis, "The End of Forever," *New York Times*, October 12, 1989, p. A29.

44. Plutarch, *Ad Principem Ineruditum*, III (780, C.).

45. An important initiative in that regard is *Shopping for a Better World* (New York: Council on Economic Priorities, 1991); with 350 pages of information on companies and products along ten dimensions, among them environmental issues.

46. Kirk Johnson, "In Schools, New Emphasis on Environment," *New York Times*, November 21, 1991, p. B1.

47. Ibid., p. B1.

48. "Exxon Faults Wildlife Group's Criticism of Oil Spill," *New York Times*, October 29, 1989, Sect. 1, p. 26.

49. Ibid., Sect. 1, p. 26.

50. Ibid., Sect. 1, p. 26.

CHAPTER 7

When Negotiations Fail: Reporting on a War*

At the height of the first world war Lloyd George, the prime minister, confided to C. P. Scott, the editor of the Manchester Guardian: "If people really knew, the war would be stopped tomorrow. But of course, they don't know, and they can't know."[1]

THE POWER OF THE MEDIA

Now that we have examined how the press might function in different settings to help promote various "peacetime" objectives, we must, out of necessity, also explore how the press might react when nations abandon diplomatic efforts to resolve conflicts, and choose to enter into war. War often occurs, in many different areas of the globe, and when it does, the press can play a critical role in what the public knows about the military conflict. It may even have a profound influence on its outcome.

The basic functions of the news media have already been documented by social science and communication researchers. One such function is its ability to help in the diffusion of information. As early as the 1940s, researchers were studying how and why different information spreads at varying speeds and in different ways across society. Media proved to be one of the principal vehicles for the transmission of information.[2] Early research in the area referred to a "two-step flow" process of information dissemination. Yet later, researchers seemed to prefer a "multiple-step" process to describe how information is circulated by the media. The latter takes into account the many transfers which may actu-

---

*A shorter version of this chapter has been translated and published in Richard C. Vincent and Johan Galtung, "Krisenkommunikation Morgen, Andere Kriegsberichterstattung," In *Krieg als Medienereignis: Grundlagen und Perspektiven der Krisenkommunikation*, ed., Martin Löffenholz (Opladen, Germany, Westdeutscher Verlag, 1992).

ally take place before information is received by some individuals.

It is also well documented that the news media can act as an agenda-setter. Here it is recognized that the media has the power to help set individuals' "agendas" by choosing the stories that will be reported, by presenting them within a certain hierarchy, and by assigning a certain amount of time to the story's presentation, all of which suggest a certain relative importance to a news item. As McCombs and Shaw have suggested: "The mass media may not be successful in telling us what to think, but they are stunningly successful in telling us what to think *about*."[3] This is not to say that all individuals are affected in the same way. It may depend on where the individuals live, which specific media they use, and various sociocultural attributes. Still, the power of the press is recognized as being instrumental in information sharing, and war news is no exception. A few examples of wartime reporting follow.

Print and electronic media have demonstrated their abilities to offer blow-by-blow narratives of a war as it unfolds. The inherent drama found in war-related activities can actually be quite high, making it a natural for mass media news. News media have been recognized for their ability to effectively present such dramas within their story telling function.

While both newspapers and visual media work are often complementary when it comes to covering war, in recent years the visual media have captured much of the attention. In Vietnam, for example, we seem to remember best a few events—South Vietnam's national police chief Brig. General Nguyen Ngoe Loan's execution of a Viet Cong officer with a pistol to the head, the Buddhist monk setting himself on fire on June 9, 1963, and the small girl escaping from a napalm attack. All were documented by the camera. The filmed account of each was available on television while still photographs appeared in newspapers and magazines. During Persian Gulf War coverage, the *New York Times* repeatedly printed photographs of the television screen during CNN telecasts when Western print media were barred access to Baghdad. Such moves demonstrate the convergence of the various media which increasingly occurs with contemporary wartime journalism. Audiences also seek multiple news sources, when available, for their information; the television images peek curiosity, while newspapers and news magazines offer greater detail.[4]

THE PRESS IN WAR

Some 150 to 160 years ago the nature of war reporting changed radically. Both the telegraph and the camera largely contributed to this change.

The telegraph was used to quickly transmit reports from a faraway bat-tlefield back to a newspaper. The camera ushered in a new era of real-ism, offering dramatic documentation of wartime events.

President Polk's message to the U.S. Congress calling for war against Mexico was sent by telegraph from Washington, D.C. to Baltimore in May 1846, and demonstrated the ability of newspapers to use the technology to accelerate their reporting process. During the Mexican War, unfortunately, telegraph lines only went as far south as Richmond, Virginia. The telegraph soon reached farther south and into the American West—to Charleston and St. Louis in 1847 and Chicago and Milwaukee in 1848; this had profound effects on national news reporting. By the time of the U.S. Civil War, the telegraph was firmly entrenched as a regular tool of the journalist. Because of the toll charges, stories became shorter and more concise.[5]

The still photograph was used to document combat in the Crimean War, and in the American War Between the States.[6] During the latter, photographer Matthew Brady moved about with no limitations. His photographs were both remarkable and shocking. But his images could not yet be used in newspapers due to limitations in the newspaper printing process (halftone reproductions of photographs were possible only in the 1870s). Instead, newspaper illustrations came from wood blocks. The drawings, though remarkably photolike, were produced by the large group of artists assigned to cover the Civil War.

The news writing styles were remarkably similar to those we find in today's newspapers. While photographs per se were not avail-able to accompany the newspaper journalist's story, the printed text could be quite descriptive. The following excerpt from the now classic report filed by Whitelaw Reid (pen name: "Agate") is a good example. It chronicles the battle of Shiloh, near Gettysburg. It was originally printed in the *Cincinnati Gazette*.

> . . . Hancock was wounded; Gibbon succeeded to command—approved soldier, and ready for the crisis. As the tempest of fire approached its height, he walked along the line, and renewed his orders to the men to reserve their fire. The rebels—three lines deep—came steadily up. They were in pointblank range.

> At last the order came! From thrice six thousand guns there came a sheet of smoky flame, a crash of leaden death. The line liter-ally melted away; but there came a second, resistless still. It had been our supreme effort—on the instant we were not equal to anoth-er.

> Up to the rifle pits, across them, over the barricades—the momentum of their charge, the mere machine strength of their com-

bined action swept them on. Our thin line could fight, but it had not weight enough to oppose this momentum. It was pushed behind the guns. Right on came the rebels. They were upon the guns, were bayoneting the gunners, were waving their flags above our pieces.

But they had penetrated to the fatal point . . .[7]

Later, when moving pictures became available, the power of the visual media became quite apparent. It helped to change views on war even more. Not only were accurate visual recordings now available to the public, but they also added the dimension of action. This helped supply another level of realism to war reporting. The response was overwhelming, and its impact enormous; the fighting military also appear to have been affected by the new medium. This point is exemplified in a *London Evening News* review of newsreel coverage of Pancho Villa's Mexican army maneuvers in 1914:

The introduction of the film on the battlefield can hardly fail in any case to have a remarkable effect upon the behavior of the troops. The soldiers will feel as individuals that the eyes of the world are upon them, and if a soldier feels tempted to run away the thought that he may be seen, bolting across the screen at home in the course of the next few days or weeks must surely exercise a great restraining effect. On the other hand, his heroic deeds will be done in the limelight and fully and permanently recorded.[8]

During World War II another medium brought faster and extremely realistic news from the front. As the public listened to the voices of broadcasters such as Edward R. Murrow, Eric Sevareid and Walter Cronkite, many radio listeners felt as if they were walking down the bombed London streets, the liberated streets of Paris, and the halls of Versailles. These were broadcasts which depicted scenes of death and destruction, courage and hope. Murrow's narrations, for example, often had a way of demonstrating the grim ironies of war. Here are two examples.

There were two women who gossiped across the narrow strip of tired brown grass that separated their two houses. They don't have to open their kitchen windows in order to converse. The glass had been blown out. There was a little man with a pipe in his mouth who walked up and looked at a bombed house and said, "One fell there and that's all."

* * * * *

Today I went to buy a hat — my favorite shop had gone, blown to bits. The windows of my shoe store were blown out. I decided to have a haircut; the windows of the barber shop were gone, but the Italian barber was still doing business. Some day, he said, we smile again, but the food it doesn't taste so good since being bombed. I went on to another shop to buy flashlight batteries. I bought three. The clerk said, "You needn't buy so many. We'll have enough for the whole winter." But I said, "What if you aren't here?" There were buildings down in that street, and he replied, "Of course we'll be here. We've been in business here for a hundred and fifty years."[9]

Today news transmissions can be instantly brought into homes thanks to satellites and other new technologies. For example, the portable, smaller format, broadcast quality cameras now available have helped to send video images to most corners of the world; we see scenes of oppressed people fighting back in Beijing, Bucharest, the Lithuanian city of Vilinius, Moscow, Prague, Haiti's Port-au-Prince, Sarajevo, and the mountains of Afghanistan. The media has had a profound effect on mobilizing oppressed societies—for example, the fall of the Berlin Wall. Radio and television reports can beam live images and sounds to audiences, and even newspapers can process stories in minimal time. The new news technologies seem to have helped create with the Persian Gulf War coverage what we might call the first instant or "participant war" we have ever known. Never before were so many individuals huddled around their television sets to watch military operations, reports of bombings, military briefings, or the latest peace initiatives. Television viewing for war information became a major activity for many worldwide, and appears to have spurred increased consumption of print sources such as newspapers, news magazines, and books on the Middle East and its political leaders.

Despite the public desire for information, media outlets were severely restricted in their access to information during the Persian Gulf War. Only in rare modern-day cases such as the 1971 Pakistan-India War has front line access been impeded to the degree it was here. The limited access was credited largely to U.S. military leaders' perceptions that negative press coverage in Vietnam turned public opinion against military objectives, as we already noted above. The press therefore faced censorship which they had not seen in U.S.-associated military actions since the days of the second World War.

Whether reporters operate under censorship or not, occasionally there are opportunities to provide revealing insights on military actions, secret motives and agendas, and personal attitudes. Even in Vietnam there were very few truly dramatic stories filed, as the odds of a camera being in exactly the right location are sufficiently low.[10] One revealing interview was reported during the early weeks of the Persian Gulf War by the Cable News Network (CNN). It provides an interesting glimpse at the method of modern warfare in which gross, destructive combat has become little more than a game to some, while the true implications of warfare are quickly forgotten. This was a pool press report, with clearance given by military censors. While the interviewed pilot is enthusiastic, his choice of analogy raises larger concerns.

POOL REPORTER:
What's the best thing you've gotten so far? Can you tell us?

PILOT OF U.S. AIR FORCE, A-10 SQUADRON PLANE:
Got a lot of good secondaries, lotto good explosions. Just kind fun. It's *great*! It's a great, ah ya-, it's like an amusement park, almost, but- except they're shootin back at ya so you gotta be real careful,- *smart* about what you do. But there's ah-, in a strange kind of way, there's a *fun-ness* [sic] about it.[11]

The notion that some perceive war as "just a game" is a view that has been echoed from time to time. The grim reality is that with modern media, this may be increasingly more likely now than in the past. This commentary comes out of Persian Gulf War writing.

"It's just unreal to be watching a war unfold like a football game," said Michael G. Gartner, president of NBC News. "You get so wrapped up in covering it that you forget it's a war and you have to stand back and [sic] sometimes and say, 'My God, this is a war'."[12]

The above examples help to demonstrate that the media can serve an important function in the delivery of war news. This is particularly critical if we recognize that many parties enter into a war in a somewhat desperate effort to resolve conflicts. News media can help promote a resolution by opening a channel of communication. While not all can "speak" through the channels of communication, the media do provide broad access to ideas and information. When administered responsibly, the news process can help stimulate community dialogue. Communication is enhanced during war by bringing readers and viewers closer to the front lines. Suddenly, faraway military actions are perceived in different ways. The glories and heroism of battlefields are juxtaposed with the harsh realities of death and destruction. Real people die—men with families, ambitions and dreams. The "enemy" is no longer a faceless target. We are reminded that they too mourn at funerals, have children, and perhaps even subscribe to the same religions as we do. The words and images are indeed powerful. Not only can news influence individual perceptions of a war, but it can also affect public opinion, both for and against a war. Given the potential power of news media in war reporting, we pose the following question: how can the media report wartime activities honestly and objectively, without falling victim to manipulation by those conducting the war? Clear, unbiased, and aggressive war reporting allows everyone to learn about the true issues, and to understand the actual costs that must be paid. By serving as a major channel of communication, the press can even help to restore peace. Regardless of the country from which a journalist hails, national interests can be best served when news is presented in as complete and straightforward a way as possible.

TEN PROPOSALS FOR WAR COVERAGE BY THE NEWS MEDIA

First, whenever there is war, the journalist should strive to tell the story from all sides. It is important to keep perspective. But, above all else, the journalist must be certain of the facts; accuracy is the key to fair and responsible reporting.

1. Report all sides/recognize own bias.
2. Push for access.
3. Seek "non-elite" sources.
4. Don't glorify technology.
5. Seek graphic footage/descriptions.
6. Personalize war stories.
7. Provide background information.
8. Avoid manipulation by newsmakers.
9. Don't make media the main story.
10. Stress/promote peace initiatives.

Figure 1. Ten proposals for war coverage by the news media.

Perhaps the classic story of a journalist lacking objectivity comes from an incident that took place just before the turn of the century. And while the case is now over 90 years old, it is still relevant for today's

media. An examination of many of the tabloids and television news programs criticized in an earlier chapter will attest to its appropriateness.

William Randolph Hearst's biographer, W. A. Swanberg, tells
the story of the *New York Journal*'s involvement in the Spanish-American
war. When reporter Frederick Remington became weary while waiting
in Havana for some activity, he telegraphed Hearst.

> Everything is quiet. There is no trouble here. There is no war. I wish
> to return.— Remington.

The publisher replied:

> Please remain. You furnish the pictures and I'll furnish the war.—
> W. R. Hearst.[13]

When the battleship *Maine* exploded in Havana Harbor, Hearst
set out on a campaign to make news, and to help persuade Americans
that war with Spain was the only alternative, even though it was apparent that it would have been foolhardy for Spain to order the ship's
destruction. The *Journal* gave an average of eight and one-half pages
daily to the story. Swanberg offers a day-by-day account of the headlines:

> February 16: "CRUISER MAINE BLOWN UP IN HAVANA HAR-
> BOR."

> February 17: "THE WARSHIP MAINE WAS SPLIT IN TWO BY AN
> ENEMY'S SECRET INFERNAL MACHINE."

> February 18: "THE WHOLE COUNTRY THRILLS WITH THE WAR
> FEVER."

> February 20 (over a drawing): "HOW THE MAINE ACTUALLY
> LOOKS AS IT LIES, WRECKED BY SPANISH TREACHERY, IN
> HAVANA BAY."

> February 21: "HAVANA POPULACE INSULTS THE MEMORY OF
> THE MAINE VICTIMS."

> February 23: "THE MAINE WAS DESTROYED BY TREACHERY."[14]

President McKinley publicly stated that the explosion on the *Maine* probably came from an accident with its own magazines, and even the U.S. Secretary of the Navy defended Spain. No matter. The *Journal* called all who advocated peace a "traitor" or a "Wall Street profiteer." The *Journal* offered a $50,000 reward to anyone who could provide evidence as to its cause, and established a fund to help erect a memorial to those lost in the explosion.[15] How different is this from the charges made by various U.S. television networks that CNN made deals with the Iraqis to influence which U.S. media organizations would be allowed access to Baghdad during coverage of events during the Persian Gulf conflict, or the charges heard across the United States that CNN was a bit too cooperative in allowing itself to be a vehicle of Iraqi propaganda in that war?[16]

The history of documentary film is filled with examples of directors and producers having difficulty separating themselves from their story. For example, the first American documentary filmmaker, Robert Flaherty, is said to have often allowed his predispositions to interfere with his films' messages. In *Man of Aran* (1934), a documentary on the lives of poor, struggling, island people, Flaherty chose to film activity on only a small portion of the island where people had to cultivate soil from hand-crushed rocks and seaweed, and then literally plant potatoes in small spaces between boulders so that they could raise food for subsistence. He chose to ignore the rest of the island where large landowners lived much more comfortably. He also had islanders retrieve whaling harpoons once used by their ancestors and then trained his subjects in the proper use of the equipment so that he could film heroic scenes for the movie's stunning climax. All because it fit better Flaherty's perceptions of reality.[17]

During the 1960s, filmmakers including Robert Drew, Richard ("Ricky") Leacock, Donn A. Pennebacker, the Albert and David Maysles brothers, Fred Wiseman, and others, reacted, in part, to the long-time concern on bias in the medium when they made documentaries for American television.[18] The movement spread worldwide.[19] These filmmakers proposed that documentaries use certain techniques to help minimize such bias. Hence, the *"cinéma vérité"* (or "direct cinema") movement was peppered with stylistic techniques such as hand-held shots, synchronous sound interviews, the absence of obnoxious movie flood lighting, enormous shooting ratios (sometimes ranging to 50:1, 100:1, and greater), and minimal editing, all designed to maximize the "reality" of the event being portrayed. Unfortunately, they too were criticized by those who noted that vérité films were also biased since the director was still making many editorial decisions both when shooting and editing. Our point is simply that it becomes extremely difficult to remove *auteur* bias, even when one recognizes the problem and attempts to resolve it.

The problem exists in all forms of reporting, be it film, print, or electronic journalism. In news there is an implied assumption of truth and accuracy. Audiences and readers have even come to interpret certain techniques of reporting as signals of straightforwardness—the presentation of opposing points of view, actual transcripts of events, reports without subtly disguised commentary, and unedited video and film footage. Journalists must be aware of these techniques, and use them responsibly.

With the new media there is increasing danger that this long-running tenet of journalism—the stress on accuracy—will be sacrificed in the reporter's or news organization's zeal to get a "scoop." This seems more likely with the "instant" reporting now possible over television and radio. Reports may be based on limited confirmation and presented without an in-depth check of accuracy. War reports are not always as balanced as a *New York Times* story that began by quoting an American general in Vietnam who said of the high Vietcong casualty rate during the first day of a combat wave: "Well, they can't stand many more like that." The report went on to note possible conflicts in the U.S. military version of events by pointing out that while the U.S. was stressing the heavy toll, the Vietcong appeared to be gaining "in morale and prestige."[20] The concern we raise is that incorrect or unbalanced reports may contribute an irreversible impact on public perceptions of events.

Recent examples of rash reports were those of ABC and NBC that chemical weapons had been used on Israel when the first Scud missiles were launched against Tel Aviv and other cities soon after the start of the Persian Gulf War. CBS aired reports of Israeli retaliation following the attack. Press reports, quoting Pentagon sources, that six Iraqi helicopters defected to Saudi Arabia prior to the start of the air battle were another. Still another was the story of how Iraqis threw newborn babies out of incubators, stole the incubators, and left the babies to die. None of these reports were true.[21] Other Persian Gulf examples of misinterpretation of events because the press was being intentionally deceived, or at least subtly misguided, involve the widely used video footage of the gigantic oil spill from Kuwait, and the "smart" bomb stories. In one frequently replayed oil spill shot we saw a cormorant floundering, covered in black oil. In actuality, CBS later revealed that the shot was recorded off the Saudi Arabian coastline, and the footage was not from the Kuwaiti oil spill at all. It came from a totally different Saudi spill, probably caused by allied bombing. It also was disclosed that the much-reported magnitude of the Kuwaiti spill was reported as being many times greater than it actually was.[22] As for the "smart" bombs, they comprised only 7% of all U.S. explosives dropped on the Iraq-Kuwait Theater, while the unguided bombs were a mere 25% accurate. Through continual replaying of selectively provided bombing footage, electronic journalists helped to perpetuate certain myths about the allied military, its abilities, and successes.[23] The question is, who's interests should the press serve—the governments, the military, or the public? By allowing themselves to be manipulated, or placing themselves in situations where they are ripe targets for manipulation, are members of the press not fulfilling their duties to their constituents? It is always difficult to serve more than one master.

When it comes to accuracy, of course, it is always interesting to observe the conflicts in casualty figures in a war. Numbers for one side may be inflated while the other may wish to deflate its total. The goal could be to intentionally mislead citizens, politicians, or members of the military within one of the countries involved in the conflict, to confuse the opposition, to affect world opinion, or perhaps, to achieve most or all of these objectives. While there are no rules as to how honest government/military leaders should be in releasing such information, greater accuracy seems to be found among those nations where a greater value is placed on freedom of expression and the support of a relatively independent press. Such systems tend to be found more often in the West. In Eastern Europe, independent journalism has only recently been discovered, while in Latin America the conditions vary. In the Middle East only Israel has such a tradition. Yet even in the West it is difficult to generalize. We are reminded of years of deception by U.S. officials in reporting American casualties in Vietnam, apparently in an effort to temper negative public opinion at home. While accuracy is sometimes difficult to achieve, war time journalists must continue to try.

Second, during wartime, the media should push for access to events, people, and issues. This can be difficult given the reluctance of many to submit to interviews, due to the perceived security risks that some military and government leaders imagine. Nonetheless, a multiplicity of sources is the journalist's most effective tool. By seeking multiple sources, journalists increase the possibility that they are reporting the true story, not just the one that some leaders would like the public to believe. Potential inaccuracies might also be uncovered. Reliability is maximized when the press fights for access to sources.

There will always be those who are reluctant to answer questions, or will try to deceive, in order to protect themselves or others. But it does not serve the public very well to make only this point of view available. The press must serve as more than an organ of public relations for a select few. Reporters must be aggressive in their pursuit of sources. They must keep asking questions. We note below efforts to dodge reporters' questions on both sides of the Persian Gulf War. The first two examples came out of Baghdad. The last one is an excerpt from the U.S. Central Command briefing on Tuesday, January 22, in Riyadh.

REPORTER:

Can we see the Filipino refugee camp in Baghdad?

OFFICIAL:

You are not allowed permission to go there. (a pause)—And there are no refugee camps in Baghdad.

* * * * *

REPORTER:

Can you explain the rationing system?

OFFICIAL:

What is rationing?[24]

* * * * *

REPORTER:

Can you give us the status of the weather, and whether or not that decreased sorties today to Iraq and Kuwait? Do you have any information about tomorrow's weather?

COLONEL GREG PEPIN:

Well, as I said earlier, weather is a factor in operations. Low clouds, fog—it affects the pilot's ability to detect the target. We want to make sure that the target is identifiable to reduce any type of collateral damage. And so it's going to have an effect, and it's—

REPORTER:

I understand that, sir, but can you tell us what the weather is like? How is the weather? Is it good or bad? I know that it's bad for the pilots when the weather is bad, but is the weather good or bad?

PEPIN:

When the weather is clear, it's good. When it's cloudy, it's bad.

REPORTER:

What do you expect the weather to be tomorrow, sir?

PEPIN:

I'm not a weatherman. I'm afraid I can't answer that.

REPORTER:

I want to go back to the weather question. You were asked a direct question about the weather, not necessarily tomorrow's weather or today's weather. It has passed. The Iraqis know what today's weather is. We were asking has the weather improved, enabling your operations to function better because we know these have been problems in recent days with the weather? Why are you unable to answer that question?

PEPIN:

I'm not a weatherman. I wasn't up there flying.

REPORTER:

Today's weather? Today's weather—past history.

REPORTER:

You're a briefer, Greg. You're a briefer.

ADMIRAL CONRAD C. LAUTENBACHER, JR.:

He just doesn't have that information.[25]

Earlier, we outlined some flaws in journalistic inaccuracy. There is one more error of accuracy, however, that should be addressed here; it is the distortion which comes through omission. We refer to the fact that some news is emphasized while other questions go unasked. Journalists have a responsibility to help set the agenda, not follow one set by others. We turn to the Persian Gulf War for illustration. Many were critical of the narrowness of news coverage during this conflict, particularly given the pre-eminence of the video medium and the emotional involvement the war offered viewers. Schiffer and Rinzler concluded:

> Media restrictions . . . served to shift the debate from vital questions—such as what the position of the United States in the Arab world will be when the troops have come home—toward wide-eyed wonderment at America's technological prowess. Detailed knowledge about the Patriot missile cannot replace information about the political and military execution of the war. As Deborah Amos of National Public Radio has remarked, "What we are seeing is too much of the war, and what we are not seeing is the context of the war."[26]

Journalists should critically evaluate issues and provide the voice of reason. As Said noted in his harsh criticism of Western journalism during the Persian Gulf War:

> The electronic war to destroy Iraq as a lesson in retributive power is now in full swing, the press managing patriotism, entertainment and disinformation without respite. As a topic, civilian 'collateral damage' has been avoided and unasked about; no one discusses how Baghdad, the old Abbasid capital, might survive the appalling rigors of technological warfare, or how the bombing of its water, fuel and electrical supplies which sustain 4 million people, is necessary to this 'surgical' war (a larger replay of Israel's destruction of Beirut). Few commentators have questioned the disproportion of 10,000-plus air sorties against a country roughly the size of California, or explained why a week into the war Iraq's air force,

artillery, Scuds and major armored forces still stand, or even how radio and television still work. That no one asks about the effect and placement of B-52 carpet bombing—a mass murder technique—is doubtless a psy-war achievement, but it is not a credit to the independent press.[27]

While throughout this chapter we provide many examples where the news media have fallen short in their war reporting, the following is a wonderful example of a more responsible approach. Here questions are raised regarding President George Bush's call for a "new world order." Such rhetoric was a key phrase in Bush's publicly stated rationale for military action against Iraq in 1991. The video essay is an important one for it poses legitimate questions about the hallowness of the concept, as employed by the President. The example comes from a CNN "Special Report" telecast on February 8, 1991. The entire report is offered in order to preserve the full impact of the telecast.

SHARYL ATTKINSON:
You've probably heard U.S. President Bush say many times that he has a vision of a new world order, nations working together in harmony. Critics say the term, *new world order*, is just a catch phrase, a cliché. CNN's Frank Sesno reports.

FRANK SESNO:
Of the many reasons given for going to the war in the Persian Gulf, one rings out for its soaring, if vague, ideals...President Bush calls it—the *new world order*.

BUSH:
It is a big idea-, a new world order-, where diverse nations—, are drawn together in common cause-, to achieve the universal aspirations of mankind. Peace- and security-, freedom- and the rule of law.

SESNO:
The President first spoke of a new world order amid the *collapse* of communism in Eastern Europe, the revolutions of 1989. But critics observe it is more than the absence of just the cold war. It is building new institutions to manage crisis and change. In Paris last November thirty-five countries signed on to the challenge. But the new world order is often invoked, seldom defined. It's lofty principles can change with the landscape, sometimes reminiscent of Woodrow Wilson's League of Nations utopia.

BUSH:
Now my *vision* of a new world order, ah-, foresees a United Nations with a revitalized peace keeping function.

SESNO:
Sometimes reminiscent of Theodore Roosevelt's "big stick" diplomacy.

BUSH:
And when we win, and we will-, we will have- (applause) We will have taught a dangerous dictator, and *any* tyrant, tempta, tempted to follow in his footsteps, that the U.S. has a new *credibility*. And that what we say, goes. (crowd noises, cheers, general approval)

CHARLES LICHTENSTEIN (FORMER DEPUTY U.S. AMBASSADOR TO U.N.):
I think the danger of saying that sort of thing, without knowing *exactly* what you mean by it is that—a lot of people, including-friends of ours, are probably beginning to be a little bit worried about what begins to sound almost like, and here again I use capital letters, Pax Americana.

SESNO:
The world's police men. U.S. officials *insists* [sic] that's not what America wants, or intends.

DICK CHENEY (U.S. DEFENSE SECRETARY):
To play policemen to the world implies that somehow you're going to get involved in every conflict, everywhere, where ever it arrives. We have *no* such- idea of trying to do that.

PETER RODMAN (FORMER NSC OFFICIAL):
We would not be succeeding if we didn't have the cooperation of many others. And I think people rightly pay tribute to the President, for- for multilateral, ah diplomacy, that can be conducted in pulling this coalition together. That I think is a model for the future.

SESNO:
But that future is clouded.-
The Soviet Union, pivotal to the new world order, has lurched to the right,- its ethnic tensions- bleeding sores, its economy collapsing, its people, like its politics, strained almost to the breaking point. It is a shaky foundation on which to build a new international structure.

The concepts vagueness lends itself to hyperbole.

JAMES BAKER (U.S. SECRETARY OF STATE):
We are really at ah,- at a hinge of history, if you will, in *terms* of the *possibility* of a new order.

SESNO:
And to criticism.

LICHTENSTEIN:
I think it is a cliché. It is, it is a catch phrase,- to describe something that's emerging.

SESNO:
To many a new world order also implies far more than the President is willing to embrace. Fundamental change with a debt ridden developing world. A new economic equation based on free trade and open markets. A far more active approach to problems of the global environment.
(gunfire)
In the environment of this war, it's clear the world has changed. But how much, and how durably, remains a question.—
President Bush's new world order is very much an evolving idea. He may be keeping it vague deliberately. In any case it is easier to invoke than it is easier to explain,- or to implement. Frank Sesno, CNN, the White House.[28]

Third, to ensure a complete story, journalists should avoid the overuse of elites as news sources. This means that efforts must be made to seek out different types of "authorities" and "experts" when writing stories.

A major problem in the use of elites as principal or sole news sources is demonstrated in another study by one of the present authors. The use of elites was examined as a narrative device in American television network news stories about air crashes. The results were that such coverage appears to lend itself to maintenance of the "status quo" in society. Knowingly or unknowingly, such source reliance may help to deliver a clear message:

Our analysis . . . suggests that these stories are well suited to develop and sustain simple, consensual notions about the social order. There is little in such stories which would provoke questioning of the social order. . . . [T]hemes imply that though a deviant event of some magnitude has occurred, we can rest assured that it was an isolated, random event which had a specific natural cause and which has been (or is being) adequately dealt with by authorities. Therefore there is no need to worry . . . People in authority are doing all they can . . . A symbiotic relationship appears to be in effect between certain societal norms and the "messages" these television news stories are delivering to viewers.

> News . . . may serve to perpetuate naive beliefs about the safety of air travel. Evidence which contradicts such beliefs is either ignored or subordinated to themes which emphasize that crashes are highly deviant events . . . The average viewer probably seeks to have his or her confidence . . . restored. The stories are structured to do this quite effectively. Viewers most likely do not want nor do they expect a detailed, critical analysis of the elites who control air travel. They simply want to be assured that these elites can continue to be trusted. The stories provide such assurance.[29]

While air crashes and war are different phenomena, each may be reported in similar ways. When critical events occur in the military theater of operation, they are often just as spontaneous as an accident or natural disaster. In addition, military leadership might easily try to control the release of information for either national security or public relations reasons. This would mean that military and government leaders may be the only news sources who are available and ready/allowed to talk. While this was especially apparent from the start of the Persian Gulf crisis, it has been a concern of wartime reporters in the United States, to one degree or another, as far back as the War of 1812.[30] The immediacy of reporting in the battle over Kuwait focused attention on the problem in 1991.

In the absence of opportunities to collaborate or weigh information and in the zeal to get a "jump" on the competition, journalists may be tempted to report the story "as is." We have already demonstrated above some of the problems which arise when news is reported too quickly, without proper checks. Such an approach involves a high level of risk.

Instead of going with a story too early, multiple sources should be consulted. These could include lower ranking officials, third-party diplomatic sources, academics, authors, members of think tanks, and other general population observers. In addition, better reporter expertise would be helpful. Just as we argued earlier that not knowing the language is a hinderance to good international journalism, limited knowledge of the subject may be even more devastating.

In many countries the model for journalism education, broadcast or print, often emphasizes trade practices rather than strong intellectual growth. Students and the profession itself help encourage this by calling for still stronger "professional" training programs. The strong interest in such an orientation can be seen by examining many college and university catalogues or by perusing almost any issue of the American journalism education journal, *Journalism Educator*. It is also often the subject of formal and informal discussions at academic conferences in the field. The danger with such a perspective is that young journalists can be trained in style, but not necessarily in substance. The style is typically "the way we've always done it" approach in which norms of the past are perpetuated over the fostering of other ideals.[31] The tendency seems so severe that numerous U.S. journalism programs are reporting major enrollment declines in their own journalism history classes when this non-"hands-on" course is not required of majors. Students reportedly see little relevance in such coursework.[32]

Ironically, some believe (including successful journalists) that a good journalist does not even need formal university training in the "art of journalism." That will come later. Rather, the argument goes, it is best to learn how to effectively *communicate*, regardless of the "channel." One key to effective communication is the possession of ideas and knowledge. This point, of course, has implications beyond the reporting of wartime events and issues. While not everyone can control, or at least gain ready access, to media, they should have the right to receive information and opposing viewpoints. Such a communication philosophy has been espoused by UNESCO in a World Information and Communication Order related-dialogue labeled the "right to communicate."[33] Suffice it to say that the media can indeed be powerful, and they should be used wisely. Journalists have the responsibility to help protect this freedom.

Fourth, the media would be wise to avoid the glorification of technology when reporting war news. Admittedly this is difficult to do. Technology tends to be important to journalists. The entire profession owes its existence to technology. It was the technological breakthrough of the printing press á la Johan Gutenberg that moved the book from a limited-audience to a "mass" medium. Quicker newspaper layouts, instant access to data bases, and instantaneous transmission of television news images have helped define and guide the journalism process of today. Yet this technological orientation may have its disadvantages. One may be that journalists are more likely to become some of the strongest advocates of technology. When it comes to reporting wartime events, journalists might be tempted to report technological developments in an elevated manner, be it Patriot missiles, AWACs, Stealth fighters, or various "Star War" technologies of today, or the German submarines and their V-2 missiles during the first and second World Wars.

This has become an increasingly greater problem in recent years. Persian Gulf War coverage has become the classic example. So mesmerized was the public by the computer chip arms technology that it appeared as if journalists often lost sight of the true story they were covering. Television viewers could follow a "smart" missile as it was propelled and maneuvered toward its target. The released footage was always of a perfect hit. Rarely did we see any human activity surrounding the target before the explosion. Yet such coverage shifts attention away from issues such as individual suffering and pain. People are inside those buildings that have been targeted. The mass destruction brought on by these bombs and missiles is phenomenal; victims close to the center are left beyond recognition, their limbs and flesh are scattered in small pieces. It is not a pleasant picture. Such harsh realities can be easily ignored when we concentrate on technology alone. The atmosphere of such coverage tends to resemble the self-glorification found when heavy arms are paraded down streets during May Day ceremonies. The latest wartime technology can be reported as information without the journalist also standing in awe of these military advances.

Fifth, as inhumane as it may appear, *the press should not avoid the use of graphic footage;* that which can be called *"blood and guts" stories*, just because they are considered repulsive by some. While repulsive, such perspectives do provide vivid glimpses of the horrors of war. War is not pretty, and its cost can be phenomenal (in terms of money and human lives). By providing such scenes, the public will be forced to address the ugly realities brought on by war. Of course, journalists must balance the presentation of such images with the requirements of good taste. This should not be an opportunity to profit from the war by displaying sensational material. "Yellow journalism" is not what we have in mind here.[34]

In the 1960s and early 1970s television was credited with helping to make the Vietnam fighting a daily "living room war."[35] Grim images were readily available for family consumption. One report stands out because it is credited with helping to change the course of war reporting about Vietnam. In 1966, CBS newsman Morley Safer shocked millions of American viewers when he reported on an operation with American Marines who marched into the Vietnamese village of Cam Ne and occupied it without resistance. The Marines then proceeded to level the village. They threw grenades and used flame throwers against the civilian population who cowered from their attackers. Thatched huts were burned. The Marines were about to torch a deep hole from which voices of women and children were clearly being emitted when the South Vietnamese cameraman, Ha Thuc Can, intervened and began arguing with the Marines. He was the only one present who spoke both English and Vietnamese (he also spoke French). He eventually persuaded the civilians to come out of the hole. A dozen or so lives were saved. Safer was shocked and dumbfounded. Somewhat embarrassed in having witnessed the whole scene, he filed the story right then and there. Not only were CBS newspeople taken aback, but so too were CBS executives, viewers, and the President of the United States, Lyndon Johnson (not everyone, including Johnson, were necessarily pleased with the story). The story was shocking; some thought it was also unpatriotic. But from that moment forward, Americans started to receive a different version of the war from journalists.[36] Years later when the United States was about to enter a different war (the Persian Gulf War), many resolved that the military should not make a similar mistake again by giving journalists the access they enjoyed in Vietnam.[37]

Also included here would be the need to portray war as the horror that it is. As many have said, "war is hell." Included in this charge would, out of necessity, be the notion that the media should not seek to glorify war and its methods. Perhaps the best example of this is when war activities are reduced to a mere "game" level. Nowhere was this more apparent than in the 1991 Gulf War where the widely televised "high tech" imagery of state-of-the-art jet fighters, and precision bombs and cruise missiles (many with miniature video cameras at the front of the war head in order to document a target "hit"), made the images more like a video arcade game than news footage. As Bella Abzug, former U.S. congresswoman, observed, "Well, I have the sense that I'm watching ah-ah Nintendo game on television rather than getting some of the more fundamental information as to what is happening."[38] She was referring to the popular home video game with which many children (and their parents) worldwide were quite familiar.

Of course, another pitfall in covering war is the temptation to make it appear too entertaining. This has become of increasingly greater concern now that television has become so influential in war coverage. With television considered primarily an entertainment medium in some societies, it is all too likely that the industry will try to package and sell war coverage in much the same way as it does other programming. We have seen this often in the United States. Television stations and networks hire market researchers to make recommendations on how the news can be more appealing (i.e., more profitable).[39] At one U.S. network, ABC, both the Sports and News divisions have been under the leadership of one person, Roone Arledge, for many years. While ABC News has flourished under his leadership, and even gained in prestige, it is nonetheless interesting how similar an American television network perceives the two types of programming. During the Persian Gulf War, the U.S. television networks, ABC, CBS, and NBC dropped plans to offer continuous war coverage when it became clear that the war would not be an extremely short one, played out in "primetime." Some programmers were said to be disappointed that the war could not be televised with the drama and imagery viewers knew from *Rambo* movies (a series of vigilante movies starring Sylvester Stallone). Some critics charge that in American media it is more and more difficult to distinguish news from entertainment. In evidence are the "happy talk" formats of local television news shows, emphasizing story and newscaster entertainment qualities rather than information; the many "soft" news programs and columns on daytime and primetime network television; radio news which has been reduced to mere "headline" service, when broadcast at all; and newspaper tabloids and "gossip" magazines. Let us look at one war news report, a Persian Gulf news story by CNN's Brian Jenkins:

> They are the gun slingers of the U.S. navy. (sound of plane landing) The flyers who shoot their fighter planes *on* and *off* a floating flattop. (plane engine) And the stagecoach that carries these 'top guns' to their showdowns in the sky is a mighty big target on the water. The gun slingers give it good protection, but the stagecoach still needs someone, riding shotgun. In Operation Desert Storm, the job of riding shotgun for the Carrier Roosevelt, belongs to the guided missile cruiser, Richmond K. Turner. And the men of the Turner insist they can knock down anything thrown in their direction . . .[40]

The above narrative offers descriptions which appear to be borrowed from a dime-store novel on the American "Wild West." It conjures up images of cowboys and shootouts. The genre is a familiar one to television, and has been a staple of its programming for many years. The choice of such language may be telling. While the reporter probably thought it was a clever association, and it is, implicit in this seemingly innocent choice of analogy is a reminder of narrative elements that seem to be well suited for television. The use of the term, "top gun," even helps to draw parallels to a Hollywood movie by the same name—a celebration of fighter pilots—starring Tom Cruise; presumably such an association was intended.

Some are concerned that graphic footage, photographs, and stories may have a negative effect on audience members. Concern has even been raised that such presentations may have had negative effects on U.S. audiences exposed to gruesome images on Vietnam week after week in the American media. Such claims have been discredited, however. Research suggests that audiences were, in fact, only rarely exposed to these images. It seems that while audiences can remember war images such as the film of South Vietnam's national police chief Brig. General Nguyen Ngoe Loan's execution of a Viet Cong officer with a pistol to the head, the Buddhist monk setting himself on fire on June 9, 1963, and the small girl escaping from a napalm attack in 1972, these images were exceptions rather than the rule. These observations were made for both television and the print media.[41]

Despite their inherently repulsive nature, some of these images have the ability to "educate" viewers to the true horrors of war. They show the "enemy" as individuals, and not as some nonhuman strategic military targets. The following descriptions of stories serve as examples. The first is from the American cameraman A.K. Dawson who was allowed to take his newsreel camera behind German lines during World War II. The second describes a CBS report filed during the Vietnam war. The third is from a Reuters report filed on the rebel uprising in Mogadiahu, Somalia on January 29, 1991.

> The camera was operated from behind the wall of a dismantled house which afforded partial protection for the operator. The film shows several men in a trench and firing steadily, when a stray bullet strikes one of them in the head. The soldier starts with the shock, and then slowly relaxing his hold on his rifle falls back and his eyes close. A companion several feet away crawls to him, administers first aid as best he can and then, taking him in his arms and boldly exposing himself to the enemy's fire, carries him away.[42]

* * * * *

> . . . CBS correspondent Robert Schakne filmed a three-minute essay on a body count after a bloody battle near the Cambodian border. Relentlessly pictured on the screen: a jumbled mound of 48 dead Viet Cong piled like slaughtered animals in a helicopter net.
>
> The lens wandered over the enemy faces as they peered vacantly through the webbing. A muddy foot dangled among the carcasses. Two GI's lumbered up with a dead VC and hurled him like cordwood atop the pile. The limp body slid off and tumbled to the ground. Finally, the helicopter lifted the net from the ground and flew off to dump its cargo into a mass grave. "In combat," Schakne told viewers, "there are no niceties. No one says a prayer here, or holds a funeral service. These had been living, breathing men yesterday. Today, they are just a sanitation problem."[43]

* * * * *

> Surrounded by pools of drying blood and dirty bandages, a man with a bullet wound in his leg sat screaming on the hospital table.
>
> On the grass outside, more wounded were brought in and laid out among those already dead, covered over with bloody sheets.
>
> The mass graves at this hospital in Mogadishu bear witness to

thousands killed in a month of street battles between rebels of the
United Somali Congress and troops loyal to the ousted Somali
President, Mohammed Siad Barre. . .[44]

The narcotizing dysfunction of mass communication holds that
exposure to some media images may have a negative effect on audience
members. Lazarsfeld and Merton suggest that "this vast supply of communications may elicit only superficial concern with the problems of
society, and this superficiality often cloaks mass apathy."[45] As a result,
the increased rate of information flow may cause us to be less willing to
take specific steps to resolve problems. While this is a real concern, we
do not appear to be in any great danger of having graphic media coverage negatively influence our perceptions of war. The number of cases in
which grim images are offered are really quite rare. If anything these
images offer dramatic reminders of the horrors of war rather than a negative campaign that closes our minds to such images. After all, death
and destruction is a byproduct of war. If people wish to support a war,
they should be reminded of its true horrors and ultimately grim outcome. People die in war. Whether they are portrayed as martyrs, patri-
ots, freedom fighters, or upholders of democracy, dead people are still
dead people. Media has a responsibility to remind their audiences of the
reality. Responsible decision making will be less likely to occur if they
do not. Even a 1942 U.S intelligence report suggested that wartime cartoon strips needed to be "straightforward (in the) portrayal of what war
involves—loss, pain, and death..."[46]

Not all journalists feel comfortable in presenting stories such as
the Robert Schanke report. NBC had the same footage as CBS, but chose
not to air it. It was reported that executives felt that it was "totally repulsive." Huntley-Brinkley executive producer Robert Northshield also
rejected the opportunity to run film of souvenir-hunting U.S. Marines
cutting off the ears of dead Viet Cong. "The evening news is viewed in a
family situation. My responsibility is to tell them about the war. But I
can't use this as a weapon and say, 'I'll show you something that will
make you sick'," said Northshield. Schakne defended such coverage by
noting that people needed to be informed. "It's nothing like a John
Wayne movie."[47] We certainly agree with Schakne.

Sixth, the press should offer meaningful and well-written stories on
"regular people." By doing so the press can offer a truly personalized
account of the war. While we argued for the use of non-elite sources
above, our point here is quite different; we are talking about human
interest stories about people who would not normally be in the limelight. They may be victims or they may be innocent observers whose
lives are cast into disarray as a consequence of a war. They may be people with little food or no shelter because of the war. Perhaps they are

families who must cope with the realities of war when members are called on to fight; and they grieve when those realities—spouses, sons, and fathers dying—hit home. They may be small children who find themselves orphaned because the war came too close to their homes, a war they are not yet old enough to understand, but with consequences that are very real indeed. Such stories allow war journalists to move beyond formal and antiseptic coverage of those facts and figures typically released through "official sources." War news could then provide emotional reference points; the experiences of war could be felt by all. Suddenly the victims of war don faces. It is no longer a vague event in some faraway land.

A wonderful example of such reporting comes from a story written by the *New York Times* reporter Chris Hedges who was one of the Western reporters held by the Iraqis following the Allied-Iraqi cease fire in March 1991. In his story we get rare insights into the Iraqi soldier as human being:

> After our interrogation we were left with our guards. Over the next four days about a dozen men would guard us. However stern as they tried to be in the beginning, their curiosity and our unceasing efforts to find out about their families and their lives won them over. . .
>
> Very few spoke English, and my Arabic, however faltering, became an invaluable bridge between us.
>
> These men were tired of the Hussein Government and nearly a decade of war. They bore me no personal malice as an American, or if they did they hid it well. Many talked about one day visiting New York, and I have a pocketful of Iraqi phone numbers that I am to call for invitations to dinners and homes, after the unrest—or perhaps, they meant, after Saddam Hussein. . . .
>
> All of the soldiers who had little to eat, made sure we ate first. Although this meant only having a piece of bread or a handful of canned vegetables, it was a generous gesture from men who had not had much solid food for days, if not weeks.
>
> We spent our four nights in Iraq in four different locations. On the third night we were in a room playing baat [an Iraqi parlor game] with the soldiers. Their AK-47 assault rifles lay against a wall and they sat on the floor with us, laughing and gesturing. An officer walked in and ordered the men back to their posts.
>
> They suddenly picked up their weapons and distanced themselves from us. All they wanted was normal human discourse, and it was them I felt sorry for as they resumed their roles as soldiers, not us.
>
> The next morning at first light I awoke to see one of the soldiers carefully laying an extra blanket over the six of us who were sleeping on the floor.

> The very weaknesses I tried to banish in myself, the longing to
> see my wife, my son and my family, I exploited in the guards. I
> learned the names of their children and their wives. I asked them
> what they wanted to do in peacetime. . .[48]

A potential problem in doing human interest stories is the possibility of misuse. There are many examples of newspaper and television journalists seeking out human interest stories for their sensational appeal, a kind of journalistic sideshow designed for viewers who wish to gawk at the miseries and misfortunes of others. The journalist must consider the ethical implications of covering some material, particularly when subjects' privacy could be violated through the reporting process (we do not refer to government leaders or members of the armed forces here; they would be considered public figures.).

Subjects should not be mistreated or otherwise abused. This can happen easily in journalism, and the next illustration comes from a different kind of warfare—urban street gang fighting. Nonetheless, it provides a good example of the larger journalistic problem of human subject abuse. Our case comes from a television news report aired almost 20 years ago on CBS's New York City owned and operated station, WCBS. It was shown on the station's local evening news program and Ed Bradley was anchorperson. The story was about a young boy who had been killed in a gang fight that day. For some reason authorities could not locate the boy's mother, but they did learn what time she normally arrived home by city bus. The police went to the corner bus stop to meet her, and the television camera crews followed. The woman stepped off the bus, and was immediately met by police and cameras. The police informed her of the murder. She went berserk, crying and screaming. The cameras continued to roll. The effects were devastating. When the program was returned to the studio there was at first silence; then Bradley made an apology about having to show such footage. The station quickly broke for commercials.

The problem with stories of this type is that a camera or a note pad do not give journalists the right to take advantage of subjects. While most journalists would probably agree, there are always the demands of deadlines, pressures from an editor, and the excitement that comes when a reporter has found and captured a unique event, highly charged with human emotions. In these situations questionable material may be used for the sake of the story. This becomes a particular problem since journalists do not have a broadly accepted set of professional standards as do other professions (minimum education, code of ethics, industry enforcement of standards, etc.).

Journalists can also show callous behavior by reporting on tragedies without making an effort to help the victims they are covering (when possible and practical). While one can argue for ethnographic protection of people and cultures, this argument hardly applies to news reporting. Saigon medical personnel claimed that reporters would come to interview civilian napalm victims during the Vietnam war thereby exemplifying an insensitive attitude. If there were none, they would leave, sometimes stepping on the sick who were there. Even if emergencies were in progress, the reporters were said to have rarely offered help.[49] Such acts not only shame the entire profession of journalism, but they also jeopardize others in their attempts to get future stories.

Seventh, the press can offer a variety of story topics including background reports. They should not simply dwell on the events of the last 24 hours. This might help the media to enhance its learning function among audience members. Possibilities for background reporting would be historical sketches on cultures, military history, geopolitics, or in-depth analyses of current issues and debates.

As noted earlier in Chapter 4, audience retention of information may be enhanced through improved story structure. A substantial body of literature speaks to reader/viewer comprehension. The research involves information processing concepts and holds that learning, which is considered somewhat inert can be enhanced when social context, the audience's earlier experience, and interest levels are considered.[50] Learning can be affected by numerous situations including clashing visual and verbal content; inadequate repetition of main story points; incomplete details on context and causation; poor labeling and summaries; brevity; confusing arrangement of similar stories; inadequate or distracting visual content; and content that is too abstract.[51] Many of these concerns can be attended to through reporting techniques such as improved analysis and synthesis of war-related issues. Such approaches are appropriate for both electronic and print journalism.

Observers often have difficulty cutting through the array of diplomatic and military events and stated objectives by parties on either side in order to identify the true causes for entry into a war. We saw this in the Persian Gulf War as government leaders and the press argued as to whether the U.S. interests in Kuwait were largely driven by: (1) a true belief in democracy and the oppression of seemingly innocent people; (2) a fear of the implications on the world oil market with Iraq in control of such a major portion of the world's oil reserves; (3) a fear of the phenomenal military buildup that was managed in such a relatively short length of time, making Iraq the fourth largest military power in the world; or perhaps (4) a combination of all of these.[52] The press can help us better explore and understand such issues. It can help us master the assortment of possible interpretations. This could ultimately lead to a better informed population, and more enlightened decision making.

We can look to other armed conflicts for similar debates about the true reasons a country enters into a war. Often these discussions continue long after the final gun has been fired. Following World War I, to take one case, diplomatic historians found that they were in considerable disagreement over what caused the United States to enter that war, given its declared neutrality from the Summer of 1914 when hostilities first began, to April 1917 when Congress supported President Wilson's request that the U.S. enter the war in support of the allies. During that period the U.S. expressed concern over the British naval blockade designed to intercept vessels of neutral nations trading with Germany. Germany retaliated with a blockade of its own, and their target area was the water that surrounded Great Britain. Wilson eventually decided that the German submarine fleet represented a greater threat to U.S. interests.

The two most widely read accounts supporting Wilson's decision and stated objectives are said to be those of the U.S. Ambassador to England, Walter Hines Page, and the President's close friend and advisor, Colonel Edward House.[53] Each agreed that Wilson's decision was wisest, and that Germany's behavior was the most serious threat to American democracy. Slightly later, however, Professor Harry Elmer Barnes came to the conclusion that "American neutrality throughout the European conflict would have been the 'peace without victory' . . . (leading to) a negotiated peace treaty made by two relative equals." Barnes goes on to suggest that if the United States had "remained neutral from the beginning, the negotiated peace would probably have saved the world from the last two terrible years of war." Thus, he was faulting Wilson on his misreadings of the situation and the outcome of the Versailles peace treaty, which had been credited with a failure to ensure peace in the region.[54]

Reporting on general topics and debates and providing background material can only help cultivate a better informed population. This, after all, is considered one of the major functions of journalism when it operates in democratic societies.[55]

Eighth, the media must be aware of attempts toward press manipulation by newsmakers. This will become a greater problem as individuals are now increasingly aware of the persuasive power of media. Much of what is reported each day falls into the categories of "press release journalism"—stories prepared by the newsmakers and shared with the news media via press releases, and similar orchestrated events such as press conferences, scheduled speeches, and news briefings. In all of these the newsmakers attempt to capture the attention of the public, or at least to control how, and to what degree, the public learns about certain events, intentions, and actions. Common users of this approach are government bodies, corporations, and public interest groups. This is perhaps the most customary vehicle for delivering official information regarding wars, whether it is information on the latest offensive, or just an update on casualty figures. Terrorist groups also have found the media to be a good outlet for "staged" events and have used it in an effort to mold public sentiments, both during wartime and in peacetime..

The media, of course, are powerful vehicles of persuasion, and have been effectively used to influence public opinion for centuries. Many examples can be cited of governments using the mass media to help promote its war cause. Documentary films and newsreels exemplify the potential media has for effective public opinion manipulation by government leaders. As John Greirson, the British filmmaker who is considered the father of documentary film, once put it, "I look on cinema as a pulpit . . . "

During World War II, documentaries and newsreels were effectively used by the Americans, the British, the Germans, the Japanese, and others. One documentary, made by the German filmmaker Leni Riefenstahl, became an exercise in the tribute and glorification of Adolf Hitler. The images of *Triumph des Willens* (*Triumph of the Will*, 1935) were almost mystical as she filmed parades of spade-touting German laborers marching past Hitler. They stood in neat rows stretched across the horizon listening to one of Hitler's electrifying speeches. The score was Wagerian-like. This powerful film encouraged many Germans to follow Hitler and his cause.

Regarding the power of the medium, Riefenstahl wrote:

> The Führer has recognized the importance of cinema. Where else in the world have the film's inherent potentialities to act as the chronicler and interpreter of contemporary events been recognized in so far-sighted a manner? . . .
>
> That the Führer has raised film-making to a position of such pre-eminence testifies to his prophetic awareness of the unrealized suggestive power of this art form. One is familiar with documentaries. Governments have ordered them and political parties have used them for their ends. But the belief that a true and genuinely powerful national experience can be kindled through the medium of film, this belief originated in Germany.[56]

As for the war effort itself, each side had its share of screen credits. In Britain, Humphrey Jennings proved to be a master at filmmaking. The most popular American-produced film series was "Why We Fight," directed by the late Frank Capra.[57] Some Japanese titles were *Sora no Shimpei* (*Divine Soldiers of the Sky*, 1942), *Marei Senki* (*Malayan War Record*, 1942), and *Gochin* (*Sunk Instantly*, 1943). In Germany there were films such as *Feldzug in Polen* (*Campaign in Poland*, 1940), *Sieg im Westen* (*Victory in the West*, 1941), and *Der Ewige Jude* (*The Eternal Jew*, 1940). A portion of one German newsreel covering a filmed (apparently staged for the camera) Goebbels speech is cited below:

GOEBBELS:
The English maintain that the German people are resisting the government's measures for a total war.

CROWD:
Lies! Shame!

GOEBBELS:
They do not want total war, say the British, but capitulation.

CROWD:
Sieg heil!

GOEBBELS:
Do you want total war?

CROWD:
Yes!

GOEBBELS:
Do you want a war more total and more ruthless than we could ever have first imagined?

CROWD:
Yes!

GOEBBELS:
Are you ready to stand with the Führer as a phalanx of the homeland behind the fighting Wehrmacht, to continue the struggle unshaken and with savage determination, through all vicissitudes of fate until victory is in our hands?

CROWD:
Yes! . . .

GOEBBELS:
You have proclaimed to our enemies what they need to know to prevent them from indulging in false dreams and illusions . . .[58]

Another case of wartime propaganda spanned two World Wars
and came in the form of the comic strip. During the First World War the
U.S. Committee on Public Information was established under the guid-
ance of journalist George Creel. The CPI created a Bureau of Cartoons,
and this office's purpose to stimulate public opinion in support of the
war. They did so by offering weekly suggestions to artists and cartoon-
ists who were drawing for newspapers.[59] The CPI was so effective overall that it was credited with ". . . stir[ing] up hatred of all things
German."[60] U.S. propaganda efforts were reorganized during World
War II. First there was the Office of Facts and Figures (OFF), and then
the Office of War Information (OWI). The OWI was concerned with all
media and its charge included the "formulation and implementation,"
". . . through the use of press, radio, motion pictures, and other media, of
information programs designed to facilitate the development of an
informed and intelligent understanding, at home and abroad, of the status and progress of the war effort and of the war policies, activities, and
aims of the government."[61] The comic strip, of course, fell under the
OWI's jurisdiction during this period, and their general popularity made
them a particularly prime medium for communicating the American
point of view. Buck Rogers fought interplanetary invaders called
"Yellow Men," and Superman addressed the U.S. Congress on the plight
of Fascism. Typically, "American forces were glorified simplistically as
'gallant men' or 'heroes all' fighting for honor and glory. Heroes such as
'Don Winslow of the Navy,' 'Navy Bob Steel,' 'Dickie Dare,' and 'Biff
Baker' effortlessly outwitted the enemy." The enemy was presented as
stereotypical: "Japanese are fierce, toothy, bespectacled, and cruel.
German officers are bald, tall, thin-faced, with a military stiffness.
German soldiers are inclined to be fat, loutish, sloppy, decidedly differ-
ent from the 'typical American boys'."[62]

A more recent case of media manipulation occurred during the
United States's military invasion of Grenada. The operation was conducted to "rescue" American medical students who were enrolled in
school there. At first it appeared that the U.S. action was extremely well-
orchestrated and executed. The U.S. "victory" was a strong asset in
Ronald Reagan's re-election campaign of 1984. It was only some time
after the invasion that the truth of the battle became known. The loss of
lives among U.S. servicemen could be attributed to poor planning.
Military morale was terribly low. Civilians of Grenada were needlessly
endangered, and the students who were saved may have never been in
any actual danger. All of this was billed as a battle to help save democra-

cy. Perhaps after Vietnam the United States needed that which would appear to be a staggering win. In actuality, it appears that the Grenada victory fell far short of such a goal.

In 1983 the U.S. Public Broadcasting Service (PBS) aired a 13-part series *Viet Nam: Television History*. It was hailed as being extremely well researched and skillfully produced. It was the recipient of numerous journalistic awards including six Emmys. Almost two years later a rebuttal program was broadcast on PBS's *Inside Story*, sponsored by the conservative group, Accuracy in Media. The program, hosted by Charleton Heston, criticized the earlier program for being less than straightforward on the role of the press in their portrayal of the 1968 Tet offensive, and then resurrected footage of Jane Fonda visiting North Viet Nam. Fortunately, the show did make some more enlightened charges, commenting on the overemphasis on U.S. troop drug and morale problems, and the underemphasis on North Vietnamese brutalities following the U.S. withdrawal. Nevertheless, major funding for the "rebuttal" came, in part, at the suggestion of friendly Reagan administration personnel. Additionally, a special screening was sponsored at the White House, and PBS officials were invited. As Time magazine noted, "Such interest at the top levels of Government . . . can hardly be ignored by a TV service depending on federal funds for its existence." So when PBS defied its policies and ran the independently produced show, critics understood, although they still lamented the move. *Vietnam* series executive producer, Richard Ellison commented: "If PBS feels that a reply to [the] series is appropriate, why does AIM get a monopoly? . . . It's a precedent that I consider dangerous in and of itself, and also it is part of a general atmosphere of pressure on the media from the right." NBC's John Chancellor echoed similar feelings: "Allowing your facility to be used for such a pointed attack from a particular ideological point of view seems to me bad journalism and bad broadcasting."[63] This and the institutional reactions/pressures that came after the Morley Safer story reported above was aired serve as valuable reminders of the constraints that are present, even in a society where a "free press" operates.[64] The danger of media manipulation, however, can even be less obvious than this.

Commenting on Vietnam War coverage, Roger Grimsby of KGO television, San Francisco, observed that "There are almost no correspondents who speak Vietnamese or who are really up on the political situation. The military are very cooperative and will take you anywhere. . . . So the military angle wins out."[65] In such an environment, newsmaker manipulation can be subtle, but extremely effective.

Ninth, a danger arises when media or newspeople become the story. In the last section we spoke of the dangers that arise when outside sources attempt to manipulate the press. Here we have potential manipulation by newspeople, whether intentional or not. The threat is a diversion of public attention from the real issues of war. While how the media cover war is indeed a valid topic, care must be taken that it does not become the only story, or overshadows other issues.

One case of media becoming the principal story occurred during the Persian Gulf War, a war that took on much of its character due to the instant and continuous television coverage it received. The leader in such coverage was the American cable news network, CNN. For a long time CNN was the only Western television organization allowed to remain in Baghdad. At times CNN provided the only coverage of critical events during the war, such as live coverage of the first night of allied bombing of Baghdad, and an exclusive interview with Saddam Hussein. So thorough was CNN's coverage that both the U.S. military and Saddam Hussein were said to have watched it constantly to learn of late breaking news that their respective intelligence communities had not yet uncovered.[66] This placed CNN in a vulnerable position for it clearly was the intention of the Baghdad regime to use the network in an effort to manipulate Western public opinion. This was possible since most movements of the crew were controlled by the Iraqi government. Still, the presence of a media voice, with or without censorship, was considered a positive that outweighed many negatives. Some Americans questioned CNN's patriotism, but others noted that the allies were perhaps just as manipulative through their press policies. The following news report reflects some of the tensions:

> The Cable News Network has added an additional caveat to its televised news reports from Baghdad informing viewers that its reporter Peter Arnett, the only correspondent from a major Western television network still working in the Iraqi capital, is unable to select or verify the news he is allowed to broadcast . . .

> A spokeswoman for CNN said that while the network had no indication that the report was anything but what it appeared to be, the network was concerned with accentuating the controls under which it operated, especially as subsequent reports may be getting increasingly graphic as the war continues . . .[67]

The other U.S. networks (ABC, CBS, and NBC) began to question how CNN had positioned itself in such an influential role for the Gulf War coverage. The U.S. television networks, which were excluded from this access, were critical of CNN:

> Friction between the broadcast networks and the Cable News Network escalated yesterday when two network news executives

accused CNN of making special concessions to the Iraqis in exchange for CNN's special access to news from Baghdad in the first three weeks of war in the Persian Gulf.

A CNN executive called the charges "desperate."

The networks also moved to limit CNN's use of reports from network correspondents by changing the rules governing the television news-pool reports . . .[68]

The danger with these issues is that people may loose sight of the larger issues surrounding a war.

Tenth, it is important for the news media to stress and promote peace initiatives in their reporting of war. The press can play a pivotal role in helping to resolve conflicts, and promote peaceful solutions. With the agenda setting abilities of the mass media, they are in a position where they can control a major vehicle of public opinion formation. Why else do so many governments show such an interest in the operation and administration of media institutions?

Reporting on war may appear to be more interesting than reporting on peace initiatives for many news organizations and correspondents. After all, the events of war are inherently charged with action, drama, and intrigue. Yet most parties who engage in war enter into it seriously believing that a resolution to the conflict can be found. This is where the press can help influence events. The following questions that seasoned U.P.I. correspondent Helen Thomas posed to U.S. President George Bush during a news conference soon after the Persian Gulf War opened are examined:

Mr. President, two days ago, you launched a war, and war is inherently a two-way street. Why should you be surprised or outraged when there is an act of retaliation? . . .

* * * * *

Why is it that any move, or yet move for peace, is considered an "end run" at the White House these days? . . .[69]

Admittedly these are spunky questions for a reporter to ask the President, but they represent the aggressiveness the press is capable of assuming. This seems to be particularly the case here where many journalists were still caught up in the euphoric climate of those early days in the allied campaign on Iraq and Kuwait. Journalists may represent the rare voices of reason at times such as these. Major contributions can be made to wartime dialogue. We consider next the introspective writing found in the *Guardian Weekly* during the early weeks of the Gulf War when many in the West were suggesting that patriotism was somehow akin to having hawkish attitudes, or at least were suppressing any talk of peaceful solutions:

> Even more unpleasant is the implication that, by seeking to avert wholesale war, the peace part was in some way failing in its patriotic duty, which ultimately is to support "our boys". It takes a very special kind of distorting mirror, reminiscent of 1914 jingoism, to believe that those who urge our boys towards the guns are giving them more sincere support than those who would rather save them from the slaughter.[70]

The author goes on to note that criticism toward Germany's reluctance to sent troops to the Persian Gulf was insane. "Do we really want to rediscover just what good soldiers Germans can be? Is it not a matter of rejoicing that the new Generation of Germans–the sons, grandsons, and great-grandsons of the Hun and the Boche–have turned out to be flower people instead?"[71]

Finally, journalists also can use the forum of electronic and print editorials to help structure an agenda for peace. Military conflicts, even when there appears to be a "winner" and "loser," do not resolve all problems. Following wars, there may be frustrations with border conflicts, prisoner exchanges, and economic rebuilding campaigns. After the Persian Gulf War, frustrations continued. The words found in a *San Francisco Examiner* editorial called for caution:

> In Erich Maria Remarque's "All Quiet on the Western Front," a soldier says, "The war has ruined us for everything." And so runs the risk for America, jubilant in its fresh and total triumph over Iraq. Winning has already gone to America's head. Now the U.S. has to avoid the temptation of becoming addicted to military solutions. America can't become the Rome of the 21st Century. Her legions can't be dispatched to the far corners of the empire to fight back the latest incursion of barbarians. The world won't allow it—and Americans shouldn't. . . .[72]

The press can also help set the agenda for peace talks and orchestrate the issues so that it includes firmer guarantees for a lasting peace. This may include a discussion of regional boundaries, economic aid, arms control, or military balance.

CONCLUSION

The press clearly can provide an effective forum for wartime information/communication. News accounts are sought by individuals seeking knowledge about war. Some hope to manipulate news content in an effort to affect a war's outcome. In such an environment, journalists must continue to operate, doing the jobs they always do, but knowing of the phenomenal consequences their reports may produce. There are pressures of accuracy, pressures of deadlines, pressures to be objective, pressures to be creative, pressures to avoid manipulation, and even pressures to be patriotic. The news reporter operates amid all of these expectations, trying to cover one of the most traumatic events there is–a conflict in which people unleash phenomenal destructive power against other people, their property, and their families including children.

It is a tall order that a journalist faces. Yet it is exactly what the press must do if it wishes to best serve the public in wartime. If a principal goal of war is to bring about peace, then the journalist is in a seminal position to help facilitate such an outcome. The press can open channels of communication so we can better learn about war events, and explore various solutions. If communication is effective, then conflicts may be resolved. Political and economic equality among countries can be fostered by equal access to information, and fair and thorough coverage by the world press. The press may be the most powerful tool we have to solve future conflicts and avert wars.

NOTES TO CHAPTER 7

1. John Pilger, "Myth-makers of the Gulf War," *The Guardian Weekly,* January 13, 1991, p. 6.

2. See Paul F. Lazersfeld, Bernard Berelson and Hazel Gaudet, *The People's Choice* (New York: Columbia University Press, 1948), for one of these early information diffusion studies. Their's was a study of voting behavior in Erie County, Ohio.

3. Maxwell E. McCombs and Donald L. Shaw, "The Agenda-Setting Function of the Press," in *The Emergence of American Political Issues: The Agenda-Setting Function of the Press*, eds., Donald L. Shaw and Maxwell E. McCombs (St. Paul, MN: West Publishing Company, 1977), p. 5.

4. The complementary relationship of various news media is well documented in the media uses literature.

5. Edwin Emery, *The Press and America: An Interpretative History of the*

Mass Media, 3rd. ed. (Englewood Cliffs, N.J.: Prentice-Hall, 1972).

6. Philip Knightley. *The First Casualty* (New York: Harcourt, Brace, Jovanovich, 1975), pp. 378-79.

7. Louis L. Snyder and Richard B. Morris, eds., *A Treasury of Great Reporting* (New York: Simon & Schuster, 1962), p. 146.

8. Editorial, *London Evening News*, quoted in *New York Times*, January 9, 1914, p. 2.

9. Quoted in Erik Barnouw, *The Golden Web: A History of Broadcasting in the United States, Volume II—1933 to 1953* (New York: Oxford University Press, 1968), pp. 140-141.

10. Although Civil War photographer Matthew Brady is said to have had an uncanny ability to predict where the next battle would occur. Soldiers reportedly dreaded the sight of his wagon (which served as a portable darkroom) for when it arrived in camp, battle often followed.

11. U.S. pool tape, portion of a CNN report, February 11, 1991.

12. Alex S. Jones, "Feast of Viewing, but Little Nourishment," *New York Times*, January 19, 1991, p. A10.

13. W. A. Swanberg, *Citizen Hearst* (New York: Charles Scribner's Sons, 1961), p. 108; citing James Creelman, *On The Great Highway* (Boston, 1901), pp. 177-178.

14. Swanberg, *Citizen Hearst*, pp. 137-38.

15. Ibid., pp. 138-40.

16. "Networks' Anger with CNN Deepens," *New York Times*, February 12, 1991, p. B1.

17. For an account of the filming see Pat Mullen, *Man of Aran* (New York: E. P. Dutton & Co., 1935; reprint ed., Cambridge, Mass.: The MIT Press, 1970).

18. Some of their screen credits from this period follow: Robert Drew: *Yanki No!* (1960); *Eddie* (1960), with Leacock, Pennebaker, Al Maysles and others; *Crisis: Behind a Presidential Commitment* (1963); *The Chair* (1962), with Leacock, Pennebaker and Gregory Shuker; Richard Leacock: *Primary* (1960), with Drew, Al Maysles, Pennebaker and others; *Happy Mother's Day* (1963), with Joyce Chopa; *A Stavinsky Portrait* (1964), with Rolf Liebermann; Donn A. Pennebaker: *Jane* (1962), *Don't Look Back* (1966), and *Monterey Pop* (1968), the last two with Drew; Albert and David Maysles: *Showman* (1962), *What's Happening! The Beatles in the U.S.A.* (1964), *Meet Marlon Brando* (1965), *With Love from Truman—A Visit with Truman Capote* (1966), *Salesman* (1969), *Gimme Shelter* (1970), *Running Fence* (1977); Fred Wiseman: *Titicut Follies* (1967), *High School* (1968), *Law and Order* (1969), *Hospital* (1970), *Basic Training* (1971), *Essene* (1972), *Juvenile Court* (1973); Michael Wadleigh: *Woodstock* (1970).

19. Alan King: *Warrendale* (1966), *A Married Couple* (1969); Wolf Koenig and Ralph Kroiter: *Lonely Boy* (1961), all from Canada; Jan Troell,

Porträtt av Åsa (1965) in Sweden; Kon Ichikawa, *Tokyo Olympiad* (1965) in Japan; Louis Malle *Phantom India* (1968) (*Calcutta* was the more widely seen shorter version) in France; and Bert Haanstra, *Zoo* (1962) in the Netherlands.

20. Tom Buckley, "Offensive Is Said to Pinpoint Enemy's Strengths," *New York Times*, February 2, 1968, p. 12.

21. R. Michael Schiffer and Michael F. Rinzler, "No News is No News," *New York Times*, January 23, 1991, p. A15; "Pentagon Is Now Denying Report of Iraqi Defections," *Wall Street Journal*, January 10, 1991; Matthew Engel, "The Tortures in Kuwait," *The Guardian Weekly*, March 10, 1991.

22. Also see "La Maree Etait Trop Belle; La Nappe Pétrollère du Siècle: FAUX," *L'Humanité*, March 11, 1991, where it is reported that the extent of the oil spill seems to have been grossly exaggerated. French journalists made offers to hire a helicopter so that they might fly over the ocean to review the extent of the spill. Each time the request was denied for "safety" reasons. We thank Belgian journalist Michel Collon for bringing this article to our attention.

23. Tom Wicker, "For Pentagon Censors, An Easy Victory, Too," *International Herald Tribune*, March 22, 1991.

24. David Pallister, "Strange News from a Baghdad Boudoir," *The Guardian Weekly*, October 21, 1991.

25. "U.S. Briefing: 'How's the Weather?' 'I Can't Answer That'," *International Herald Tribune*, January 23, 1991.

26. R. Michael Schiffer and Michael F. Rinzler, "No News is No News," *New York Times*, January 23, 1991, p. A15.

27. Edward W. Said, "Ignorant Armies Clash by Night," *The Nation*, February 11, 1991, pp. 1, 160.

28. CNN, February 8, 1991.

29. Richard C. Vincent, Bryan K. Crow and Dennis K. Davis, "When Technology Fails: The Drama of Airline Crashes in Network Television News," *Journalism Monographs*, no. 117 (1989).

30. Formal censorship is know to have existed during the Civil War; Andrew Jackson restricted news dispatches from lines of battle in the War of 1812. During the Persian Gulf War, reporters excluded from the military-sanctioned "news pools" were known to "independently" report events despite restrictions to the contrary; see: John Kifner, "Reporters Get Out of the Pool to Get Their Feet Wet," *New York Times*, February 9, 1991, p. A7.

31. The concern does not seem to be confined to broadcast and print journalism. Other areas of communication studies have also been faulted. See Michael Burgeon, "Instruction about Communication: On Divorcing Dame Speech," *Communication Education*, 38 (October 1989),

pp. 303-308.

32. Wm. David Sloane, "Journalism Historians Lost in the Past, Need Direction," *Journalism Educator* 42 (Autumn 1987), pp. 4-7, 48. Other U.S. communication studies programs known to the authors have made similar decisions when weighing the role of "theory-based" classes in the curricula.

33. L. S. Harms and Jim Richstad, eds., *Evolving Perspectives on the Right to Communicate* (Honolulu, HI: East-West Communication Institute, East-West Center, 1977; distributed by the University Press of Hawaii); Desmond Fisher, *The Right to Communicate: A Status Report*, Reports and Papers on Mass Communication, No. 94 (Paris: Unesco, 1982).

34. Here we refer to an earlier period of American journalism when sensationalism was the norm in reporting. Names such as Hearst and Pulitzer are associated with the tradition.

35. Michael Arlen first used the phrase; see Michael Arlen, "The Falklands, Vietnam, and Our Collective Memory," *The New Yorker*, August 16, 1982, pp. 72-73.

36. David Halberstam, *The Powers that Be* (New York: Alfred A. Knopf, 1979).

37. Philip B. Davidson, *Secrets of the Vietnam War* (Novato, CA: Presidio, 1990), p. 810; William M. Hammond, "The Press in Vietnam as Agent of Defeat: A Critical Examination," *Reviews in American History* 17 (June 1989), pp. 312-323.

38, CNN, January 25, 1991.

39. Fred Friendly gives many examples of the tensions that existed between the CBS news department and network executives, advertising people, etc. under Edward R. Murrow and himself when each headed CBS news; see Fred W. Friendly book, *Due to Circumstances beyond Our Control...* (New York: Random House, 1967).

40. Opening of report, CNN, February 11, 1991.

41. Oscar Patterson, III, "An Analysis of Television Coverage of the Vietnam War," *Journal of Broadcasting* 28 (1984), pp. 397-404; Oscar Patterson, III, "Television's Living Room War in Print: Vietnam in the News Magazines," *Journalism Quarterly* 61 (1984), pp. 35-39, 136.

42. A.K. Dawson, cited in Francis Collins, *The Camera Man* (New York: Century, 1916), p. 9; and Raymond Fielding, *The American Newsreel: 1911-1967* (Norman, OK: University of Oklahoma Press, 1972), p. 120.

43. "How Bloody Can It Be?" *Time*, December 25, 1967, p. 75.

44. "In Somalia, Graves and Devastation," *New York Times*, January 30, 1991, Sec. A, p. 1.

45. Paul Lazarsfeld and Robert Merton, "Mass Communication,

Popular Taste, and Organized Social Action," in *The Communication of Ideas*, ed., L. Bryson (New York: Harper's, 1948), pp. 95-118; reprinted in *The Process and Effects of Mass Communication, rev. ed.*, eds., Wilbur Schramm and Donald F. Roberts (Urbana, IL: University of Illinois Press, 1971), pp. 554-578, see p. 565.

46. Special Intelligence Report No. 45, Bureau of Intelligence, OWI, June 17, 1942, p. 3, RG 44, Entry 171, Box 1844; reported in Steve M. Barkin, "Fighting the Cartoon War: Information Strategies in World War II," *Journal of American Culture* 7 (Spring/Summer 1984), p. 115.

47. "How Bloody Can It Be?" *Newsweek*, December 25, 1967, p. 75.

48. Chris Hedges, "A Reporter in Iraq's Hands: Amid the Fear, Parlor Games," *New York Times*, March 12, 1991, pp. A1, A7.

49. See William M. Hammond, "The Press in Vietnam as Agent of Defeat: A Critical Examination," p. 313.

50. Richard C. Vincent and Dennis K. Davis, "Trends in World News Research and the Implications for Comparative Studies," Paper presented at the 39th annual conference of the International Communication Association, San Francisco, May 26, 1989. See also Dennis K. Davis and John P. Robinson, "News Flow and Democratic Society in the Age of Electronic Media" in *Public Communication and Behavior*, ed., George Comstock (New York: Academic Press, 1989); and Doris Graber, *Processing the News* (New York: Longman, 1984).

51. Gill Woodall, "Information Processing," in *The Main Source: Learning from Television News*, eds., John P. Robinson and Mark Levy (Beverly Hills, CA: Sage, 1986).

52. All of these were stated in a NBC interview, reported by the *New York Times*: "Our objective is to get Saddam Hussein out of Kuwait, and destroy that military capability that he's used to invade Kuwait and to threaten the other nations in the Middle East." See "U.S. Aims Include Elimination of Baghdad as Regional Power," *New York Times*, January 22, 1991, p. A9.

53. Burton J. Hendrick, *The Life and Letters of Walter Hines Page: 1855-1918*, 3 vols. (Garden City, N.Y.: Garden City Pub., 1922); Charles Seymour, ed., *The Intimate Papers of Colonel (Edward E. Mandell) House*, 4 vols., (Boston: Houghton Mifflin Co, 1926-1928).

54. Charles A. Beard, *The Open Door at Home: A Trial Philosophy of National Interest* (New York: The Macmillan Co., 1934); Charles A. Beard, *The Devil Theory of War: An Inquiry into the Nature of History and the Possibility of Keeping Out of War* (New York: Vanguard Press, 1936; reprint ed., Westport, CT: Greenwood Press,1969).

55. See, for example, Theodore Peterson "The Social Responsibility Theory of the Press" in *Four Theories of the Press*, eds., Fred S. Siebert, Theodore Peterson and Wilbur Schramm (Urbana, IL: University of

Illinois Press, 1963); other traditions are also discussed.

56. Leni Riefenstahl, *Hinter den Kulissen des Reichsparteitagfilms* (Munich: N.S.D.A.P., 1935), pp. 15; translated by Erik Barnouw, *Documentary: A History of the Non-Fiction Film* (London: Oxford University Press, 1974), p. 103.

57. Humphrey Jennings: *First Days* (1939), with Harry Watt and Pat Jackson; *London Can Take It* (1940), with Harry Watt; *Listen to Britain* (1942); *The Silent Village* (1943); *The 80 Days* (1944); *A Diary for Timothy* (1945). Other notable titles include Harry Watts's *Target for Tonight* (1941), and Roy Boulting's *Desert Victory* (1943). "Why We Fight" series, directed by Frank Capra: *Prelude to War* (1942), *The Nazis Strike* (1942), *Divide and Conquer* (1943), *The Battle of Britain* (1943), *The Battle of Russia* (1943), *The Battle of China* (1944), *The War Comes to America* (1945). Other American titles: John Ford's *The Battle of Midway* (1944); William Wyler's *Memphis Belle* (1944); John Huston's *Report from the Aleutians* (1942), *The Battle of San Pietro* (1944), and *Let There Be Light* (1945)].

58. *Deutsche Wochenschau*, No. 651, the Goebbels Sportpalast speech; reported in Erik Barnouw, *Documentary: A History of the Non-Fiction Film*, pp. 143-144.

59. Barkin, "Fighting the Cartoon War: Information Strategies in World War II," pp. 113-117.

60. Special Intelligence Report No. 28, Bureau of Intelligence, OWI, June 17, 1942, p. 4, RG 44, Entry 171, Box 1844; quoted in Barkin, "Fighting the Cartoon War: Information Strategies in World War II," p. 113.

61. Executive Order 9182, June 13, 1942; R. Keith Kane to G.S. Pettee, "Information Policy," Sources Division, Bureau of Intelligence, OWI, April 8, 1942, RG 44, Entry 171, Box 1849; reported in Barkin, "Fighting the Cartoon War: Information Strategies in World War II," p. 114.

62. Special Intelligence Report No, 15, Bureau of Intelligence, OWI, 11 March 1942, Appendix B, pp. 2, 6-9; Special Intelligence Report No. 45, Bureau of Intelligence, OWI, June 17, 1942, RG 44, Entry 171, Box 1844; reported and summarized in Barkin, "Fighting the Cartoon War: Information Strategies in World War II," pp. 113-115.

63. Richard Zoglin and Peter Ainslie, "Taking AIM Again at Viet Nam," *Time*, July 1, 1985, p. 47.

64. CBS president Frank Stanton was reported to be very uncomfortable after the Morley Safer story was aired. He was very close friends with Lyndon Johnson. See David Halberstam, *The Powers that Be* (New York: Alfred A. Knopf, 1979).

65. "The Press: Room for Improvement," *Newsweek*, July 10, 1967, p. 76.

66. Interestingly, Hussein's reliance on CNN has also been suggest-

ed as having played a major role in his staggering military defeat. It is suggested that Mr. Hussein miscalculated Western response. When watching the network's coverage of Congressional debates over American policy on the Gulf, for example, he may have interpreted the debates as a country divided on whether to go to war. "He didn't realize that there could be democratic debate, but when the decision was taken, it would be over," Egyptian President Hosni Mubarak remarked to Egypt's Parliament. "He didn't believe there could be a war." See Elaine Sciolino, "Hussein's Errors: Complex Impulses," *New York Times*, February 28, 1991, p. A10.

67. "CNN Warns on Censorship," *New York Times*, January 25, 1991, p. A9.

68. Excerpt from Bill Carter, "Networks' Anger with CNN Deepens," *New York Times*, February 12, 1991, p. C11.

69. White House Press Conference, Washington, D.C., January 18, 1991. "End run" seems to be a reference to a move common in U.S. football, in which the offence uses a strategy designed to elude opponents by running to the outside of the playing field. Transcription by authors.

70. Ian Aitken, "Thank God the Germans Don't Want to Fight," *The Guardian Weekly*, February 3, 1991.

71. Ibid.

72. "Caveat for Pax Americana," editorial, *San Francisco Examiner*, March 10, 1991, p. A18.

CHAPTER 8

Epilogue

Our inventions are wont to be pretty toys, which distract our attention from serious things. They are but improved means to an uniproved end, an end which it was already but too easy to arrive at... We are in great haste to construct a magnetic telegraph from Maine to Texas; but Maine and Texas, it may be, have nothing important to communicate."
— *Henry David Thoreau, Walden; or, Life in the Woods* [1]

THE NEWS MEDIA IN A CHANGING WORLD

Information exchange in our society seems to get more sophisticated and complex with each passing year. As a result, the manner in which information is produced and distributed has become increasingly important. The many emerging technologies available for data transmission help underline the significance that information flow now plays in our lives. The news media, of course, is one particularly effective channel for information transmission. Attention to technology, unfortunately, may make it even more difficult for media to control the context in which news is reported as the process becomes faster and possibly more ornamental.

Various news people and critics have voiced concern about the changing nature of news gathering and reporting. We take U.S. television as an example. Throughout the country there is a trend to move away from network news programs as many local television stations believe they can do national/international news reporting just as well (read: "more profitably") by utilizing network "feeds" (a package of hundreds of secondary network news stories received daily). Along with this trend comes a growing practice to provide shorter news stories (60 to 90 seconds or less) consisting of extremely short shots (2-3 seconds and less) and "sound bytes" (spirited video clips up to 10 seconds in

235

length, which may or may not characterize what was said in a covered speech). Some have suggested that this approach to television reporting is an attempt to simply replicate an MTV (Music Television) format in news programs. Following the recommendations of news consultants (social science/marketing researchers such as Frank Magid, Lou Harris, and others–sometimes referred to as "TV news doctors") station management often makes changes in program formats and in on-air and behind-the-scenes personnel to enhance the entertainment quality/appeal (again read: "profitability") of these shows.

At worst, we are seeing a further degradation of a system that radio and early television personality Fred Allen once quipped was mere "chewing gum for the mind." Yet local anchors and reporters in many markets often do not have the ability to do optimum-level investigative and analytic reporting. As a result, their reports have a greater potential to be one dimensional and nonaggressive when dealing with issues of national and international importance. As ABC news producer Greenfield observed recently in a Gannett Center for Media Studies talk, the Reagan White House administered a "Local Program Network" of presidential interviews in which local anchors were granted meetings with the President. A "Sam Donaldson" might have the ability to ask tougher questions than "the local anchor in Des Moines" when you consider the "flattery problem." This is why presidents "like to talk to these people."[2]

Added to all of this, consider that even the networks are eliminating regional news bureaus based in many foreign capitals. Gone are the regional desks. Now Latin America is covered from Miami, Asia from Los Angeles, the Middle East from London, Paris, or New York. What is this doing to our ability to seek out and process information throughout the world? How can we be sure that we have access to the best and least biased information reports possible? The concern, of course, goes beyond television news and other media systems well outside the immediate boundaries of the United States.

The news media find themselves in a volatile time. While in many countries the media are increasingly concerned with cost effectiveness, we also see the nature of news gathering in dramatic transition due to the convergence of technology. News reporting has become faster, often instantaneous. The opportunity to do thorough, analytic and prosocial reporting may be more difficult than ever.

First, the agendas of politicians, private business people, and the public are all potentially threatened by the press and the way it operates. Groups from government to the military, and business leaders to terrorists are now more aware of the powers of the media, and try to manipulate news in order to help promote specific group "causes." Some news

people are still skeptical of the U.S. bombing of Libya which came at 7
P.M. Eastern Standard Time, for example. This was perfect timing for
the heavily viewed evening hours of U.S. network television. Because of
the new speed by which media images/reports can be delivered, it
makes an effective vehicle for public relations and propaganda.

The increased speed under which media operate may be another
way that media are losing control of events. News events are taking control of the media. The need to get a story out quickly is just too great. If
you do not do it, a competitor will as when CNN scooped the other
American television news networks with its Persian Gulf coverage.
ABC, CBS, and NBC, scrambling to find ways to respond, used counter-
measures in an effort to win back audiences (ABC and CBS, as an illustration, sent anchors to Saudi Arabia and Kuwait to originate broadcasts
on location in an effort to intensify the feeling of immediacy.). It is not
just television; print journalists are writing their stories on laptop computers and sending them back to the office via modems and mobile telephones when they travel. Gone are the days related in the Morley Safer
story (Chapter 7) when it took some 36 hours or more for film to be
flown to Los Angeles and then transmitted via very expensive wire
transmissions to New York. This process allowed plenty of time for the
reporter to check his notes, reflect on the story, and confer with editors
and producers in New York prior to a story being aired. As Greenfield
warns: "what you become is not a reporter but a narrator." He tells of an
ABC broadcast following the assassination of Gandhi. A well-known
correspondent was flows into New Delhi. Thirty minutes after landing,
that correspondent was on the air with a report thanks to satellite technology. "But what does a reporter learn in the 30 minutes that he is on
the ground in New Delhi?"[3]

Second, some argue that the boom in information technologies
will lead to an abundance of information sources which should/would
decentralize the power of media institutions and allow consumers direct
access to primary data. Tofler and others are correct in recognizing the
increasing importance of these new information sources.[4] The jury is still
out, however, on whether they will replace existing media, just as pre-
dictions that computers would lessen our paper needs have not yet been
realized (in fact, our paper consumption has increased since the advent
of computers). The convergence of voice and data transmission technologies will undoubtedly change the nature of existing media. But sym-
biosis is a process in which it is acknowledged that media can be rede-
fined, not eliminated. We have seen this happening ever since the "plastic" arts (photography and moving pictures) of the late 19th century
allowed existing arts to pursue avenues other than realistic expression.[5]

The information society has already led to a severe "information

overload." We see what happens when information is simply dissemi-
nated with no attempt to analyze and synthesize, as in the U.S. television affiliates example above. And the news learning/processing literature cited earlier suggests that audiences are failing to retain much of the
news they now see. It is reported that one-half of the viewers who watch
television news have only a cursory recall of half of the stories seen.
Similarly, about one-third of the viewers can remember little or nothing
about stories viewed, and the most informed third of the audience can
report main elements for only one-third of the newscast.[6] How can more
information alone help if the basic way that information is collected and
organized is digressing, or, at best remains the same? The questions
which we must address are much larger than those posed thus far. To
argue that electronic data banks will be the answer runs contrary to
attempts we have seen where regional news agencies are created by simply "pooling" stories, without editorial intervention. This is a clearinghouse, not a news *agency*. Without a mechanism to critically assess and
edit information, to truly "pool" resources of various Third World press-
es, such regional press agency ventures appear to be destined to failure.
Similarly, electronic data pools and services are of little use in enhancing
information flow.

We return to the Thoreau quote offered at the beginning of this
chapter: "We are in great haste to construct a magnetic telegraph from
Maine to Texas; but Maine and Texas, it may be, have nothing important
to communicate." By having the technologies or the communication
institutions it does not mean that there automatically will be something
worth communicating. We do not mean to isolate Maine and Texas, of
course (although it is interesting that they are the two states George
Bush considers home). We can just as easily substitute Washington, New
York, London, Paris and Moscow. So often attention is given to the
mechanisms for communicating messages, but little interest is given to
the content of messages. It has been our hope that we might help change
this by calling attention to some flaws in the news media, and helping to
set an agenda for its change. These also have been concerns of the World
Information and Communication Order debate. The NWICO hoped to
direct attention to international news flow inequities, and sought to generate a discussion on salient issues. Yet the debate became too political.
UNESCO was not equipped to fully address the issues. The questions
raised in UNESCO meetings, though, were for the most part appropriate. They needed, and still need to be asked. The world press must find
ways to transcend its shortcomings. It must strive to provide thorough,
expanded, and unrestricted accounts of world events in as fair and equitable a way as possible. We can use media to help promote dialogue
between people and nations. Free information flow is the key to a more

understanding world population. We strive for *global glasnost*.

GLOBAL GLASNOST

The title of this book is *Global Glasnost*. The notion of "glasnost" has been around for some time and is said to go back to Tsarist Russia, when George Parrot first called for glasnost as a way to improve central decision making under Nicholas I (1825-1855). Others are also said to have used it, or versions of the term, often in different contexts, including both Lenin and Khrushchev.[7] Mikhail Gorbachev announced his party's information policy in 1985. He acknowledged that it came from the word *golos* (meaning "voice" which can be translated as "candor," "forthrightness," "accessibility," and "directness") and it was to be the goal of the Communist Party's new information policy. "The better people are 'informed,' the more consciously they will act, the more actively they will support the party, its plans, and its goals."[8]

Yet we can see how "glasnost" seems to have different interpretations when it comes to the role the news media might play in its adoption. As Gorbachev has noted:

> Democracy should not be confused with anarchy and permissiveness... It is not allowed to convert a magazine, a newspaper, the mass media, [or] public fora into a medium of information about personal views. Authentic democracy is indivisible from...responsibility...[and] from strict adherence to the laws and norms of socialist community.[9]

So a global glasnost implies that new channels of communication will emerge and these channels will be marked by candid dialogue. We would change Mr. Gorbachev's words slightly. Instead of support for the party, we envision the support of societal goals. All of humanity can benefit from this new world order. A responsible press is the vehicle that can help us achieve these goals.

Throughout this book, we have been looking at some of the inadequacies of international news flow and implications of this for the world community. We believe that by improving news flow the world's people can gain a better understanding of one another. We espouse a *global glasnost*. To come to a better understanding of fellow humans, of course, is the essence of communication.

In addition to analyzing world news trends, we also have proposed an agenda for better journalism. With greater effort, journalists may be able to rectify some of the ills found in international news flow that our world leaders have been unsuccessful in changing thus far. Yet our proposals have bordered on the hypothetical. We have cited examples to support different proposals, but it took some effort to find them. They do not represent the status quo.

To demonstrate some of the possibilities for news reporting that promotes *glasnost*, we turn to an event that already has received wide attention by the world press. We revisit those events in an effort to point to some pitfalls to which journalists may fall victim. We look at the events that transpired on June 3-4, 1989 in Beijing, China.

WHAT HAPPENED IN BEIJING ON JUNE 3-4, 1989; WHAT HAPPENS NOW?

Two months after the Chinese student demonstrations and government crack down in early June 1989, one of the present authors traveled to Beijing. He was aware of the Western press accounts of events, but he was curious to learn what really happened. What he was able to uncover, from the best sources he could locate in Beijing, was that the events of early June had been greatly exaggerated in the Western, particularly the U.S., press. Furthermore, what was happening some 2 months after those events that captured much of the world's attention was of equal political importance, but it went largely unreported.

During those early days of June, the official number of those executed was only 31. However, independent, unconfirmed estimates run as high as 8-9,000, even 10,000; 4-5,000 were shot to the neck in Beijing, some very close to the Marco Polo bridge, with their feet and hands tied. Students and intellectuals were not executed, but the military were—for disobedience.

Estimates of the number arrested are as high as 100,000, including student leaders Wang Dan and Liu Xiaobo (actually a university lecturer). The scenario seems to include court cases, possibly confessions and self-criticism, and then punishment ranging from exile to distant, despondent places in China for life, or at the least losing the coveted residence permit for Beijing.

Why? It is because this was a real threat to a regime whose socialism had failed, and whose capitalism is failing. It was much more than merely the nonviolent demonstration coming out of the death of Hu Yaobang on April 15, the reaction of the students to the party obituary, Dang's reaction to the students reaction, or the famous *People's Daily* editorial of April 24 that lead up to the Tian'anmen pro-democracy demonstrations. In the demonstrations were some 1 to 1.5 million people, 2.5 million on May 17, and when we include the masses on Chang'an Avenue, 3 million on May 18! Then there were the disastrous events of June 3 and June 4.

So what exactly did happen? Chinese government reports and other sources contacted seem to agree, roughly speaking, on the following:

1. The major initial violence directed against the military was on June 3. Peaceful, verbal efforts to dissuade the military from entering and enforcing the martial law order of May 20 had failed. Large scale, atrocious anti-military violence resulted around 10 P.M. For this day the number of military killed in Beijing is given as "some dozens" (possibly 2 dozen), some burnt alive, disemboweled, castrated, or eyes gouged out, and one hung alive. The military killed now have status as martyrs, as "Guards of the Republic." The number of wounded military is given as 5,000; 1,300 vehicles burnt or destroyed including buses and trucks, some tanks, and armored cars.

2. The violence of June 4 may have been reactive; an act of revenge. The estimates of the total number killed in Beijing is from 200-300 to about 1,000; this includes the "some dozens" of military. The number of students killed is given as 36, made up of six from the People's University, three from Qinghua, three from Beijing Technical University, and then seven universities with two each (among them Beida and the People's Normal University) and ten universities with one each. The rest are "civilians," meaning essentially workers, the *laobaixing*, and bystanders. The number of wounded is given as around 2,000. The total number of casualties given by the Chinese Red Cross (2,500-6000) may not distinguish sufficiently between dead and wounded. The figures given here may be too low, but not by much. Thus, all of this attests to the notion that there was indeed a massacre in Beijing on June 3-4.

3. There was no large-scale massacre at Tian'anmen Square. There was sporadic killing (the highest estimate we have seen is 30-40),[10] but not a massacre in the sense of killing anything that moves, with any means (this is also Taniguchi's point, his great advantage was that as a Japanese he could more easily hide among the Chinese in the square). No-one has been able to demonstrate that there was a "Tian'anmen massacre," although this formula has become standard. Tanks did crush the tents, but there is no reason to believe that anybody was inside given that many students had retreated at 4:40 a.m. and that nobody can be expected to continue sleeping when volley after volley of warning shots

are fired and tanks are moving in making the ground shake. The massive killing was done somewhere else, at four or five places along the major Chang'an avenue (also close to Beijing Hotel where the foreign television news teams were) and, possibly, in the south of Beijing. The report from the U.S. Embassy also reinforces this point. Taniguchi calls this a "large-scale massacre committed in the suppression of demonstrating students at Tian'anmen Square," not the "Tian'anmen massacre." Maybe no-one wanted to desecrate Tian'anmen Square, a major symbol in Chinese history? Perhaps someone wanted that bloody symbol?

Conclusion: The figures have been vastly inflated by the phrase repeated so often, "hundreds, possibly thousands." The Chinese authorities were not Orwellian, changing history by insisting that the first large-scale violence was the attack on the military. Perhaps others were. Sloppy reporting on the western side, establishing "facts" that were fictitious, angered Chinese authorities who appealed to "finding truth from the historical records" (a rule that certainly also would apply to them). This is certainly no excuse for the atrocities, but erring on this important point (symbolically) makes it too easy for the Chinese authorities to reject other points made by Western media.

One source of the sloppiness seems to be the overreliance on the Student Broadcast Station in the middle of Tian'anmen square, thereby neglecting the basic rule of all good journalism: always check with the other side or sides in the conflict, irrespective of where your sympathies are. In addition, the students were systematically distorting reality. Thus, the station launched deliberate lies: that senior leader Deng Xiaoping and Premier Li Peng had stepped down, that Li was shot in the leg and Deng had died. These were later confirmed as lies in a *McNeil-Lehrer Newshour* program by one of the Chinese graduate students studying in the U.S. Other fabricated rumors included: a student killed in a bus accident had been killed by the police; a student had been fighting between the 27th and the 30th army corps of the PLA; the Foreign Ministry had declared independence from the government; and Shanghai has seceded from the "false central authorities."[11]

Two themes appear to emerge from the official films and from the photo exhibition in the Beijing Art Gallery, probably holding some of the key to the disaster; again this was checked with very different informants who were in agreement. In advance of the historical account, this method, reporting only consensus across conflict gaps, is not the worst.

The soldiers were very young, some even born before 1972, with the faces of children. They were attacked for the first time in their lives, stones and bricks thrown at them, their vehicles set afire. Blood was streaming down their faces, they were collapsing with anguish, with fear of death and extreme pain in their faces. Of course, the officers were older and experienced; but this was the general impression. The "martyrs" were also young, small boys, probably mainly from the countryside.

And then the same young, almost childlike faces appeared in the photos/movies of the students, holding hands, courageously and defiantly linking arms, retreating orderly. They were in their late teens, or very early twenties, many of them with spectacles differentiating them from the soldiers. So history has again shown one of its ugliest sides, young boys killing young boys. Those without spectacles were killing those who had them.

But who did the killing on the student side? Again photos and films are revealing. They appear to have been very active, jumping upon vehicles, as they hammered and poured gasoline. They were very agile, and no doubt competent technically, knowing how to destroy vehicles, even tanks. They were definitely not "late teens, early twenties," but probably more in their late twenties, early thirties. We have heard them described as coming from "all walks of life, workers, unemployed academics" by people sympathetic to the students. Some, not many, were plain criminals. There seems to be agreement that the students participated much less in such activities and rejected the people who behaved violently. There is some speculation that they were agents provocateurs from the government and that the young soldiers were even sacrificed to create this pretext. This seems doubtful; it would have been very risky for the government, which, moreover, appears to have been both confused and also remarkably restrained during the 6 weeks prior to the tragic climax. One wonders what government would have waited that long.

The second theme is the idea of the two periods in the "events;" a first period from mid-April until around May 28-29, and a second 1-week period planned to last to 20 June, but ending disastrously (this is what the government calls the counter-revolutionary phase). Several informants agree on these basic differences. During the first nonviolent period the participants were mainly Beijing students, supported by the Beijing population; in the second violent period participants were students from the provinces (possibly 200,000) and people from Hong Kong and further abroad. The cost of keeping the demonstrators at Tian'anmen was calculated at 100,000 yuan per day, paid by the population in the first period, and possibly from millions of dollars Hong Kong collected at the two universities in the colony during the second period (including the tents, from Hong Kong). There is little mention of Taiwan, but there is always a possibility of a CIA connection. Evidently, the whole "rebellion" changed character with a disastrous outcome.

The atrocities in Beijing, Chengdu, and Kunming might have been avoided had the authorities entered into serious dialogue with the students (as they did in Shanghai and Tientsin), held partly on television for the general public, and partly in government and party headquarters. All over Beijing, in early August, there were signs for *Law and Order*, the slogan of iron-clad authority. "Stability" occurs very frequently in Deng's speeches about the "turmoil" and the "counterrevolution." The pro-democracy, rule of law, human rights movement was defined away as a counter-revolutionary effort to topple the government; however, much in their campaign against bureaucracy and corruption was found praiseworthy.

Act I ended on June 4. Act II has been ongoing since then, with the full power of the government imposing itself with mass arrests, mass executions, well publicized trials, and sentencing. The foreign press is by and large tired of the issue. Foreign governments returned to the market race in China, joining Deng Xiaoping in the deep countryside. It is easy to say what the Chinese government should do: enact general amnesty, let bygones be bygones, let the dialogue begin. But this is not the habit of states, capitalists, socialists, and others.

There must be an Act III somewhere, that holds a future for China. However, where would that be?[12]

SUMMARY OF CONCLUSIONS

We began this work with an examination of some major trends in the structure and process of international news information and communication. As we noted, there appears to be less relative emphasis on former Center nations and somewhat more on former Periphery ones. It is not clear whether such a trend will lead to permanent changes in the character of what is regarded as news itself. More power to the Periphery, both on the printed page, in the loudspeaker, and on the television screen, and in the production of news, does not mean that the product has changed. The product might, in fact, even have worsened as the lines separating information, advocacy, and entertainment become increasingly blurred. While communication has become more relevant to global problems, these global communication efforts often become counter-productive. Hence, it appears that little progress is being made toward global and human journalism. Changes can be observed in the *structure* of news, but the *product* remains essentially the same. The time seems ripe, then, for a new journalism. It must be global and human, void of visible and invisible repression, and reflective of its social com-munication abilities. Above all, it must be responsive to human concerns and responsible to norms of decency and objectivity. This is all that the 1976 Nairobi UNESCO General Conference apparently had in mind.

We have explored the research environment in which news flow and international news content has been examined. It seems necessary that the academic community increase the attention it gives to many of the new research technologies, some that are exclusively qualitative in approach, and others that combine both qualitative and quantitative research techniques into the same study. The results are that many now choose to look beyond the superficial "flow" of news items, and instead examine deeper themes and messages, often influenced by the fields of sociology, psychology, linguistics, literary studies, and rhetorical analy-sis. One of these approaches employs narrative analysis in order to gain a better understanding of the storytelling functions of news. We argue that through this and other newer approaches to news analysis, our understanding of international news would benefit. By studying the news as discourse, we should have better individual frames of reference in general, and more profound insights into how the discourse defines the news script. The script, of course, defines what has to be done to an event in order for it to become news.[13]

Additionally, future international news research needs to con-sider constraints on coverage of foreign news which arise from domestic production practices in various nations. These production constraints may foster less useful schemas or encourage the activation of inappro-priate schemas. Such problems can easily arise even when production practices meet certain minimal standards for balance or objectivity. It may prove useful to compare production practices in various nations, identifying those that seem especially useful in communicating interna-tional news and criticizing those that nurture misunderstanding.

We have seen how complex the relationship actually is between economics and information-communication within the new internation-al order. Whereas before they both worked unambiguously in favor of the First World, they are now more ambiguous. However the struggle between the First and the Third worlds is, to a large extent, being won by the Fourth. We conclude that whereas the old international order was based on much economic exchange, with exploitation and not much dia-logue, one relatively viable new international order might be based on more dialogue and less economic exchange (this would not exclude high levels of activity within the great trade blocks, however). The most likely "development" still appears to be that which is based on much rhetoric that sounds like dialogue and on the structure of the old international economic order, only located at new places.

Finally, we then looked at different news areas/ issues — peace, development, the environment, and war–in an effort to explore various trends found in reporting on these topics, and to provide a journalistic agenda for future newswriting. For each, we recognize that the media shapes images. People often act on the basis of media-mediated images rather than reality. Thus the role of media becomes a major concern. The way the media mediate becomes a major factor. As media images become increasingly instantaneous due to lightweight computers, "electronic carbons," electronic "paint boxes" (such as the AVA system), CONUS trucks, hypercard systems, Local Area Networks (LANs), non-linear tape editing (such as the Avid system), electronic data bases (like Nexis and Lexis), microwave relays, satellite transmissions, and other new technologies, our ability to actually participate in distant events improves. The spontaneous images of the Persian Gulf War from CNN and other news organizations, noted in Chapter 7, certainly attest to this burgeoning trend. The continuous flow of news images will only increase, and our inability to discern between news and reality will become greater.

The media have the power to shape images. This is not only apparent in much of the media research conducted to date, but also in the vast sums spent on development of media systems by various governments and private enterprises, and the confidence that sponsors have placed in using media as a channel of advertising. These trends will undoubtedly continue.

Media can be used to improve economic, social, and political balances throughout the world. It can help promote peace, foster development, protect the environment, and reduce the probability of wars, to name some objectives. These will not happen automatically, though. The media make powerful tools of influence and change, but they must be properly guided in order to achieve these goals.

Now is the time to make another attempt to foster a World Information and Communication Order dialogue. The debate is not over, and major issues have not been resolved. UNESCO should find ways to once again help lead the debate. It will require backbone, but it can be done. The first step, of course, would be to depoliticize the process somewhat. The attempt to serve too many masters may have been where UNESCO went wrong the first time around. It also appears that world religious leaders, missionary groups, and other humanitarian organizations can increasingly play a role in the Information and Communication Order discussions. The best way to help people overcome oppressive conditions and attitudes is to make them equal participants in the world community. A better understanding and control of the news media process can be the key to insuring that equity.

NOTES TO EPILOGUE

1. Henry David Thoreau, *Walden; or, Life in the Woods* (Reprint: Garden City, NY: Doubleday, 1970).

2. Jeff Greenfield, "Technology and News," talk given at Gannett Center, New York; in *Demystifying Media Technology: A Gannett Center Reader*, eds., John V. Pavlik and Everette E. Dennis (Mountain View, CA: Mayfield Publishing Co., forthcoming).

3. Ibid.

4. Alvin Toffler, *The Third Wave* (New York: Morrow, 1980); and others.

5. See John Fell, *Film and the Narrative Tradition* (Norman, OK: University of Oklahoma Press, 1974).

6. Doris Graber, *Processing the News*, 2d ed. (New York: Longman, 1987); John P. Robinson and Mark R. Levy, *The Main Source: Learning from Television News* (Beverly Hills, CA: Sage, 1986); Dennis K. Davis, "News and Politics," in *New Directions in Political Communication*, eds., David L. Swanson and Dan Nimmo (Newbury Park, CA: Sage, 1990), pp. 147-184.

7. Tomasz Goban-Klas, "Gorbachev's Glasnost: A Concept in Need of Theory and Research," *European Journal of Communication* 4 (1989), p. 248; he makes these observation, in part, on an analysis of books by W. Bruce Lincoln and a work by Natalie Gross. See W. Bruce Lincoln, *Nicholas I. Emperor and Autocrat of all Russians* (1978); (Polish translation: Warsaw: PIW, 1988); W. Bruce Lincoln, *In the Vanguard of Reform* (DeKalb, IL: Northern Illinois University Press, 1983); Natalie Gross, "'Glasnost:' Roots and Practice," *Problems of Communism* (Nov.-Dec. 1987), pp. 69-70.

8. *Pravda*, March 15, 1985, p. 3; as translated by Tomasz Goban-Klas, "Gorbachev's Glasnost: A Concept in Need of Theory and Research," *European Journal of Communication* 4 (1989), p. 247.

9. *Pravda*, April 17, 1987; as translated by Tomasz Goban-Klas, "Gorbachev's Glasnost: A Concept in Need of Theory and Research," *European Journal of Communication* 4 (1989), p. 251.

10. Junichi Taniguchi, "An Eyewitness in China," *Japan Times*, July 31, 1989.

11. *China Daily*, August 12, 1989.

12. Robin Munro, in "Who Died in Beijing, and Why," *The Nation*, June 4, 1990, pp. 811-822:

> To conclude, we should turn to two Chinese activists from last year's democracy movement, both of whom witnessed the final

clearing of the square, for an answer to the question posed at the outset: Why does it matter where the massacre took place? Kong Jiesheng, a famous novelist and essayist, says: "Now, when the power-holding clique in Beijing is still unrepentant about the June 4 massacre but also sorely vexed by the criticisms and sanctions imposed·by numerous countries, rebukes from outside China based on ill-founded concepts have given those vicious thugs precisely the 'spiritual shield' they so desperately need. It makes plausible their lengthy refutations of outside criticisms as being mere 'stuff and nonsense' and 'much ado about nothing'"–the very phrase used by General Secretary Jiang Zemin when asked by Barbara Walters, on ABC's 20/20 on May 18, about "the massacre in Tiananmen Square."

But Lao Gui should have the last word: "Because of hatred of the murderer, one sometimes cannot resist exaggerating the severity of the crime. This is understandable. . . But those butchers then take advantage of this opportunity 'to clarify the truth,' using one truth to cover up ten falsehoods. They exploit the fact that no one died during the clearing of Tiananmen Square to conceal the truth that some deaths and injuries did occur there earlier. And they use the fact that there was no bloodbath in Tiananmen Square to cover up the truth about the bloodbaths in Muxidi, Nanchizi and Liubukou. Why do we give them such an opportunity?"

13. For further discussion on news as discourse, see book by authors Johan Galtung and Richard C. Vincent, "Glasnost"—U. S. A.; Missing Political Themes in U.S. Media Discourse (Cresskill, N.J.: Hampton Press, forthcoming).

AUTHOR INDEX

249

SUBJECT INDEX